The Lifelong Activist

The Lifelong Activist

How to Change the World Without Losing Your Way

HILLARY RETTIG

LANTERN BOOKS

A DIVISION OF BOOKLIGHT INC.

2006
Lantern Books
One Union Square West, Suite 201
New York, NY 10003

Printed in the United States of America

Library of Congress Cataloging-in-Publication Data

Rettig, Hillary.
The lifelong activist : how to change the world without losing your way / Hillary Rettig.
p. cm.
ISBN 1-59056-090-6 (alk. paper)
1. Social reformers—Life skills guides. 2. Political activists—Life skills guides. 3. Social action. I. Title.
HN18.3.R47 2006
303.48'4023—dc22
2006009735

Dedicated with love to my parents, Gloria and Julius Rettig

ACKNOWLEDGMENTS

I wish to thank George Lewis for more than twenty-five years of love and friendship, as well as for his comments on the manuscript. Also, our Sudanese sons Daniel Mamour Agok, Phillipps Lual Baguoot, Aleer Galuak Deng and Dau Nun Deng, and our nephew, Angok Adier Angok, for sharing their lives with us. *Meth e ran pioc path ben tene warkendit.* And also Orbit, Comet, Elvis, Hawkeye and Neutrino, for more unconditional love than any mere human could ever provide.

I also wish to acknowledge the love and support of my sisters, Diana Presser and Lisa Rettig-Falcone, as well as of Larry Presser and John Falcone. And I am truly privileged to be the aunt of three very special individuals: Paul Busch, John Falcone III and Julia Falcone.

I am grateful to Melanie Joy, John Thompson, Patrick Tyrrell and Adam Weissman for their detailed critiques of the ideas in this book, which is much improved by their input.

I also wish to thank my friends and mentors Lois Arthur, Lisa-Claudia Brown, Brent Hymer, David Karp, Bill Merklein, Lisa Norling, Lydia Ross, Michael Stiefel, Vincent Suppa, Joe Valof and Bill Wollheim for their wisdom and generosity of spirit.

Also, Aryenish Birdie, Hilary Friedman, Ché Green, Stephanie Mittak and Nicholas Read for their close readings of, and detailed comments on, parts of the manuscript.

Finally, I wish to thank my editor, Martin Rowe, who supported this project from the beginning.

In dreams begin responsibilities.

—**William Butler Yeats** (famously quoted by Delmore Schwartz)

Be regular and orderly in your life like a bourgeois, so that
you may be violent and original in your work.

—**Gustave Flaubert**

TABLE OF CONTENTS

INTRODUCTION

I wrote this book because I believe that progressive activists are the world's most precious resource. We tackle the most difficult and important problems—including hunger, war, disease, poverty, violence, cruelty and exploitation—and work to further humanity's evolution in the direction of compassion and kindness. Conservatives may create more wealth, but we create more of the values, including justice, equality and freedom, that make life worth living. As history has repeatedly shown us, and as we are unfortunately witnessing in the United States today, wealth without the tempering of progressive values and mores leads inevitably to corruption and despair.

Imagine how different the world would be if there were twice—or ten times!—as many progressive activists as there are now, and if those activists were happy and effective and enjoying long full-time or part-time careers[1]. Entire societies and cultures, and quite possibly every society and culture, would be transformed.

That's why I wrote *The Lifelong Activist*, a guide to building a sustainable activist career. It is aimed at you, the activist, volunteer or other politically active person who is considering your long-term career and life options. My goal is to empower you to live a happy life that includes an effective and sustainable activist career, and in particular to help you avoid the burnout that afflicts so many activists.

This is not a typical book on activism, perhaps because my background is different from that of many activists. Although I've long been involved in progressive causes, including labor, feminism, and, most recently, animal rights and vegetarianism, I have chosen to earn my living as an entrepreneur, business journalist and business coach. Prior to writing *The Lifelong Activist*, I spent three years working as lead business coach at a Boston nonprofit, where my team and I helped more than 1,000 economically disadvantaged people of diverse backgrounds start or grow businesses, professional art careers and nonprofit organizations. In that position, I was able to witness firsthand what causes intelligent and dedicated people to succeed and what causes them to fail. That is the knowledge I bring to this book.

That knowledge is, in a nutshell, that **the secret to success as an activist, as well as in life itself, is to live a life that is as much as possible an expression of your core values.** *The Lifelong Activist* is a guidebook for doing so, and it is based on the premise that you succeed by making *conscious choices* about your life, specifically in the crucial areas of your mission, time, fears and relationships. Self-actualization—a term coined by the late psychologist Abraham Maslow that refers to the cultivation of your unique strengths, talents and character—should be your primary goal, since the more self-actualized you are, the more creativity, energy, focus and other positive attributes you will be able to bring to your activism and other endeavors. Self-actualization is also, as I discuss in Part IV, entirely congruent with your progressive ethic and mission.

Self-actualization begins with breaking free of other people's inappropriate influence and control over your life. Some of these people might mean well, while others might mean ill; still others might not care about you at all but are simply pursuing their own agenda. Some might even be other activists trying to bully you into working on their cause or meeting their standard of ideological purity. You need to break free of all of these inappropriate influences so that you can start to build a life in keeping with your values.

Perhaps because of my background, aspects of this book may challenge, and even anger or upset, some activists:

- My business background, naturally, influences my perceptions and advice, and so you may see more approving references to money, materialism, hierarchies and competition than you are used to seeing, or like to see, in a book aimed at progressives.
- I believe that activists need to place a high priority on money—or, more specifically, on creating a sustainable income for themselves. I understand that this can be difficult in a society whose values are opposed to your own. But our society's capitalist structure isn't changing any time soon and you still need to earn a living. The good news is that you probably have more choices than you realize: Chapters 12 through 15 in Part I will help you sort through them, and through your feelings and thoughts regarding money.

• I also believe that an activist should live the lifestyle he or she wants to live even if that lifestyle seems "unacceptably" bourgeois or materialistic. We are not machines and can't program our likes and dislikes. Moreover, a life built on self-denial is bound to be an unhappy one, and an unhappy life, besides being tragic in its own right, is likely to lead not to lifelong activism but to burnout.

So, go ahead: buy the car, the clothes, the electronics, the gym membership or the vacation. Or buy all of them, if that's what it takes to makes you happy. This may require that you get a non-activist job and do only part-time activism, but that's fine: I'd rather see you be a happy part-time activist than a miserable, deprived full-time one. Chances are, you'll get more done as a happy part-timer, anyway—and you may even get to do some "bonus" activism at your day job. Enjoy your life fully, and without guilt, shame or other negative emotions.

I want to be very clear, however, that I am not advocating a bourgeois or materialistic lifestyle. I am not advocating any lifestyle in particular. I advocate, rather, that you build a happy, sustainable lifestyle for yourself based on your values and no one else's. It's usually better, for a host of personal and societal reasons, to live as simply as possible, putting the bulk of your time and energies into your inner development and vocation(s), instead of into buying and maintaining a lot of stuff. But do what you need to do to be happy.

To those readers who are offended by these or other points I make in *The Lifelong Activist*, I urge you to stay with the book and glean whatever useful information you can from it. My goal is to help and empower as many activists as possible, and that obligates me to tell what I perceive to be the truth even if some readers find it to be controversial or even painful.

Your task, therefore, is this: to work to visualize and create a more liberated *self* at the same time you work to visualize and create a more liberated society. Picture yourself as someone who does activism as part of a happy, healthy and well-balanced life, and then work, using this book as a guide, to make that vision happen. Get past the stereotype, if it afflicts you, that activists are supposed to be ultra-serious and humorless. Get past the stereotype that they are supposed to suffer for their cause. Get past the stereotype that they are supposed to be poor. Envision a new mode of activism for yourself that is built on joyous involvement with the world. As Julia Butterfly Hill says, "Activism is so much more than just a response to something that is wrong. Activism is a celebration of life itself. It is a manifestation of the miracle of being alive. And isn't that something to celebrate!"

I hope you find *The Lifelong Activist* helpful as you build your activist career, and I invite you to contact me and let me know your thoughts on the book or any aspect of your life or activism.

Peace and Freedom for All,
Hillary Rettig

lifelongactivist@riseup.net
www.lifelongactivist.com

PART 1

MANAGING YOUR MISSION

PART I: MANAGING YOUR MISSION

CHAPTER 1

Who Are You?

Who are you?

That question should be at the heart of your quest to build a sustainable activist career—actually, it should be at the heart of your quest to build a happy and productive life. It is a question that every human being should give deep thought to throughout her or his life.

Socrates famously said, "An unexamined life is not worth living." (Actually, it was Plato, quoting his teacher, Socrates.) Gloria Steinem, in *Revolution From Within* (see Bibliography), talks about a long period in her life during which she consciously resisted such self-examination:

> I continued in this way for decades while pressures grew. . . I organized and traveled and lectured; I campaigned and raised contributions and solicited ads to keep [*Ms.* magazine] going; I turned my apartment into a closet where I changed clothes and dumped papers into cardboard boxes; and I only once in twenty years spent an entire week without getting on a plane. But at home or away, I often awoke with sweaty palms and a pounding heart, worried that I was going to mess up some public event, fail to find enough money to pay the printer and meet the payroll, or otherwise let down this movement. . . .

She further recalls, "When my friends asked about my state of mind or emotions, I made them laugh—and despair—by turning Plato on his head. 'The examined life,' I explained, 'is not worth living.'" Despite her jokes, however, she reports having felt "burnt out many times" during this long period, and "like a soldier who is wounded but won't lie down for fear of dying."

I'm of two minds about Steinem's story. On the one hand, there's no question that she paid a terrible personal price for her activism: decades of anxiety and self-denial. On the other hand, there's also no question that she was spectacularly effective. Along with her feminist colleagues, she transformed our culture and politics in ways that have improved life for hundreds of millions of women and men in North America and around the world. It's sometimes hard to remember how difficult things were for women before the second wave of feminism ushered in by Steinem and her colleagues, but here's a sampling: employers routinely discriminated against women both in hiring and in pay; women were often fired from jobs simply for marrying or becoming pregnant; many schools provided little or nothing in the way of athletics programs for girls; many banks wouldn't lend money to unmarried women or to married women without their husband's approval; and behavior that we now consider sexual harassment or even rape was considered socially acceptable.

Steinem and her colleagues were largely responsible for changing all of that, but many of them, including Steinem herself, paid a heavy personal price for devoting their lives to activism. Was it worth it? Steinem doesn't address this question directly in her book, but I suspect her answer would be "Yes." (And as a direct beneficiary of this liberation, I can only say "thank you.")

What if, however, Steinem had achieved less than she had? What if, like most activists, she had achieved *much* less? Because, let's face it: Steinem was a superstar. Through some combination of talent and luck, she was able to achieve vastly more than most activists, even activists who make a comparable or greater personal sacrifice. Most activists have to content themselves with creating a relatively small amount of social change, although those changes add up, of course, and also provide the context in which the occasional big change can happen. And some so-called "small changes" can make a huge difference in the life of an afflicted or oppressed individual and, hence, are not really small at all.

It's not just true for activism, it's also true for sports, business, art and any other human endeavor: most people are not superstars, most change happens in small increments, and those increments are often achieved only after substantial personal sacrifice.

So, imagine that you are an "ordinary" activist. You've worked for years or decades on an important cause, enduring poverty, isolation, disapproval from family and community, and the depression and (sometimes) trauma that comes from being a constant witness to society's evils. In other words, you've made the usual sacrifices that activists make and endured the usual things they endure. But you haven't achieved a vast amount of liberation, or even a little liberation. Maybe you've just held the line against one small evil. Or maybe, despite your best efforts, the line moved backwards.

Were your years or decades of sacrifice worth it?

Objectively, it is clear from history that even small changes are meaningful. In *Bury the Chains: Prophets and Rebels in the Fight to Free an Empire's Slaves* (Boston: Houghton Mifflin, 2005), Adam Hochschild describes how a tiny group of "superstar" abolitionists, including Granville Sharp, Thomas Clarkson, John Newton and former slave Olaudah Equiano, was responsible for the historic evil of slavery being banned not just in England but indirectly around the world, and in little more than a hundred years. But that group, he repeatedly emphasizes, was supported by the work of thousands of other activists who were doing pretty much what activists continue to do to this day: holding demonstrations, giving speeches, writing letters, doing legislative work, speaking through the press, providing financial support, selling socially-conscious products (for instance, the famed "Am I not a man and a brother?"–inscribed Wedgewood medallion), and risking life and liberty taking direct action to help individual slaves. The vast majority of these activists are unknown to history, and yet, working alongside the superstars, they halted one of history's most monumental evils.

On a non-objective, more personal level, the answer to the question of whether your sacrifice was worth it depends on the answer to this one: *Who are you?*

This section of *The Lifelong Activist* is devoted to helping you answer that question.

CHAPTER 2

More Questions . . .

The tough question asked in the last chapter was:

> **Imagine you are an activist who has sacrificed years or decades for a cause, and has achieved a non-spectacular result. Was your sacrifice worth it?**

As discussed, the answer lies in the answer to this more fundamental question: Who are you?

Ask a group of activists whether a decades-long sacrifice for non-spectacular results was worth it, and you will get a spectrum of answers. Some will emphatically say, "Yes, it was." Others will just as emphatically say, "No, it wasn't." And many others will answer somewhere in the middle.

Moreover, everyone will have a different reason for her or his answer. Some will say "Yes" because they see activism as an inherently difficult challenge in which you shouldn't expect to achieve a dramatic result—although it's nice when it happens. Others will say "Yes" because they see the activist life as its own reward. And still others will say yes for some other reason entirely.

The people who answer "No" will offer similarly diverse reasons.

Actually, the question "Was it worth it?", lacking nuance and specificity, isn't very useful. Here are some more useful ones:

- What specifically was the nature of your sacrifice?
- What specifically was the nature of your achievement?
- Could you have somehow reduced the level of sacrifice without compromising your achievement?

- Could you have somehow increased the amount you achieved without increasing your level of sacrifice beyond what you were willing to accept?

You won't be able to answer these questions for some hypothetical example, or for someone else's career (like Steinem's). But you can look back on your own activist career and answer them—and doing so is the very first step to Managing Your Mission.

So, set aside some time, find yourself a quiet place to think and write, and do the following Activist Project Histories exercise.

EXERCISE

Activist Project Histories

Choose two or three of the most important activist projects you've worked on over the past few years, and, for each, answer the questions below in as much detail as possible. *It's a good idea to select not just projects you consider "successes," but at least one you consider a "failure," as we often learn more from our so-called "failures" than our "successes."* (The words "success" and "failure", and their derivatives, are in quotes throughout *The Lifelong Activist* for reasons that will become clear in Part III.)

- What was the project's goal?
- What was your role in the project?
- How did you get involved in the project?
- What did you like about the project?
- What did you dislike about the project?
- Was the project successful?
- What result was achieved?
- How could that result have been improved?
- Could the result have been achieved more easily? (Or more quickly and/or cheaply?) If so, how?
- What talents or skills of yours were used in this project? How were they used?
- What talents and skills of yours were not used? Why not?

- What personal result (i.e., experience, information, contacts, career advancement) did you get from the project?
- How could that personal result have been improved?
- How could your own work on the project have been improved?
- Which parts of the project did you *most* enjoy working on? Why?
- Which parts did you *least* enjoy working on, or not enjoy at all? Why?
- What sacrifices did you make in other areas of your life to do this project?
- How did you feel about those sacrifices at the time?
- How do you feel about them now? Looking back, were they worth it? Should you have sacrificed less or more than you did?
- Did participating in the project harm you in any way? If so, how?
- Would you do a project like this one again? Why or why not?
- If so, what changes would you make, either in the project itself, or in your life outside the project?

Some tips for completing the Activist Project Histories are provided in the next chapter.

CHAPTER 3

Tips for Completing the Activist Project Histories

1. **Answer Each Question as Thoroughly as Possible**

    It's important to answer each question as thoroughly as possible because your answers will serve as the raw material for your Personal Mission Statement (see Chapter 17), a statement of values and purpose that you can use to plan and organize your life, and the more you write, the more you will have to work with. (If you don't like to write, the next tip may help you get over that hurdle.)

2. **Format Doesn't Matter**

    It doesn't matter if your answers are in paragraph, list, narrative or some other format. Just get the information down as easily as possible. And don't worry about grammar or spelling; you're not showing your Activist Project Histories to anyone. (See #6, below.)

3. **Don't Rush It**

    Take as much time as you need to complete your Activist Project Histories. At the same time, don't obsess over details or aim for perfection. As you will learn in Part III, perfectionism is always the enemy, so just write as much as you can *easily* in answer to each question before moving on to the next.

    It's a good idea, after you've finished writing, to set aside your Activist Project Histories for a week or two. Then return to them and look at them with fresh eyes. See if you can add to, or clarify, what you have written.

4. **Get Specific**

    Don't just say a project was successful or unsuccessful: write down why, and what exactly was and was not accomplished. If you can quantify any "successes" or "failures," so much the better.

    Don't just say a project used a certain skill of yours: give an example of how the skill was used. And don't just say you screwed something up: write down how. Whenever possible, your points should be substantiated with a specific example.

5. **Ask Others for Their Input—But *Only* After You've Finished Writing**
It's great to get input from mentors, colleagues, family and friends; and what they say may pleasantly surprise you, since others often rate our achievements higher than we ourselves do. But only approach them after you've finished getting your own thoughts down on paper. You don't want their thoughts to prematurely influence your own.

6. **Don't Show Your Activist Project Histories to Anyone Else**
It's hard to be completely honest if there's even the slightest chance someone else will see your Activist Project Histories, so make a pledge to yourself that you won't show them to anyone.

And, finally, the most important instruction of all:

7. **Be Honest and Objective**
Honesty and objectivity are key, because only honesty will lead you to a valid Personal Mission Statement. Being honest is also harder to do than it sounds, since most of us have trouble being objective about our own life story and the situations we find ourselves in.

Chapters 4, 5 and 6 will tell you how to do it.

CHAPTER 4

How to Tell the (Absolute) Truth

To create really useful Activist Project Histories, you have to tell as close to the absolute, objective, unvarnished, "microscopic" truth as possible.

This is harder to do than it sounds.

All kinds of things stand in the way of our telling the truth, including: strong negative or positive emotions surrounding a situation; a tendency to overemphasize a situation's good or bad aspects; myths, clichés and stereotypes surrounding our work; and a tendency toward generalization and oversimplification.

Here are some tips for getting past these and other barriers:

Learn Not to Self-Censor

We often self-censor when we believe our thoughts or feelings are somehow unacceptable. What I have seen from working with my students is that most people self-censor a lot, in big and little ways.

You may, for instance, start to write that you hated having to call up strangers for a get-out-the-vote project. That feeling strikes you as unworthy of a "true" activist, however, so you mentally correct (i.e., self-censor) it by thinking, "Wait a minute! If I'm really an activist, I shouldn't mind making a few calls."

Just write, "I hated calling strangers."

Or, you may start to write that you hated working with a certain person. That feeling strikes you as unacceptable, however, so you mentally correct (i.e., self-censor) it by thinking, "How could I hate that person? She's a famous, brilliant, important activist, and I learned so much from working with her. So what if she has a temper?"

Just write, "I hated working with her and her obnoxious temper."

Don't censor your positive feelings, either. If you start to write, "I loved having the summer off. It was great taking a break from activism," but then start to self-censor it by thinking, "I should be committed enough to my cause to never want any time off," just write, "I loved taking a break."

Or, if you start to write, "I loved creating the posters and other artwork for the event," but then catch yourself starting to self-censor by thinking, "Aw, that was just stupid, silly stuff. Other parts of the project were much more important," just write, "I loved creating the artwork."

Always write the absolute truth in your Activist Project Histories, even if that truth makes you feel guilty, embarrassed or ashamed. Remember that your feelings are always valid, even if they don't meet your own or someone else's standard of seriousness, appropriateness or ideological purity.

Head vs. Heart? Heart Wins

If you study the previous examples, you will see that frequently a strong and honest feeling is obscured by an intellectualization or rationalization. So, "That other activist was obnoxious, and I hated working for her," gets obscured by layers of rationalization about how brilliant and dedicated the activist was, and how much you learned from working with her.

We often try to intellectualize or rationalize away feelings or thoughts we feel are unacceptable or inappropriate. Try not to do this, as it is one of the most fundamental forms of self-denial. In other words, if there's a conflict between what your heart (your feelings) and your head (your intellect) are telling you, go with your heart.

Your heart often speaks in a softer voice than your head, and you may need to slow down and stay quiet to hear it. Just concentrate on your feelings, including your physical feelings. If thinking about a certain situation makes you physically tense or even physically ill, that's obviously a warning sign. Conversely, if thinking about a situation causes you to burst out into a big smile, that's obviously a very positive sign. Your brain may leap in and try to cover up whatever it is you are feeling, but don't let it.

Watch Out for "Shoulds" and "Shouldn'ts"

If you catch yourself thinking things like . . .

- "I should have done more work on that project."
- "I should have given more money to that cause."
- "I should have stood up for myself more when talking with that opponent."
- "I shouldn't have taken the night off to be with my friends."
- "I shouldn't have bought that new coat."

. . . the very next thing you should do is ask yourself, "Why? Why should (or shouldn't) I have . . .". It may be that you're right: you should or should not have done the act in question. But it is also very possible that what you did was quite okay, and this "should" and "shouldn't" stuff is pure pointless self-criticism and Monday morning quarterbacking.

As you will learn in Part III, criticizing yourself because you didn't act perfectly is a destructive habit.

If you're oppressed by a "should" or "shouldn't" statement, try repeating it a few times in your mind. Whose voice do you hear saying it? Is it yours? Or is it your Mom's or Dad's? Your partner's? Some other activist's? Or someone else's? Once you know who, specifically, is "scolding" you, you can often then figure out whether he or she is making a valid point or just trying to manipulate you into acting according to his or her agenda.

Embrace Complexity and Contradiction

Most of your projects will have both positive and negative aspects, and include elements of both success and failure. Try to capture all of these contradictory aspects and don't worry about reconciling them or coming to some kind of artificial, oversimplified conclusion. So, instead of just writing, "I hated working for low pay," write, "I loved doing activism full-time, I loved most of my colleagues, I thought my boss was OK—but I didn't like working for low pay. Actually, I didn't mind the low pay so much as not having health benefits. That really screwed me up when I got into that accident with my bike."

Avoid Preconceptions, Clichés and Stereotypes

Many of us also have bought into the many clichés and stereotypes surrounding activism. You may believe, for instance, that . . .

- All activist work, no matter how difficult and unrewarding, and no matter how meager the result achieved, is inherently worthwhile.
- Activism is supposed to be difficult or unpleasant.
- Activists are supposed to be suffer.
- Someone who has suffered discrimination or oppression has an automatic pass to be obnoxious or hard to work with.

Try to get past preconceptions, clichés and stereotypes such as these, so that you can record your honest experiences and feelings about your work. One key here is to listen to your "heart" voice, as discussed above.

CHAPTER 5

Honesty vs. Burnout

Why is telling the truth so important? Because honesty is a preventative of, and antidote to, **burnout**. Here's a definition of burnout:

> **Burnout is the act of *involuntarily* leaving activism, or reducing one's level of activism.**

Note the word "involuntarily." Someone who makes a conscious decision to do less activism, either because her life priorities have changed or because she's tired and needs to take a break, is not burning out: she is making a wise choice.

But, let's face it: most people seem to leave activism involuntarily, and that's a problem on many levels. When an activist burns out, she typically derails her career and damages her self-esteem and relationships. She also deprives her organization and movement of her valuable experience and wisdom. The worst problem, however, may be that when an activist burns out she deprives younger activists of a mentor, thus making *them* more likely to burn out. And so it's a vicious circle, with burnout leading to more burnout.

No one knows exactly how many activists burn out each year but the number must be very high. (One indicator is the high employee and volunteer turnover rates in most activist organizations.) To picture how great a loss this represents, imagine how different, and how much better, the world would be if there were just twice as many activists out there as there are now. That's twice as many campaigners for peace and justice, the environment, sustainable agriculture, labor, corporate accountability, gender equality, racial equality and other progressive movements. And then, imagine if all of those activists were happy and effective and enjoying long careers. It would make a huge difference.

Now, imagine if we were able to really lick this burnout thing and there were *ten times* as many happy, productive activists as there are now. That means, basically, that everyone who does activism in their teens and early twenties continues to do it, in some form, throughout their lives. ("Ten" is a guess, but a conservative one, I think. The ratio of younger to older activists could be up around twenty-to-one or thirty-to-one or even higher.)

Life would improve dramatically for perhaps every living thing on the planet.

That is why it is imperative that all activists work to self-actualize: so that we can prevent burnout in ourselves, and help prevent it in others.

As an activist, you probably see burnout all around you: activists leaving activist work, or staying in it but doing a crappy, half-hearted job. (I call the latter "passive burnout.") Burnout is so common that it sometimes seems like an inevitable consequence of activist work. It isn't, however: it is an entirely avoidable phenomenon. Burnout can have many causes, but perhaps the most common is this:

> **Burnout is caused by living a life in conflict with your values and needs.**[1]

When I say "living a life in conflict with your values," I am not accusing you of being a bad activist. For all I know, you're a terrific activist, and whether you are or not, I know you're doing your best, as are we all. What I'm talking about is a failure to create a life for yourself that reflects who you are as an activist and a complex, multidimensional human being. People make this mistake for all kinds of reasons, including:

- They don't know they are supposed to consciously build a life around their values and needs.
- They do know, but don't know how.
- They let others control their time and priorities.
- They have emotional or other barriers to success.
- They are overly focused on one area of their lives, such as activism or a relationship, to the exclusion of other important areas.

Some of these reasons may seem better, or nobler, than others. The problem, however, is that **living a life in conflict with your values, and where your needs aren't being met, no matter how noble your reason for doing so, is an energy-draining, soul-sucking experience that almost always leads to burnout.**

The Cure for Burnout

The only cure for this kind of burnout is to be truthful about who you are, what your values are and what your needs are, and to start reorganizing your life around that truth. You may have a romantic fantasy of sacrificing your all to save the world the way Gloria Steinem did, but if you're not the kind of person who can remain effective while enduring decades of deprivation—and few of us are—you'll probably fail at that unrealistic goal and simply burn out.[2]

Once you come up with your Personal Mission Statement, your next step is to *live* that Statement, which brings us to another common cause of burnout:

> **Burnout can also be caused by the perception that you have been working too hard, or sacrificing too much, for too small a result.**

The word "perception" is significant, as it is our perceptions, as much as or more than the actual facts, that often determine our level of satisfaction or dissatisfaction with a particular situation or outcome. Your Personal Mission Statement will help you identify what level of sacrifice you are prepared to make for your activist career, what level of success you hope to achieve, and whether those expectations are realistic.

CHAPTER 6

Three More Facts About Burnout

A large fraction of my activist and other students were experiencing burnout by the time they took my classes. From witnessing them, discussing their experiences with them, and from my own research, I have concluded these three things about burnout:

1. **Burnout is a Process**

   It typically starts small and gets worse. Sometimes it happens quickly, and a person who was perfectly happy doing activism a month ago suddenly wakes up one morning and realizes he can no longer stand it. Usually, however, it happens slowly, over a period of years or decades.

2. **Events Don't Cause Burnout—It Always Comes from Within**

   Often there appears to be a precipitating event that leads to a case of burnout, such as a failed campaign or a fight with a colleague. Sometimes it's a personal event such as an eviction notice or relationship break-up.

   In cases such as these, it is tempting to come up with a simple cause-and-effect explanation for the burnout, but such an explanation is usually not accurate. Because burnout is a process, often what appears to be the precipitating event is really just the last straw: in other words, the person was mostly burned out before the event even happened and, being burned out, lacked the resiliency or will to cope with the crisis and carry on with his activism. Often, the event merely serves as a convenient excuse for doing what the activist has been wanting to do anyway.

   For all the activists who burn out, however, there are others who keep on doing their activism despite having many other personal and professional commitments. And there are many activists, especially in the developing world, who keep on doing their activism even in the face of horrendous persecution and personal risk. When you ask these activists how they can keep on doing their activism, they often respond something like this: *How could I stop? This is who I am. I wouldn't feel right if I didn't do it.* In other words, their activist work doesn't drain them; it sustains them.

For activism to be sustaining, it has to derive from your values and also occupy the right place in your life. If you are an activist who is feeling burned out, your challenge will be to figure out what type of activism is right for you, and where that activism fits in with your other priorities. Coming up with your Personal Mission Statement using the process described in this part of *The Lifelong Activist* will help.

3. **Burnout Often Happens at a Subconscious or Semi-Conscious Level**
    Often, we're not really aware that we're burning out. We may not be aware that we're in a bad mood a lot of the time, or that we're not getting as much work done as we used to. Or we may be aware of these symptoms, but not recognize them as symptoms. Or we may recognize them as symptoms, but of the wrong problem.

    That last one happens all the time and it's a real pickle. Obviously, if you misdiagnose a problem, then you're not going to be likely to solve it— and a misapplied "solution" can even make things worse. Many burned-out and burning-out activists, for example, misidentify their problem as laziness, lack of commitment or lack of discipline. Their solution—to try to work harder—often makes them feel even more burned-out than before.

    The vast majority of burned-out activists are not lazy. They are not uncommitted. They are not undisciplined. They are, in contrast, some of the most energetic, committed and disciplined people around. They are, however, blocked from using their energy and talents in the service of their movement; and the block is invariably caused by trying to live a conflicted life where one's actions do not derive from one's values and needs.

    The solution, once more, is honesty: about yourself, your situation and your needs. So, let's return to your Activist Project Histories, and, in particular, to what may be your toughest honesty-related challenge: facing up to "bad news."

CHAPTER 7

How to Handle Uncomfortable Truths

You are likely, in the process of doing your Activist Project Histories, to uncover lots of gratifying information about your talents, skills and accomplishments. Unfortunately, you are also likely to uncover some "uncomfortable truths." You may discover, for example, that:

- You are not as committed to activism, or to your cause, as you thought. (Maybe you have other priorities right now. Or maybe you're just exhausted.)
- Or, conversely, you are *more* committed to activism than you realized. (And, therefore, you should be doing even more of it than you are doing now. And how are you going to do that while continuing to earn a living and take care of your loved ones?)
- You have stronger materialistic cravings than you previously thought. (You really would like a nice car, new clothes or a bigger apartment. Or maybe you are just tired of living hand-to-mouth.)
- You would like to have more fun. (But how can you possibly take a night off, or a few nights off, when there are suffering people and/or animals out there who need you?)
- Your desire to do activism is partly rooted in your "selfish" personal needs or insecurities. (You want everyone to think you're cool, or sensitive, or super-committed. Or, you like it when your activist ideals and lifestyle get under your parents' skin.)
- You have questions about the validity of your cause. (You're no longer sure whether it's completely in the right.)
- You are no longer committed to the organization you are working for. (You don't like the people or their approach.)
- You're not as good an activist as you thought. (You're not good at certain key skills, such as talking about your cause without annoy-

ing people. Or, you haven't really accomplished that much relative to all the time and effort you've put in.)

- You haven't really done as much activism as you thought. (So, what have you *really* been spending your time on, all these years?)

Confronting uncomfortable truths such as these can cause sadness, shame, guilt, regret and other negative emotions. It's important, however, not to give in to these. The way to handle uncomfortable truths is as follows:

1. **Don't feel bad! Congratulate yourself, instead!**
   Confronting the truth about oneself is hard, gutsy work. Many people can't do it, and many, perhaps most, don't even try. So give yourself a lot of credit. Recognize that all of the so-called terrible things you are learning about yourself are not terrible at all (see Points 2 and 3), and that they don't mean that you are a bad or uncommitted activist. Also remember that this process, painful as it may be, will ultimately lead to your becoming a better activist and a happier, more fulfilled person.

2. **Don't judge yourself harshly.**
   Many of us seem to believe that if we just criticize ourselves enough, we will be motivated to change our bad habits. The truth is, however, that self-criticism almost never works. In fact, as you will learn in Part III, it usually backfires. So, try not to indulge your habit of self-criticism, and instead seek to compassionately observe your failures and limitations without feeling bad about them.

3. **Remember to look at the big picture.**
   In Part III, I devote an entire chapter to negativity, a self-sabotaging habit that many people are prone to. Negativists, as I call them, tend to be unduly harsh on themselves for their perceived failures or shortcomings, and also to blow them way out of proportion. They also tend to minimize, or not even acknowledge, their achievements and strengths. Negativism will really undermine you, so avoid it, and strive to keep a balanced view of your successes and failures.

4. **Talk to someone else.**
   Because many of us are negativists, it's often helpful to get a second opin-

ion from a supportive mentor, colleague or friend. Often that opinion will be more balanced than our own, and can help us keep our "failures" and limitations, as well as "successes" and strengths, in perspective.

And, finally:

5. **Consult a professional.**
    If you are finding it really difficult to cope with your unpleasant truths, please consult a mentor, therapist, coach, spiritual counselor or other advisor.

The goal, as always, is honesty, or, to put it another way, objectivity. You want your Activist Project Histories to accurately reflect the entire spectrum of your achievements, "failures," "successes," strengths and weaknesses.

EXERCISE

Return to your Activist Project Histories and see if they are objective representations of your experiences and feelings. In particular:

- See if there are any achievements you've omitted or underemphasized.
- See if there are any uncomfortable truths you've omitted or under- or over-emphasized.

If so, rewrite the document so that your experiences and feelings are more accurately and objectively conveyed.

CHAPTER 8

The Importance of Focus/Creating Your Activism Goals List

Once you've completed your Activist Project Histories, you should set them aside for a while. Spend the next two or three weeks giving your brain a rest and allowing some of the insights you've gained to settle in. Treat yourself well, and if you've got the money for it, buy yourself a little present. Absolutely no guilt or remorse allowed after the purchase! This is a reward for a job well done.

After you've rested, return to your Activist Project Histories. Now, your goal will be to review what you have written with the aim of determining which activist movement and which type of activism you should be working on. That's right: singular "movement" and singular "type of activism." In general, you should focus most of your efforts on one activist movement and, within that movement, on one type of activist work, be it electioneering, legislation, community education, running a shelter or sanctuary, guerrilla art or theater, letter-writing or something else. That doesn't mean that you should just be doing that one activity: it means you ought to be doing that activity and all the other activities needed to support it. If, for instance, you're focusing on community education via tabling and demonstrations, you're probably also going to need to: manage your volunteers, do publicity, create posters and other artwork, build coalitions with other groups, negotiate with the people you're targeting (and maybe law enforcement), solicit funds and materials donations, follow up with those who sign up for more information, and many other tasks.

Focusing is crucial because it takes a huge amount of time and effort even to do one seemingly "simple" thing, like a demonstration, well and completely. Many activists are so busy bouncing from one movement to the next, or one type of activism to the next, that they don't have the time or energy to do a great job at any of their activities. That's a shame, because great activism is *way* more effective at creating social change than merely good activism.

Activist Henry Spira even came up with name for unproductive workaholic activist behavior, "hyperactivism," which he defined in an article in *Satya* as "the phenomenon of doing without achieving." He asks, speaking about the animal rights movement in particular, "How can so many activists with so many resources achieve so little?" He offers several answers, including that, "Campaigns . . . have evolved into mindless rituals without beginning or end."

Don't fall into the hyperactivist trap of thinking that if you're not rushing around every minute of the day, you're wasting time/uncommitted/lazy, etc. Quantity is not the sign of a good activist, quality is: quality of work, quality of professional and personal relationships, and quality of outcomes. And you don't achieve a quality result by spreading yourself too thin.

More on workaholism in the next chapter.

Focus to Avoid Burnout

Here are other reasons why focusing is important:

1. Transitions are wasteful. Every time you switch between movements or types of projects, you lose time and energy.
2. Working in too many movements, or on too many types of projects, means that you will probably have to manage unwieldy amounts of information and people.
3. By focusing, you'll gain deep expertise in whatever type of activism you are doing—expertise that will help make you an even more effective activist.
4. Because of your expertise, you'll attract other experts. Therefore, you'll probably make many more valuable contacts and connections as a specialist than as a generalist. And, finally,
5. Focusing will lower your stress level. This is particularly true if you've been rushing around trying to do too many things at once. After you focus, you'll have less to do, so you'll be able to take a breather when you need it.

Professionals in many fields, including medicine, law, science and technology, become specialists in order to have a successful career in which they can achieve a lot without becoming too stressed. You should be a specialist, too. Even though focusing on one movement and type of activism may initially seem constricting, it is actually very liberating. You'll be able to do a great job, and see many positive results from your activism, while at the same time living a balanced life. And instead of being burned out, you'll wake up each morning rested and recharged and rarin' to go.

Budgeting Your Time

Above, I said that you should focus most of your efforts on one activist movement. So what does "most" mean? There are no hard and fast rules, but I'm going to suggest you spend 80 percent of the time you devote to activism working in your chosen movement, and the remaining 20 percent working in a different movement.

You always want to spend some time working in another movement because, by doing so, you'll get to form the kinds of linkages and coalitions that are vital to effecting broad social change. Also, you'll get to "cross-pollinate"—exchange useful and empowering ideas, information and insights with activists in the other movement.

Needless to say, all of your activist work should be done in the context of a larger strategy aimed at achieving a defined and important goal. That goal could be something like:

- I want to help get at least **20 percent more** Democratic or Green candidates elected to state and local offices in my state over the next **five years**.
- I want to help **at least three** town governments in my state increase the amount of conservation and recycling they do, so that their energy use and solid waste production are **cut in half** over the next **ten years**.
- I want to get vegetarian options added to **all** elementary, middle and high school lunches in my state by the year **2012**.

Note the highlighted words: "20 percent more," "at least three," "cut in half," and "all." Good goals, as you will learn in Chapter 18, are quantified. Also note, "five years," "ten years," and "2012." Good goals are also deadlined.

Many activists make the mistake of working on activities that are not linked to a defined goal, with the sad result that, even if they do good work, their efforts don't result in much social change. The way to avoid this painful mistake is to take strategy seriously and work with other activists who do the same. Books such as Randall Kehler, Andrea Ayvazian and Ben Senturia's *Thinking Strategically: a Primer on Long-Range Strategic Planning for Grassroots Peace and Justice Organizations* (Amherst, MA: Peace Development Fund, n.d.) and Kim Bobo, Jackie Kendall and Steve Max's *Organize!— Organizing for Social Change: Midwest Academy Manual for Activists* (Santa Ana, CA: Seven Locks Press, 2001) are good places to start.

When you choose a primary and secondary movement, and a specific type of activism, to focus on, that doesn't mean you have to stay with those choices forever. Your interests may, and probably will, take you in a different direction later on. So don't worry that by focusing you are making a life-defining choice. You are just making a choice that is going to make you much more effective in the short term.

Focus, by the way, happens on multiple levels. There's the "macro" level of focusing mainly on one movement at a time. Then there's the "micro" level of focusing mainly on one type of activism within that movement at a time. And finally, there's the "nano" level of focusing on one task at a time. Here's what the late Peter S. Drucker, the world's most famous management guru, said about nano-focus in his classic book *The Effective Executive* (see Bibliography):

> **If there is any one "secret" of effectiveness, it is concentration. Effective executives do first things first and they do one thing at a time. . . . This is the "secret" of those people who "do so many things" and apparently so many difficult things. They do only one thing at a time. As a result, they need much less time in the end than the rest of us.**

It's just as true for activists as for businesspeople.

How to Choose

If you're lucky, you'll feel a strong emotional pull toward one particular movement and type of activism. If not—if you feel pulled in several directions at once—you have two valuable resources that will help you choose: your Activist Project Histories and your mentors.

So, go back and review your Activist Project Histories, asking yourself these questions:

- **Which movement or cause did you most like working on? [Note: not necessarily the one you considered most important.]** Was it gay rights, labor, environmentalism, antiglobalization, transparency in government, poverty reduction, fair housing, antiwar, animal rights/animal welfare or something else?
- **What type of work did you most like doing? [Ditto.]** Was it electioneering? Organizing and running demos? Legislative work? Building websites? Door-to-door canvassing? Guerrilla art and/or theater? Letter-writing? Something else?
- **What type of organization did you most like being part of?** [Ditto.] Big or small? National or grassroots? Hierarchical or flat? Majoritarian or consensus decision-making?
- **Which role did you most like taking on? [Ditto.]** Did you like working independently or as part of a team? How big a team? Did you like being a leader or coordinator, or did you prefer to let someone else handle that role?

Now go back beyond your Activist Project Histories, to your earliest activist experiences, the ones you landed in almost by accident back when you didn't really know that what you were doing was called "activism." And then look back even beyond that, to your childhood. Often in our early years we express our true passions, which we then tend to lose track of as we get older and busier. For example, as a child I was always deeply passionate about, and concerned for, the animals in my life and animals in general. As an adult, I did many other kinds of activism, but it wasn't until I started doing animal activism that my activism truly began to feel like a comfortable "fit" and extension of my core values. Animal activism very quickly took me deeper into activism than any of my previous activist experiences, and I was more effective at it as well. I wish I had returned to this childhood passion earlier.

Next, talk to mentors. (More on how to find and work with mentors in Part III, Chapter 26.) This is actually a vital step to take at any pivotal stage of your career—or, more precisely, at every stage of your career. Review the conclusions you've drawn from your Activist Project Histories with them and see if they agree. In particular, ask them what talents, skills and resources they think you have that you might have missed; and also which skills they think you need to improve.

There's one more important question you need to consider as you plan your activist career: **how much activism do you really want to do?** I discuss that one in the next chapter.

EXERCISE

Activism Goals List

After carefully reviewing your Activist Project Histories and talking with your mentors, write down the answers to these questions relative to the primary activist movement you wish to be working on:

- Which activist movement would you like to focus on?
- What type of activism would you like to focus on?
- What goal (quantified and deadlined) would you like to see result from your activism?
- What type of organization would you most like to be part of?
- What role would you most like to assume?

Please answer each question in as much detail as possible.

Then answer the same questions for your secondary (coalition-building) movement.

We'll call this document your Activism Goals List.

Remember that your answers to this and the other Goals exercises in *The Lifelong Activist* are not meant to be set in stone. You're simply taking your best guess as to what you want to be doing in the future, and you can always change your mind later. Planning should be a fun, low-stress activity, almost a game, so don't get nervous over it.

CHAPTER 9

How Much Activism Do You Really Want to Do?

Many activists, and especially many young activists, see the enormous amount of injustice and suffering in the world and conclude that their only moral choice is to devote their lives 100 percent to activism. These activists tend to see all activities other than activism as a waste and a distraction. They also often scorn the easier types of activism, choosing instead to plunge themselves directly into the most difficult and dangerous aspects of the struggle.

There are several problems with this viewpoint, beginning with the fact that no one can devote 100 percent of their time to activism or any other activity. We are all human beings with a minimum set of human needs—to be fed, clothed, rested and sheltered—that consumes many hours a day. This may seem like a small point, but these tasks are essential and if you stint on them to devote more time to your activism, you probably won't function well either as an activist or a human being. Eating junk food, going without sleep, skipping medical appointments and ignoring other personal needs are common ways activists stint on the essentials.

Another problem is that most of us have needs that go well beyond the minimum. We want our bodies to be not just fed and rested, but healthy and fit. We want not just to endure in isolation, but to be part of a sustaining social network. We want our living situation to offer not just safety and protection, but a measure of comfort. And many of us also have important intellectual, creative, cultural, spiritual and other needs.

Many activists try to deny their personal needs so that they can focus more intently on their activism, but in my experience and (especially) that of my students, that strategy never works well. These activists tend to feel progressively more deprived, and progressively less happy, until they eventually burn out.

Please note that I am *not* arguing in favor of a bourgeois or materialistic life. Nor am I arguing against a lifestyle in which the activist lives humbly and buys as little as possible. As mentioned in the Introduction, I advocate only that people build lives for themselves that derive from, and reflect, their innermost values.

It is a problem when an activist makes choices out of guilt or shame, or to fit in with a certain crowd. It is also a problem when an activist succumbs to behavior that in any other field would be considered workaholism. **Workaholism is an addictive behavior in which you work excessive hours largely as a means of avoiding having to deal with stresses or problems in your life, and especially in your personal life.** Not everyone who works long hours is a workaholic, but many people who do are.

Workaholics usually have lots of good excuses to justify their long workweeks. A workaholic businessperson might say: "I'm providing for my family," "No one else can do what I'm doing," and "This is a once-in-a-lifetime opportunity!" And a workaholic activist might use any of those excuses, or some familiar activist-specific ones: "The cause needs me," or "My sacrifice is nothing compared with that of other activists [or those who are suffering]." Examined closely, however, the workaholic's excuses rarely make sense, especially given that most workaholics tend to work inefficiently. They get less done during their monumental workweeks than well-adjusted people do when working normal, or even light, schedules. Why should a workaholic work more efficiently when wrapping up at 6:00 p.m. simply means that she has a long, leisurely evening ahead of her during which to contemplate her troubled relationship, growing mountain of credit card debt, incipient alcoholism and other problems? If she stays at the office until 10:00 p.m., even if she's doing nothing but shooting the breeze with her coworkers, she can probably manage to avoid thinking about these painful topics.

Workaholics also often claim that their need to work excessive hours is only temporary, but despite that claim, the long workweeks never seem to end. That's because the real reason for the long workweeks is not the stated one, but to help the workaholic avoid dealing with other areas of her life.

How do you know you're making a healthy decision to work long hours, as opposed to an unhealthy, workaholic one? The following table may help:

HEALTHY	WORKAHOLIC / UNHEALTHY
You work from a plan or schedule.	You have no plan or schedule.
You have generally good feelings about your work productivity. Even if others try to throw tons of work at you, you only take on what is reasonable.	You constantly feel besieged, stressed, overworked, under-performing, etc. When others throw work at you, you try to do it all.
You feel good at work and outside of work.	You only feel good at work. OR, you feel bad at work (stressed or under pressure) but worse everywhere else.
You feel rewarded (either monetarily, or through outcomes, personal satisfaction or other means) commensurately with your efforts.	You don't feel you are being rewarded commensurately with your efforts.
You set limits, and make sure your other life needs—health, relationships, money—are being met.	You don't set limits. No matter how much activism you do, it's never enough. Because of this, you sacrifice your other life needs—health, relationships, money—to your activism.
You work because you want to—and your work gives you pleasure.	You work out of guilt, shame, fear, obligation, confusion, or some other negative emotion. Or you work because someone else wants you to do it, or to fit in with a particular crowd.

What it Really Takes to Change the World

Many activists seek to model their careers after those of famous activists such as Gloria Steinem, Martin Luther King, Jr., Mohandas Gandhi, Nelson Mandela, or the nineteenth- and twentieth-century abolitionists, suffragists and labor unionists. There's nothing wrong with that. The only problem is that, often, we don't know what those careers really entailed, and are modeling ourselves after a vague romantic ideal.

If you really want to model yourself after your heroes—hopefully without paying the terrible price many of them did—then at least take that goal seriously. Read their biographies, read histories of their movements and study up on their philosophies, strategies and tactics. You'll see exactly what it takes to accomplish what they accomplished. If you think you have it within you to do the same, then go for it.

Activist and journalist Todd Gitlin, in his terrific book *Letters to a Young Activist* (see Bibliography), offers one clue as to what it takes:

> I knew hundreds of New Leftists, but in the course of a decade I don't think I encountered more than half a dozen who had the personalities for strong political careers—the patience, self-sacrifice, willingness to calculate what is winnable, toleration of small talk, interest in people, capacity to size up people's strengths and weaknesses and to make deals. New Leftists were undisciplined, unruly, talky, frequently narcissistic, ambivalent about politics in the first place. For myself, I would rather have written poetry than knocked on doors in poor neighborhoods.

Nowhere in that passage, you'll note, does he mention subordinating everything else in your life to activism. In fact, many of the qualities he does mention, including patience, toleration of small talk and interest in people, are best cultivated in the context of a well-rounded life. Most of us think of a super-activist as being a super-intelligent, super-visionary, super-passionate and super-hard-working person. Intelligence, vision, passion and hard work are surely important, but they are not enough, and may be not even the most important things.

So, if you want to be a hero, I say go for it—but do it with your eyes open. Understand the nature of the challenge you are taking on, and work with integrity to meet it.

If, after study and reflection, however, you decide that you don't want to sacrifice your all on the altar of your activism, then, first of all, please accept my congratulations. It takes courage to let go of a romantic ideal.

Next, be optimistic. By shedding the ideal, you leave yourself in a much better position to embrace a realistic vision of activism for yourself. You are going to be much more likely to build a lifelong and productive activist career, and much less likely to burn out, than your starry-eyed and workaholic colleagues.

EXERCISE

Reread the Activism Goals List you created in Chapter 8 and make sure that it presents a reasonable set of goals for you to pursue, given your values, needs, situation, talents, resources and willingness to sacrifice.

In particular, see if it reflects an unrealistic romanticized or "heroic" view of activism. If so, rewrite it so that it is more realistic, and the goals you list, attainable.

CHAPTER 10

Health and Fitness

Health is one of those things we tend not to worry about too much when we're young, but that becomes increasingly important as we age. At any age, however, bad physical or emotional health can be a drain on your productivity, and, of course, a blot on your overall happiness. And ongoing neglect of your health can lead to catastrophe.

For these reasons, "self-care," meaning the care and nurturing of your physical and emotional being, should always be your top priority. Although this sounds selfish, it is actually quite practical. By spending a few hours each week maintaining your physical and emotional health, you ensure that you have maximum energy and motivation to devote to working on your activism and other goals.

Self-care includes things like getting good nutrition[3], lots of exercise, lots of sleep and regular medical and dental checkups. It also includes things like therapy (if you need it), maintaining a good social network, and creating a safe and comfortable physical environment for yourself. It also includes making enough money so that you can meet your obligations to yourself and others, and live the kind of lifestyle that makes you happy. And for some people, self-care also includes following an intellectual, creative, spiritual or other practice. (Most of these topics are discussed in more detail in the following chapters.)

Self-care also means dealing with any problems related to your physical or emotional health as quickly as possible. If you currently suffer from any such problems, consult a professional and work on your cure in a committed and decisive way. Health problems can impede your progress every step of the way, and often get worse if left untreated, so please don't ignore them.

EXERCISE

Health & Fitness Goals List

Write down a list of your goals related to your physical and emotional health in as much detail as possible. Don't forget to include . . .

- nutrition
- exercise
- sleep
- medical checkups
- emotional health (i.e., your "issues")

We'll call this document your Health & Fitness Goals List.

Here are some tips for when you create this and the remainder of the Goals Lists I'll be discussing:

First, be sure to be specific. Under "nutrition," for example, don't just write "eat better," write down what, specifically, "eating better" means, i.e.: "cut back on caffeine, stop eating candy, stop drinking soda, stop going to McDonald's for lunch, eat more whole wheat, etc." We'll call those "sub-goals." And no, you don't tackle them all at once. (See below.)

Next, when writing about a behavior you wish to stop, be sure to indicate the behavior you want to replace it. Don't just say you want to stop going to McDonald's for lunch, for instance; say where or what you're going to do instead—i.e., "go to the local soup-and-salad place," or "bring a healthy lunch from home."

And, finally, be sure to prioritize each set of sub-goals. This is because, as Drucker advises, you should only work on one sub-goal at a time. In other words, you should only be working on your most important nutrition, exercise, sleep, physical health and mental health sub-goals, not just because you won't have time to do much more, especially when this Goal List is combined with the Activist and other Goal Lists you'll be creating, but also because, as I'll discuss in Part III, you'll see the best results that way. Only after you achieve a sub-goal should you re-prioritize your list of the remaining subgoals and then focus on the next most important one.

CHAPTER 11

Relationships

"Relationships" is a big, complex topic, which is why Parts IV and V are entirely devoted to it, and some chapters in Parts II and III as well. So what I offer here is just an overview of some very important points designed to help you appreciate the true scope and importance of your relationships in your quest to self-actualize.

First, let's acknowledge that **humans are social animals**. We exist in a web of relationships with other humans, and non-human animals, too. If those relationships are nurturing and supportive, they help us succeed. If they are dysfunctional and destructive, they drag us down. As you have probably seen in your own life and those of the people around you, few things will have more impact on your success or failure than the people you choose to associate with.

There is an article I discuss with the students in almost all of my classes, regardless of the subject matter being taught. It is from the November 7, 2003 *Wall Street Journal*, and its title is, "Expectations May Alter Outcomes Far More Than We Realize." It discusses the large body of research that shows that people's performance is linked to the expectations of those around them. The article quotes Robert Rosenthal, a professor of psychology at the University of California, Riverside:

> Expectation becomes a self-fulfilling prophecy. When teachers have been led to expect better intellectual performance from their students, they tend to get it. When coaches are led to expect better athletic performance from their athletes, they tend to get it. When behavioral researchers are led to expect a certain response from their research subjects, they tend to get it.

Psychologists call this the "expectation effect" or "Pygmalion effect." The article goes on to describe an experiment in this area:

> Elementary-school teachers were told that one group of kids had done extraordinarily well on a test that predicts intellectual "blooming" and so would make remarkable academic gains. The test seemed prescient: after a few months, the "bloomers" it identified had achieved statistically significant gains over the other students. In reality, there was no such test. The kids the teachers thought were bloomers included students from every ability level as measured by a nonverbal intelligence test. So did the supposed nonbloomers. "The only difference was in the mind, and expectations, of the teacher," says Professor Rosenthal.

The lesson is clear: we tend to live up, or down, to the expectations of those around us. **So, no matter how talented or dedicated you are, if you are hanging around people who constantly put you down, or who demean your values, you will be far *less* likely to succeed. But if you are hanging out with people who are supportive—who think you're marvelous and who at least respect, if not agree 100 percent with, your values—you will be far *more* likely to succeed.**

The other reason it's important for you to form healthy relationships is that **your effectiveness as an activist is tied directly to your ability to create and manage quality relationships with other activists, your audience, and even your opposition.** Recall Todd Gitlin's comment, quoted in Chapter 9, about the importance of "people"—oriented qualities such as patience and a tolerance for small talk.

In Peter Singer's biography of animal rights activist Henry Spira, *Ethics Into Action* (see Bibliography), Singer describes Spira's 1975–1977 campaign to convince the Museum of Natural History in New York City to stop conducting cruel research that involved mutilating cats to test their sexual response. A key breakthrough was a surprisingly sympathetic article on the campaign that appeared in *Science*, a magazine one would normally expect to support the vivisectors. Singer quotes the article's author, Nicholas Wade, on Spira:

> I think he was effective because he was such a friendly, outgoing, moderate sort of person. He wasn't strident. He didn't expect you

necessarily to agree with everything he said. But he was very bubbly and full of ideas, and just interesting to listen to. So I found him an engaging character to cover. I thought he had lots of good points, so I was ready to run with them and bounce them off his adversaries.

Spira eventually won that campaign, and went on to win many others.

EXERCISE

Relationships Goals List

Write down a list of your goals related to your relationships, in as much detail as possible. Don't forget to include . . .

- Family relationships
- Intimate relationships
- Relationships with friends
- Relationships with neighbors, classmates and other acquaintances
- Relationships with bosses, teachers and other authority figures
- Relationships with other activists, including mentors
- Relationships with your audience
- Relationships with your opposition
- Relationships with neutral parties

We'll call this document your Relationships Goals List.

CHAPTER 12

Money

True story: one time, I was working with one of my students, trying to help her develop her Personal Mission Statement. I asked her what I thought was a simple question: "How much money do you need to live on?"

Her response was to burst into tears.

No doubt about it: money is an emotionally laden topic for many people. That's especially true in our society, where it is often used as a barometer of a person's intrinsic worth. Money can be a particularly tough topic for activists, who may be deeply acquainted with the inequities and evils inherent in the capitalist system, and yet are forced to live within that system.

Nevertheless, you are a human being with material needs, and those needs must be met, and some of them will require money. My major point in this chapter will be the same as that of every other chapter: that you need to make *conscious* decisions about how you will live your life—decisions based on your values—and then you need to follow through on those decisions. For many activists, this seems harder to do with money than in other areas of life. I explain why in the next chapter, but first let's talk about what poverty is and why it is a problem.

The Problem with Poverty

Poverty is the condition of not being able to get your important needs met, whatever those needs may be. What's "important" is largely, but not entirely, up to you. Everyone needs food, shelter and the other necessities of life—including, I would add for U.S. activists, health insurance.[4] Beyond these necessities, everyone has his or her own list of what's important, be it a nice apartment in a good location, nice clothes, a nice car (or at least a reliable one), great music, great sports or outdoor gear, a gym membership or all of the above.

The problem with poverty is that it is not a viable long-term strategy. While a few years of bohemian poverty can be fun, few people can really tolerate poverty over the long term. Poverty is uncomfortable. It is also time-consuming. (For example, waiting on line at a free clinic, or having to take a ninety-minute bus ride to work every morning.) It saps your energy and, ultimately, limits your options. Not for nothing are the two most common adjectives used to describe extreme poverty "grinding" and "crushing." Poverty wears you down and wears you out.

The situation gets even worse when, as is often the case, you're not just poor, but in debt. Now, the metaphor is drowning, as in "drowning in debt," or "I can't get my head above water." Few situations are more debilitating than chronic debt.

Poverty and debt deplete you, and ultimately sap your ability to do activism or anything else.

Poverty and Age

As bad as poverty and debt are when you're young, they are even worse when you get older. The novelist Robert Musil perhaps put it best: "In every profession that is followed not for the sake of money but for love, there comes a moment when the advancing years seem to be leading into the void."

Remember, from Chapter 9, that list of things that are important to you? It tends to get bigger in middle age, when it might include many of the appurtenances of a middle-class lifestyle, including a comfortable house in a safe neighborhood, a college fund for your kids, a retirement fund for you and the ability to take care of your parents should they need help. All this, by the way, has nothing to do with selling out, and everything to do with common sense, meeting your obligations to yourselves and others and not being a burden on your loved ones. It also has to do with building the kind of happy, stable life that fosters a sustainable and productive activist career.

Of course, you can make choices, lots of choices. You can buy a small house or a co-op, instead of a big house with a big mortgage and big heating bills. You can drive an old car, or not use a car at all. You can have one kid, or no kids, instead of two kids. And you can ask that kid to attend a state college for a couple of years before transferring into the Ivy League. These kinds of compromises are recommended by the authors of two excellent books on money management, *The Millionaire Next Door*[5] and *Rich Dad, Poor Dad* (see Bibliography for both). Every activist should read them.

Even if you strive to live the most frugal lifestyle possible, you will still need money. And let's not forget the possibility, which we all hate to think about, of catastrophic bad luck, like being involved in a serious accident, becoming very sick or being victimized by a crime. Although it sounds callous to mention it, it would be irresponsible not to: money will make your recovery from these and other calamities much easier.

Money and Your Activist Career

To live in unnecessary poverty and debt is a form of denial, and denial is anathema to your goal of building a sustainable activist career. **An important step to building such a career, therefore, is to own up to your present and future financial needs, and acknowledge, once and for all, that you're not some kind of cosmic exception to the universal rule that all humans have material needs and need some kind of stable income to meet them.**

This can be tricky stuff, psychologically. Like my student who burst into tears at the mere mention of the "m-word," you may find it hard to own up to your materialistic side. If you do, it may be because you harbor some of the dysfunctional attitudes toward money I discuss in the next chapter.

CHAPTER 13

Why Are Activists Poor?

Another book I recommend to all my students is *Money Drunk, Money Sober* by Mark Bryan and Julia Cameron (see Bibliography). It discusses how many people become poor because of their dysfunctional (and, as the title implies, addictive) attitudes and behaviors toward money. These "money addicts" fall into several categories, including . . .

- **The Compulsive Spender:** someone who gets an emotional "high" from spending.
- **The Big Deal Chaser:** a gambler who thinks he is always just around the corner from a big win, and so he doesn't worry about managing his money or staying out of debt.
- **The Maintenance Money Drunk:** someone whose expenses keep growing, so she has to keep working harder and harder just to pay the bills.
- **The Poverty Addict:** someone who sees poverty as a virtue.
- **The Cash Codependent:** someone who impoverishes himself by giving money to a money addict.

You probably recognize one or more of these types of "money addiction" either in yourself or in other activists.

Jerrold Mundis, author of the classic debt-recovery book *How to Get Out of Debt, Stay Out of Debt, and Live Prosperously* (see Bibliography), makes the same point:

The core problem is simple: Repeated debt results from dysfunctional (or distorted) attitudes and perceptions about money and self. They are generally subconscious; we don't even realize they're there. Yet they rule our behavior and actions with the power of a dictator. It's essential to recognize them for what they are.

His list of dysfunctional attitudes toward money is longer than Bryan and Cameron's and includes: I Don't Understand Money; When the Going Gets Tough, the Tough Go Shopping; I'm Entitled; Look at Me, Ma, I'm on Top of the World; Money Corrupts (equivalent to Bryan and Cameron's Poverty Addict); $200 Worth of Love; Waiting for Godot (equivalent to The Big Deal Chaser); I'm a Special Case; Good People Help Others; and Yeah But I Still Want to Be a Kid.

Another interesting book is *Why Are Artists Poor?* by Hans Abbing[6] (see Bibliography), an artist and economist at the Erasmus University in Rotterdam, The Netherlands. Abbing takes 367 pages to answer his title question: "Why are artists poor?" I will distill an important part of his answer, relative to activists, into just five words: "Because they choose to be."

This isn't true for all activists, of course—especially not those who were born into poverty, or who suffer from a disability or illness that limits their ability to support themselves. But it is true for a great many activists who were born into middle- or upper-class families but have, in the course of their adult lives, dropped into poverty. Their poverty is voluntary.

I get more push-back from activists on the subject of voluntary poverty than on any other. Some point out that our society makes it extremely hard to earn a living doing activism; others, that there is a long list of employers they cannot work for ethically and jobs they cannot take. Some tell me that they cannot in good conscience participate in a capitalist system. All well and good, and I truly respect anyone who tries to take an ethical approach to earning a living.

At the same time, however, I think it's important to acknowledge that these activists are indeed making choices. I do this not to shame or blame them, but as a way of empowering them to see their situation more clearly, so that they can make even better choices in the future. **"In dreams begin responsibilities," William Butler Yeats said; and if it is our privilege as activists to dream of a better world, it is also our responsibility to do the hard work of figuring out how to integrate our dreams into the real world around us, not only as a means of taking care of ourselves and those whom we love and are responsible for, but as a crucial step toward building that better world we all dream of.**

I also find that many activists are poor for reasons other than ethics.

Even activists with the most stringent ethical requirements should still be able to address these common causes of poverty:

1. **Lack of Information**

   Personal finance is a specialty requiring knowledge of, at the very least, household budgeting, money management and investing. You also need knowledge not just of how to do these things, but the particular options you have for doing them, so that you can make wise choices.

   People who are good with money tend to have made it a priority to acquire this knowledge. They get it from books, magazines, television shows, savvy relatives and friends and professionals.

   People who are bad with money tend to just ignore the whole issue— and become poor as a result.

   Needless to say, if you don't have a lot of money to work with, you need to be even *more* informed about how you handle the small amount you have.

   A good start to correcting this problem would be to read the money-related books listed in the Bibliography.

2. **Lack of Commitment to Money Management**

   Yes, I know: personal finance is about the most boring thing around, and a distraction from your vocation. Still, it is like flossing your teeth: something you should do whether you like it or not.

   Thomas J. Stanley and William D. Danko, the authors of *The Millionaire Next Door*, conducted research that showed that people who are good "accu-mulators of wealth" spend an average of 8.4 hours per month managing their investments, while people who are poor wealth accumulators spend only around 4.6 hours. In other words, the more time you spend managing your money, the more money you are likely to have.

   If you hate the whole topic of personal finance, I suggest taking a Zen approach: delve deeply into it and try to become one with it. Do a lot of reading, take a class, buy (and use) Quicken or another personal finance program, and talk with friends and family members who are good at it. (This could wind up to be a nice bridge-building activity you do with your folks.) You may discover that your dislike of personal finance was actually due to fear and confusion, and that, as you become more knowledgeable, the topic itself becomes more interesting and fun.

   If not, well, sorry: you still have to do it.

3. **The Difficulty of Juggling a Vocation and a Job**

Another reason activists "choose" poverty is because it's hard not to be poor when your vocation (i.e., activism) doesn't pay well—or at all. That often means you'll have to take a day job along with your activism; and holding two jobs, no matter how common a phenomenon in our over-materialistic and wage-depressed society, remains a difficult balancing act.

4. **"Poverty Addiction"**

Are activists "supposed" to be poor? I don't think so. **I hope you understand by now that choosing to be an activist and choosing to be poor are two separate choices, and that choosing poverty will generally make you a worse activist, not a better one.** *Money Drunk, Money Sober* coauthors Bryan and Cameron were not writing specifically about activists, but I suspect that their description of the Poverty Addict category of money addiction will sound very familiar to some readers:

> Repelled by the materialism of the American Dream, we strive for lives of austerity, only to find we have crossed an invisible line and become addicted to self-deprivation.
>
> Lack of money gets us high: we feel martyred, anxious, virtuous, self-righteous and, yes, self-pitying. While smugly judging the "money-grubbing" all around us, we ourselves are ruled by money as well.
>
> Obsessed with judgments of the shallowness around us, we fail to deepen and mature ourselves. In a sense, we remain children acted upon, not acting. Refusing to earn, to own, to husband and nurture our lives, we take spiritual pride in what amounts to an eternal adolescence, refusing to grow up and take responsibility for changing a system we may despise or accepting a world as it is and setting down roots. This would rob us of our position as outsiders, judges, and saints . . .

Ouch!

This is harsh stuff, so I won't comment further, except to urge you to take your time in pondering this and the other information in this chapter, and to be relentlessly honest in determining whether any of it applies to you.

The solution to poverty addiction, according to Bryan and Cameron, is as follows:

> Poverty Addicts need to unhook their sense of virtue from having no money and stop blocking their creativity with worry. . . . [I]t [is] necessary to set out minimums that [you] must spend in order to maintain a sense of health. . . . [There is] an unexpected shift in spiritual consciousness often occurs when we begin self-nurturing. A universe . . . that had long felt like a harsh and hostile place begins to be transformed into a gentler and more loving habitat. Many recovering Poverty Addicts have noted with some astonishment that as we begin to give to ourselves, we begin, also, to receive unexpected gifts from the universe.

In fact, recovering from a poverty addiction means not just receiving gifts *from* the universe, but giving them *to* the universe in the form of more powerful and sustained activism. Consider these facts:

1. Your being poor isn't helping your movement or anyone else, except those who might want to exploit your poverty.
2. As you start to recover from your poverty addiction, you will begin to accumulate resources, including money, time and energy. You can then use those resources to be a more effective and influential activist than you ever were when you were poor.
3. You can also use your money to help build the green economy and to model your progressive values for those around you. You can, for instance, buy a hybrid car to replace your gas-guzzler, or solar panels for your home.

In the Money Goals List exercise at the end of this chapter, and elsewhere, too, please take the radical step of imagining a life for yourself that's not lived in opposition to the acquisition of wealth, and in which the wealth you do acquire is used not just for your own betterment, but that of the world around you.

Dysfunctional attitudes toward, and behavior around, money are a serious impediment to long-term happiness and success, so if you have this problem I urge you to address it quickly and decisively. Whether you have an obvious problem or not, however, I urge you to consult the money-related books listed in the Bibliography, and discuss your financial situation with trusted and knowledgeable relatives, friends or advisors. And if you feel strong guilt, anger, fear or shame around the topic of money, I urge you to discuss those feelings with a therapist or other professional.

Activists choose poverty by choosing not to deal with the types of issues outlined in this chapter. But there is one choice that activists make that, perhaps more than any other, leads to poverty. I discuss that in the next chapter.

Free Help for Your Money Problems!

Many nonprofit agencies provide free or cheap personal finance classes and coaching. If you are in debt, talk to a *nonprofit* credit counselor or attend a Debtors Anonymous meeting. (Many so-called credit counselors are actually businesses that prey on people in debt, so be sure to choose a reputable nonprofit organization.) Those who are in debt should also read *How to Get Out of Debt, Stay Out of Debt, and Live Prosperously*, which is based on the Debtors Anonymous philosophy and methodology.

EXERCISE

Money Goals List

Write down a list of your goals related to your lifestyle and material needs in as much detail as possible. First, figure out what kind of lifestyle you would like to be living . . .

- Next Year
- In Five Years
- In Ten Years
- In Twenty Years
- In Thirty Years

- In Forty Years
- In Fifty Years
- In Sixty Years
- In Eighty Years. (If this sounds ridiculous, it isn't: lifespans in the Western world, at least, are continuing to rise. See, for instance, "100th birthdays may soon be the norm in rich nations: researchers," from *TodayOnline*, February 21, 2006, which reports on research presented at a meeting of the American Association for the Advancement of Science. And, yes, increased longevity presents an additional, very strong argument for managing both your health and your money.)

More specifically, think about what you would like to own and what you would like to be able to do at each of those points in your life. Start by thinking about how much, and what kind of, activism you want to do, and what kind of impact you could make if you had a generous amount of money and time to devote to your activism. Then, think about other life goals, including health, relationships and other interests, including art, travel, sports, entertainment, etc. If you have or want to have children, think about the kind of life and opportunities you would like to give them. Also think about others you want to be able to take care of, including perhaps your parents as they get older. We'll call this document your Money Goals List.

CHAPTER 14

The Worst Choice: Not Having a Well-Paid Career

Activist Mickey Z. wrote a book about the jobs activists and artists take to make ends meet. It was titled, after a line from the poet Charles Bukowksi, *The Murdering of My Years* (Brooklyn, NY: Soft Skull Press, 2003).

I think that title reflects a fair amount of ambivalence, don't you? And the activists Mickey quotes in his book do tell their share of stories of mind-numbing wage-slavery "spiced" with institutionalized racism and sexism. Mickey also quotes some heavy hitters, including Noam Chomsky, Aristotle and Oscar Wilde, to support his contention that having a job is a deleterious experience for activists and artists.

Nevertheless, I believe that the problem many activists have with jobs is not so much with the idea of a job itself, but with the kinds of jobs many activists tend to get: crappy jobs that pretty much guarantee they're going to be miserable, not to mention poor. So, in my view, it's not really a "murdering" of your years so much as a "suiciding." I'll discuss this further below, but first let's talk about the *other* crappy strategies activists use to support themselves, including:

- Enduring unstable living situations involving flaky or irresponsible roommates
- Staying in failed, but financially sustaining, love relationships
- Borrowing money from family members
- Living at home with parents
- Running a time-intensive but low-paying, business or nonprofit organization

These strategies often backfire, taking up way more time and energy, and creating way more stress, than a good job would have in the first place. Taking money from family members seems a particularly bad bet: I've never met an adult activist, or anyone else, who didn't pay a high psychological price for letting their parents or siblings support them.[7] (Letting your spouse or partner support you, however, is an entirely different arrangement that sometimes works.)

It's hard to do good activism, or anything else, when you're broke. So, instead of the above-mentioned crappy strategies, try this one instead:

1. **Think In Terms of "Income," Not "Money"**
   In *Why Are Artists Poor?*, Abbing comments, "When a certain amount of money comes in, artists suddenly lose interest in earning more money." Often, with artists and activists both, it takes only a little money to trigger that loss of interest—too little money, really, to avoid poverty.

   Your need for money is substantial and ongoing, and therefore, your source of money should also be. Occasional small windfalls are not enough: you need a stable, predictable and adequate income. "More than adequate" is better still. Your income should also come with health insurance and other benefits if at all possible.

   Incomes should be low-maintenance, meaning that you shouldn't have to spend too much time worrying about your income going away, or working to ensure that it doesn't. Otherwise, what's the point? Obviously, this is not entirely within your control, but you do have the ability to choose, for instance, a permanent job at a company that's in good financial condition over a temporary job at one that looks shaky.

2. **Think In Terms of a "Career," Not a "Job"**
   Many people use the words "job" and "career" interchangeably, but it's helpful to consider the differences between the two concepts. The table on page 52 summarizes some of them. The last row on the table, Random vs. Planned, is particularly interesting.

   Let's talk about that last point, random vs. planned. Many activists are so ambivalent about the idea of getting a job, or so pessimistic about their prospects for getting a good one, that they gravitate to the bottom of the job pool, going for the easy-to-get (read: crappy) jobs. And they don't invest in education or other assets that could help improve their long-term employability.

   Settling for random, low-paying jobs, instead of planning for, and then building, a career, is *the* big mistake, the one that practically guarantees you'll become poor, or poorer.

   So, don't think in terms of your next gig, or even your "day job." Give up the fantasy that an ongoing string of temporary "non-solutions" to

JOB	CAREER
A short-term stopgap	A long-term strategy
Static; going nowhere	A path or progression; even a context
Boring / dull	Interesting / fun
Pays poorly	Pays better, and sometimes very well
Utilizes few of your skills	Utilizes many of your skills, and teaches you new one
You have little control over your situation	You have more control, and sometimes a lot more
You have little influence over the people you work with	You have more influence, and sometimes a lot more
Randomly selected	Planned; often requires an up-front investment in education, tools, etc.

your money problem will somehow lead you out of poverty and into a happy and productive life. Think, instead, of building a career that will satisfy your long-term need for cash in the easiest and most enjoyable way congruent with your values.

There are lots of resources that will help you do this, including the classic career-planning guide, *What Color is Your Parachute?* (See Bibliography.) If you attended college, your college probably has a career service that you can use even if you've already graduated, and there are also lots of paid and nonprofit career coaches. Also talk with your mentors and trusted friends and family members. They may identify talents you didn't know you had—or knew you had but undervalued—and also point you toward opportunities you weren't aware of.

3. **If You Want, Build Your Career Around Activism**

Nothing I've said, by the way, implies that you can't do activism for your paid career. If you want to be a professional activist, I say go for it! Not only is that a wonderful gift you are giving me and the rest of the planet, but I truly believe that what you will lose in material benefits, you will gain many times over in creative, intellectual, social and spiritual ones.

If you are planning to do activism as a paid career, here are three things to keep in mind:

a) **Don't believe the myth that there are no activist jobs out there.** I've never seen a movement that had no open jobs. True, the exact job you want may not exist; or it may exist, but not at the salary you would prefer or in the town where you would like to live. But some job exists, and it's up to you to figure out how badly you want it, and what sacrifices you are prepared to make to get it.

Job scarcity is not a particular hardship of activists, by the way: many other workers also wind up compromising, sometimes in painful ways, for the right job, particularly in a bad economy. I admit, however, that there may be many fewer good jobs in activism than in most other fields.

Still, I have found that truly dedicated, focused and effective activists can usually find a way to get paid to do activism. (Hint: you must not only do good work, but make sure that the right people—those in a position to offer money or jobs—find out.) It has also been my experience that many activists who claim that there are no activist jobs out there don't even bother looking, or do so in only a half-hearted manner. If you really want a job in activism, then you should be going after it gangbusters. That means networking like mad, talking to everyone you know, aggressively going after whatever opportunities do exist—and, yes, relocating and making other painful compromises, if necessary. Ambitious activists, like ambitious people in any field, don't wait for opportunities to arise so much as they create them.

b) **Don't let people abuse you.** It is an unfortunate fact that many activist organizations are bad employers. They not only pay badly, which we can accept up to a point, but treat people badly. Yelling, harassment and mind games are commonplace, as are the kinds of poor management that result in rampant chaos and disorganization, constant killer deadlines and abusive work schedules.

Of course, activist organizations aren't the only employers who treat people badly. But there's something particularly demoralizing and obnoxious, not to mention hypocritical, about an organization that purports to be dedicated to progressive values such as justice, compassion and equality, and yet mistreats its workers.

Don't let *anyone* treat you badly, no matter how exalted their reputation or noble their aims. If you must make a temporary "deal with the devil" to work for an abusive employer—perhaps for the connections, credential or learning experience—make sure that it is only temporary, that you are prepared for what you're getting into, and that you have an exit strategy.

Better by far to take a non-activist job than to work for an activist organization that abuses you. If more activists made that choice, then maybe more activist organizations would be impelled to treat their employees, interns and volunteers better.

c) **If jobs are truly scarce in your movement, then broaden your search while retaining a focus on your core values.** You could, for example:

- Work in another movement. Not only will the work be satisfying, but you'll have the opportunity to build linkages between that movement and your own.
- Teach or do social work.
- Work for a charity.
- Do political work.
- Work in the media.
- Work in a "green" industry such as renewable energy, sustainable building or organic agriculture.
- Do something involving fair trade.
- Work in a compassionate, or at least neutral, field. Someone who works as a nurse, medical technician or physical therapist may not be explicitly promoting progressive values, but they are not harming anyone, either. In fact, they are only helping. . . .

So many choices! Just make sure to choose carefully, so that your career doesn't swamp your other interests, including activism.

CHAPTER 15

More Career Advice

Here are some more tips. . . .

4. **If You Don't Want to Be a Full-Time or even a Part-Time Activist Then Don't!**
If you can't, or won't, be a full-time activist, don't worry about it. I only ask
that you not drop out of activism entirely. A few hours of hands-on
activism a month, even if it's "just" writing letters, is good for the planet
and good for *you*. But if you can't even spare those few hours, then it's perfectly OK just to write checks. Some people might judge you for that, but I
sure wouldn't; money is necessary to the success of every activist venture.

   **There is no one right way to be an activist, and anyone who tries to
tell you there is, or who calls you a sell-out, is not only wrong, but probably speaking out of their own confusion, conflict and unhappiness.**
The truth is, we need progressive values represented *everywhere*: in every segment of society, every geographic region, every industry and every government organization. Someone who works daily to promote progressive values in a non-activist milieu might even wind up having a bigger impact
than someone who works full-time as an activist. As I write this, in summer
2005, a big news story is winding down about Microsoft Corporation,
which had caved to pressure from the Christian Right and reneged on its
longstanding support for a bill under consideration in the Washington state
legislature banning discrimination against gays and lesbians in housing,
employment and insurance. Internal activists (employees), as well as outside ones, applied weeks of pressure, and Microsoft eventually returned to
its former stance in support of the bill.

   Microsoft is a hugely influential company—a bellwether, really—and I
predict that, in the fight against bigotry in America and elsewhere, this victory will one day be considered pivotal. Microsoft's gay employees and
allies, *simply by being located within Microsoft and being willing to take a brave
public stand for their values*, played a key role in that victory. Who can say

that their time would have been better spent working full-time for an activist organization?

If you do decide to pursue a non-activist career, do it without guilt or shame, and go after success aggressively. I hope you will make a lot of money that you can use to live a life congruent with your values, and donate generously to progressive causes. I also hope you will be an effective ambassador for progressive values in whatever milieu you find yourself in. In the end, your donations and "diplomacy" could yield as great, or greater, a result than any full-time activism you might have done.

5. **When Looking for Non-Activist Work, Don't Undersell Yourself**
In *Why Are Artists Poor?*, Abbing points out that many artists continue to struggle to have a professional art career long after they are burned out on art. They do that, he says, because they don't know what else to do with themselves—or, more precisely, because they don't think they are fit to do anything other than art.

Many of the activists I talk to feel the same way. They have been immersed in activism for so long that they have no idea what else they could do, and are too intimidated to even try to apply for a serious non-activist job. And so, they grind along with their activism—often in a half-hearted, burned-out, ineffectual way—getting more and more miserable.

These activists, in my view, are selling themselves short. Activists in general tend to be the kinds of informed, clever, creative and self-motivated people that many employers like to hire. Many activists, in fact, have technical and interpersonal experience and skills that make them desirable candidates for a wide range of jobs. So, if you are sick of activist work, but don't know what else to do with yourself, consult some of the career-related resources mentioned in number 2 in the previous chapter, and don't be afraid to push the envelope and see where, outside of activism, your skills and talents can take you.

6. **Whether Your Career is in Activism or Some Other Field, Move as Far Up the Hierarchy as Possible**
Aim high.

The reasons are simple: the higher you go, the better off both you and your movement will be. At a higher level, you will get paid more and have more interesting and fun work. You will also have more of an opportunity to influence others.

Aiming high means planning high. It generally begins with getting the highest level of education you can. Don't stop at a B.A. when you can get an M.S.W., M.Ed., M.B.A., M.P.A. or law degree. Don't stop at those degrees if you can get a marketable doctorate. Try not to take too big a break, or any break at all, in between these steps; statistically, many people who take long breaks from school wind up never returning. (If you absolutely hate the idea of going to graduate school, then feel free to ignore this advice, since there's no point in going to school if you're not going to be motivated.)

The question naturally arises: how do you pay for this expensive degree? Assuming your family can't or won't help out, there are more options than you might think:

- **Go part-time.** All around you, people are working their way through graduate school a course or two at a time. Most would probably prefer to attend full-time, but they recognize that attending even part-time is way better than not getting the advanced degree at all.
- **Attend a community college or other inexpensive college.** While prestige degrees undoubtedly open many doors, just having a degree from an accredited school, even if it's not in the Ivy League, is often enough to help you move up the hierarchy.
- **Work for a university.** They usually aren't the highest-paying employers, but they often offer free or discounted classes to their employees. Even many non-university employers offer a tuition reimbursement benefit, so seek out one who does.
- **Take out a loan.** Most student loans offer a very low rate of interest, and financial advisors therefore tend to see them as a good strategy. If you're going to go into debt, however, be sure to have a concrete career goal in mind that will allow you to both live comfortably and pay back the debt.

Once you're out of school and working, take your career advancement seriously. Figure out which *leadership* role you want—it doesn't have to be at the very top of the organization, but it should be at a level where you get to interact with, and influence, many people within and outside your organization, and where you have control over at least some money and other resources. Next, figure out how you are going to get there. And next, work on getting there. Throughout your professional life, continue to educate yourself; consult mentors and others who can advise and support you; and work assiduously to overcome any personal or professional barriers to your success.

Of course, whether you work for a progressive organization or not, moving up the ladder inevitably involves ethical and other compromises. In his classic activist text *Rules for Radicals* (see Bibliography), Saul Alinsky tells how, for many years, the graduating class at a local seminary used to visit him to ask his advice. One year, the class asked him how they could maintain their progressive values while operating within the conservative culture of the Catholic Church. Alinsky writes: "That was easy. I answered, 'When you go out that door, just make your own personal decision about whether you want to be a bishop or a priest, and everything else will follow.'"

So, let me modify my advice: move as far up the ladder as you can without unacceptably compromising your values. But be very clear what your values are and what constitutes "compromise." Sticking to a low-level position out of laziness or obstinacy does neither you nor your movement any good.

7. **Don't Start a Business Simply as a Way of Earning a Living**

Some activists, and especially those with art, construction, programming and other skills, think they can beat the system by starting a small or freelance business. The thinking, which is shared by many non-activists, is that they'll be able to earn money doing the work they want to do and doing it on their own terms: flexible hours, no boss, no long commute, etc. And think how much time there'll be left over for activism!

As someone who has coached hundreds of people in entrepreneurship, I can assure you that it usually doesn't work that way. Business is way harder than it looks, and it is way harder than most jobs. If your business is like most, you will wind up working fifty or more hours a week, mostly on marketing, sales, bookkeeping and management. And for all of this work and stress, your take-home pay will likely be minimal and/or erratic, at least for the first few years.

If business were your priority, then it might make sense to make these kinds of sacrifices. But if activism is your priority, then what's the point? Far better to get a job with a fixed salary and benefits, and leave the management headaches and long workweeks to your boss.

There are two exceptions to this rule:

- If you happen to be the kind of talented and lucky graphic designer, construction worker, etc., (a) whose skills are in constant demand, (b) who can command a lot of money for those skills, and (c) is a disciplined time and money manager, then you might, just might, be able to pull off entrepreneurship. If not—if you are constantly scrounging and scraping for work, not to mention begging people to pay you for work you've already done, or if you can't seem to manage your time or money well—then I think you should give entrepreneurship a pass and go out and get a job. Many of my students took this advice after years of struggling as a freelancer and were much happier as a result.

- If you want to build a business based on progressive values, such as a green, organic or fair-trade business, that's terrific. Just be sure you understand the degree of hard work required for such a venture to succeed. Also remember that, even in a progressive business, profit must rank very high among your priorities, a reality that often mandates difficult compromises.

For more clarity on this issue, discuss your entrepreneurial plan with mentors who have built businesses themselves. They should help you understand the pros and cons of entrepreneurship, and whether you are suited to it.

8. **Don't Start a Nonprofit Organization Unless It's a Necessary Strategy for Advancing Your Cause**

Often, when doing activism, you want to call yourself by an organizational name just so you look more serious and professional. Three activists who decide to call themselves The Downtown Centerville Fair Housing Coalition, for instance, are likely to be taken far more seriously than if they had just presented themselves as three concerned individuals.

But should the activists choose to legally incorporate and register as a 501(c)(3) charitable organization (a.k.a. nonprofit corporation)? That's a tougher call. The minute you legally incorporate, you add a lot of paperwork and management chores to your workload, including complex tax filings and mandatory board meetings. (And the incorporation and nonprofit status application processes themselves are a pain.) Sure, you gain fundraising advantages, and possibly some personal financial protection in the event that you get sued because of your activism, but for many activists these advantages won't be worth the extra time, expense and hassle of legally incorporating. This is especially true because activists can often arrange to do their fundraising and other work under the "fiscal sponsorship" of an existing 501(c)(3) organization that assumes much of the administrative burden.

For more clarity on this complex issue, talk with mentors who have built nonprofit organizations themselves, as well as lawyers and accountants who specialize in helping nonprofits. Foundation officers and other donors are also good people to consult. If you have a donor willing to back your fledgling organization with a grant, that's a very positive sign, since it means the donor not only has faith in what you are doing, but in you as a manager. If, however, you have no strong connections to the funding community, that's a strong sign that your professional network is not yet developed enough for you to start your own organization. Use your time as an employee to make some contacts, and also to learn what it really takes to build and run an activist organization.

9. **Remember: Your Career Should Be Fun**
With everything else we've discussed, it is easy to forget one crucial fact: your career should be *fun*. It's something you're going to be devoting a large part of your waking hours to, and so it should be a positive experience.

I'm not saying it should be an ongoing series of parties or laugh-riots; that's setting the bar too high. I'm only saying that the individual jobs you take should be interesting and pleasant, and the people you work with should also be interesting and pleasant. Otherwise, you're paying too high a price for your career.

One aspect of this, obviously, is choosing the right career and jobs. But another is cultivating your ability to derive satisfaction from a wide range of circumstances. If you're the kind of person who has to have a great many needs met before she can feel happy or at ease, then that rigidity is going to cause you problems, not just at work, but in your activism and elsewhere. Far better to be laid-back and adaptable, with the ability to derive happiness from a wide range of circumstances.

This adaptability will open up a much wider range of jobs to you. It will also make building your career, and the rest of your life, much easier.

EXERCISE

Referring back to your Money Goals List, plan a career that will fund the lifestyle you outlined in that document. Always keep in mind, when evaluating career options, that there are probably a lot more out there than you are aware of. Don't be too rigid or narrowly focused! You should also consult a wide range of people, including career counselors, teachers, mentors and family members, for career advice. If you've been out of the job market for a while, start preparing yourself for reentry. Put together a good resume and an interview wardrobe. Then go out and interview for a few jobs, just for the practice. Do your best to prepare, but don't worry if you don't do well; that's what practice is for! The goal is to be well prepared for when a position that you really do want opens up.

CHAPTER 16

Other Needs

In Chapter 9, I discussed the fact that all humans have diverse needs. All of us have the "big three" of Health, Relationship and Money needs, but many of us also have intellectual, creative, cultural and spiritual needs, to name just a few other categories.

These needs represent important aspects of our character and personality, and should not be ignored in the name of some higher-seeming goal like activism. Instead, they should be acknowledged, nurtured and celebrated. Doing so will not only make you a happier, more fulfilled person, but a better activist, since:

1. A happy activist is generally a better activist.
2. Your explorations in these areas will deepen your understanding of people and the human condition, thus making you a more powerful and effective advocate.
3. You can promote your progressive values to people you meet while engaged in these endeavors.

The following exercise will give you the opportunity to document these types of important needs.

EXERCISE

Whole Person Goals List

Write down your goals for all important areas of your life that weren't covered in the previous exercises. This could include intellectual, creative, cultural and spiritual goals. We'll call this document your Whole Person Goals List.

CHAPTER 17

Your Personal Mission Statement

By now you've created the following **Goals Lists**:

- Activism Goals List
- Health & Fitness Goals List
- Relationships Goals List
- Money Goals List
- Whole Person Goals List

You need to take five more simple steps to create your Personal Mission Statement—a statement of the goals you wish to pursue in every important area of your life.

1. Study each List, and create a one- to three-sentence **Mission Statement** *for that List.* That mission statement should summarize your overall philosophy regarding, and goals for, that area of your life.

- Study the goals listed in your Activism Goals List, and from them create a one- to three-sentence Activism Mission Statement.
- Study the goals listed in your Health & Fitness Goals List, and from them create a one- to three-sentence Health & Fitness Mission Statement.
- Study the goals listed in your Relationships Goals List, and from them create a one- to three-sentence Relationships Mission Statement.
- Study the goals listed in your Money Goals List, and from them create a one- to three-sentence Money Mission Statement.
- Study the goals listed in your Whole Person Goals List, and from them create a one- to three-sentence Whole Person Mission Statement.

2.　Put each Mission Statement at the top of the relevant List.

3.　Combine all of the Lists (with the Mission Statements on top) into one document. That's your **Personal Mission Statement**.

4.　Study your Activism, Health, Relationships, Money and Whole Person Mission Statements and come up with a single paragraph that summarizes and encompasses them all. This will be the core **Mission** that summarizes your current "life philosophy" and goals. Put that at the very top of your Personal Mission Statement.

5.　Stick a **date** on the document, both to record when you created it, and also because you will be revising it periodically, and it's helpful to know which version you're working with.

That's it—you're done! Congratulations on having created something wonderful and rare, that you can use to move to your new level of growth and success.

Note that this process is actually the reverse of that recommended by many authors and life coaches, who will tell you to begin with a formal mission statement and then derive some specific goals from it. I like starting with the goals, however, because they are often more concrete and authentic than a formal mission statement spun out of thin air. Such formal missions tend to be over-intellectualized and over-rationalized, and the goals that one derives from them often tend to be unrealistic and not a true reflection of the person's core values. Hence, my method of beginning with the goals.

When Things Don't Fit Together

If, when working backwards from your goals, you come up with a Mission you're not entirely comfortable with, or that doesn't seem to reflect the real you, that is an important clue that you need to do some more thinking around your values and goals. (It's fabulous, by the way, that you encountered this problem "on paper," where it's easily corrected, rather than in real life, where it's often not.) Keep reworking your Goals Lists, Mission Statements and Mission until everything synchs up and feels like a good fit.

Also, look for goals that contradict each other or are mutually exclusive. If, for example, one of your Money goals is to own a fancy house similar to the one your sister the corporate lawyer owns, but one of your Activism goals is to do full-time activism, then you've set yourself up for a tough, perhaps impossible, challenge. See if you can come up with a plan for achieving both goals, and if you can't, alter one or both goals so that your overall Mission is realistic and achievable.

The process of synchronizing your Goals and the Mission can be painful, but it is also very valuable. Don't rush it.

Remember, also, that your Mission (and Mission Plan—see next chapter) are "living" documents that are not fixed in stone, but designed to be regularly reread, pondered and revised. Revisit them at least every six months and make whatever changes are needed to reflect your new situation.

CHAPTER 18

Your Mission Plan

Now that your Personal Mission Statement is completed, you can create a plan for achieving your goals.

Perhaps you've worked with plans in some of your campaigns or in your day job. If so, you know that planning often spells the difference between success and failure in a complex endeavor. If the idea of "planning your life" sounds weird, don't worry about it; many people do just that. Planning is, in fact, one of the primary tools that successful people use to ensure that they achieve their important professional and personal goals.

Planning is very powerful, which is why having even a small, sketchy plan is vastly better than having no plan at all. Generally speaking, however, the more detailed your plan, the better; but you can always start with a sketchy plan and expand it later on.

Whatever the size of your plan, here is some information you should include in it:

- The **steps** you need to take to achieve each goal. Think "baby steps": each small and *easily* achievable. (More on the importance of taking baby steps in Part III.)
- The **resources** required for each step. This could be money, your time, others' time, information, or tools such as a better computer.
- Wherever possible, **quantitative benchmarks** for success. If you were working on an electoral campaign, your plan would probably specify how much money you needed to raise, and by when; how many volunteers you needed to recruit for each district, and by when; what the poll numbers should look like at different stages of the campaign; and how many votes from each district you need to get your candidate elected. That way, you could tell at every stage of the campaign whether you were on track for success.

It works the same way for your personal goals. If, say, you want to own your own home by the time you are forty, you need to know how much that house is likely to cost, how much the down payment on the mortgage is likely to be, and how much money you need to save each year to amass that down payment. You also need to know how large an income you will need to get the mortgage approved by a bank—and, of course, to pay back the loan—and how and when you will achieve that income. Everything that *can* be quantified *should* be quantified.

- As the above examples indicate, you also need to indicate a **deadline** for each step. As the saying goes, "a goal is a dream with a deadline." If you don't make, and try to meet, deadlines, you're just messing around. Everything that *can* be deadlined *should* be deadlined.

- A truly savvy plan also focuses on the **risks, problems and obstacles** you might encounter. Don't just list these, but write down how you intend to avoid or solve them. For example, how will your plan to buy a house be affected if you go through a long period of unemployment? And what could you do to avoid that problem?

  No one likes to dwell on the negative side of things, but good planners force themselves to think long and hard about the potential risks, problems and obstacles they are likely to encounter on the way to achieving their goal. They encounter these obstacles, and make their mistakes, "on paper," so that they can either avoid them, or know how to deal with them, in real life.

There are entire libraries devoted to the topic of planning, but we don't need to get that fancy here. Begin with your Health & Fitness and Whole Person Goals Lists—because they are likely to be shorter and simpler than your Activism, Relationships and Money Goals Lists—and start writing down the steps, resources, quantitative benchmarks and deadlines for achieving each goal, as well as any potential risks or obstacles you might encounter and how you will avoid or deal with these. Use whatever format you like—paragraph, list, chart, etc.—just as long as the plan is easy to create and easy to follow later on.

Then, when you've finished with your Health & Fitness and Whole Person plans, you can move on to Activism, Relationships and Money. These are likely to be longer and more complex, so take your time and, if necessary, do them in stages, a little at a time. Don't feel pressured to create a fabulous plan; planning should always be a fun, low-stress activity, and even your very first, rudimentary drafts of these plans are likely to be very useful to you as you start to work toward your goals.

As with your Mission, you are likely, when doing your Mission Plan, to run into conflicts. Perhaps one of your goals requires more resources than you think you can put together, or perhaps you are starting to realize that there simply isn't enough time to accomplish all of your goals. Again, it's great that you encountered these problems "on paper" as opposed to in real life. As was the case with your Mission, resolving these conflicts will be a very valuable exercise.

Combine your Activism, Health & Fitness, Relationships, Money and Whole Person Plans into one document—call it your **Mission Plan**—and you're done! The next step is to go out and make that Mission Plan happen, which is what the rest of *The Lifelong Activist* is all about.

You now understand that success as an activist, and happiness as a human being, comes from pursuing a Mission that is a natural and honest extension of your values, and that burnout and unhappiness frequently result from pursuing a Mission that's not. You've created Goals Lists that illuminate your values, a Personal Mission Statement that organizes them, and a Mission Plan for achieving them.

The remainder of this book presents tools that will help you live that Plan. It tells you how to Manage Your Time (Part II), Manage Your Fears (Part III) and Manage Your Relationships (Parts IV and V). So let's move right along to . . .

PART II. MANAGING YOUR TIME

PART II

MANAGING YOUR TIME

PART II. MANAGING YOUR TIME

CHAPTER 1

The Value of Time

In my classes, I frequently run a little experiment. First, I ask the students to tell me what is meant by the expression, "Time is money." The answers are generally along these lines:

- "Time is very valuable; it's as valuable as money."
- "You can use time to earn money."
- "You can use money to buy time—to hire help around the house or at work."
- "If you waste time, you've lost the money you could have earned during that time."

I then ask the class to raise their hand if they believe the expression is true. Most do.

"Let's test that," I say. "How many of you, in the past month, participated in a meeting or phone call that went way past the point you thought useful? And yet, you didn't leave that meeting or call, and so you wound up wasting half an hour or more of your time?"

In most classes, nearly every hand goes up.

I then ask a second question: "How many of you, if an acquaintance or stranger walked up to you and asked you to give them fifty dollars, for no particular reason, just because they wanted it, would give them the money?"

In most classes, there's a moment of silence as students ponder this odd scenario. Then, *no* hands go up, and everyone starts to laugh.

The lesson is clear: even though most of us believe that time equals money, and some of us actually go around using that expression, we tend to value our time *far less* than our money. Many of us, in fact, are perfectly happy to waste loads of our "valuable" time not just on superfluous meetings and conversations, but on things like video games and junk TV.

Undervaluing your time is a terrible mistake because **time, as it turns out, does not equal money: it's far more valuable than money.** The fact that relatively few people understand this is probably why so many people, including so many people with lots of money, live unhappy, unfulfilled lives.

Time is more valuable than money not just because it is a finite (limited) resource, but because time, invested properly, can bring rewards that money never can.

Picture two people, both trying to get physically fit. The first guy has lots of money but no time, while the second guy has not much money but lots of time.

The first guy uses his money to join a fancy health club, hire a personal trainer, and acquire lots of fancy sports equipment. But he doesn't make the time to actually go to the gym, work with the trainer or use the equipment.

The second guy can afford only a used set of weights from a garage sale. But he uses them for an hour a day, plus runs for another forty minutes.

Guess who's going to get fit?

We're all familiar with the parent who never spends any time with her children, but tries to compensate by buying them expensive stuff. Is she likely to win her children's affection through her presents? Not in any meaningful way. She can only do that by spending time with them.

There is also no question that time is more valuable than money when it comes to activism. We've all seen situations where buckets of money were thrown at a social problem, or at an activist or nonprofit organization, with little or no result to show for it. We've also seen situations where activists achieved amazing things on a shoestring budget. That's because, in activism as in life in general, time is far more powerful than money. You can get much further with a little money and a lot of time well spent, than with a lot of money and only a little time well spent—or with a lot of money and a lot of time badly spent.

Activists, in my experience, are less likely than most people to trade their time unthinkingly for a superficial material benefit. But, like most people, they are not particularly good at using their time in a focused manner to achieve their goals.

Time Management = Life Management

Time management is important because it really is "life management." The basic premise of time management is this:

Time Management Premise

The things you spend time on, and devote quality attention to, are the things you will improve at or make progress on. In contrast, the things you *don't* spend time on, or devote quality attention to, are the things you will *not* improve at or make progress on.

This is one of the most fundamental pieces of wisdom you will ever encounter. It means, basically, that **how you spend your time determines where you will end up**. Spend a lot of time and quality attention on your health and fitness, and you will end up healthy and fit. Spend a lot of time and quality attention on your activism, and you will end up an accomplished and successful activist. Spend a lot of time and quality attention on television and video games, however, and you will end up accomplished at these low-value activities.

"Quality attention" means not just putting in your time, but putting in your *mind*: being focused on, and thoughtful about, the activity at hand. Of course, it's possible to devote forty, or eighty, hours a week to something and not really be focused on it. In that case, your odds of making progress are little better than they would have been if you hadn't devoted time to it at all.

Time, invested properly, will help you achieve the Activism, Health & Fitness, Relationships, Money and Whole Person goals you set for yourself in your Personal Mission Statement. A lifetime spent working toward these important goals, as opposed to the wrong goals or no goals, will most likely be one of accomplishment, peace and joy.

CHAPTER 2

How Successful People View (and Use) Time

Given what you learned in the previous chapter, it will probably not surprise you to learn that one of the key traits separating successful from unsuccessful people is how they manage their time. More specifically: **successful people control their time, while unsuccessful people let others control their time for them.**

Let's illustrate this with two hypothetical examples: Alyssa and Chris, women in their mid-thirties who are very politically aware and passionately committed to progressive values. Both are married, with two school-aged children.[1]

> **Alyssa** works nine hours/five days a week at an office job. (One hour for lunch.) The job is located 45 minutes from her house, so she also has a 1.5-hour daily commute. She drops the kids off at school in the morning, and her husband, who also works full-time with a long commute, picks them up from their after-school program on his way home from work. At home, one parent helps the kids with their homework while the other cooks dinner. The family eats together, and then, after the kids go to bed, Alyssa and her husband "veg" in front of the television while doing laundry or other chores, or some office work that they brought home.[2]
>
> Both Alyssa and her husband average around six hours of sleep a night. This leaves them perpetually sleep-deprived, which in turn often leaves them feeling crabby; and so they tend to squabble a lot with each other and with the kids. Being sleep-deprived also means that they don't do as good a job at work as they would like, and that a lot of stuff that needs to get done around the house simply doesn't.
>
> Alyssa belongs to a couple of grassroots activist groups, but she

is always behind in her commitments to them, and misses many meetings. She originally planned to do her activist work on Sunday afternoons and one or two evenings a week, but it's been years since she's kept to that schedule. In fact, she spends most of her free time either napping or zoned out in front of the television.

The truth is, Alyssa has done very little activism in the past five years, a situation that leaves her unhappy and unfulfilled. She hasn't even been able to write many checks to activist organizations, because her husband's and her incomes barely cover their own expenses.

Alyssa sounds like a typical rushed American and underachieving activist, doesn't she? Now here's Chris, another married mom who also has two young children:

Chris used to have a job and commute similar to Alyssa's, but she decided that the commute was taking up too much of her time, so she found a job closer to home. She also chose a workplace that is family-friendly and has lobbied her boss for flex-time, so that she now works a thirty-six hour week comprised of four 9.5-hour days (including a thirty-minute lunch break, required by law). This means, of course, that she has a three-day weekend. Her husband has also selected a job with a shorter commute and flexible scheduling.[3] Because of their easier schedules, Chris and her husband have a much easier time than Alyssa and her husband in meeting their kids' and their household's needs. The jobs pay less, but Chris and her family are willing to make sacrifices, including:

- Living in an inexpensive community, as opposed to an upscale, gentrified one.
- Living in a small home with a small yard. This means that many expenses are lessened, including mortgage, repairs and maintenance, heating, electricity and grounds maintenance.
- Minimizing the number of possessions (furniture, appliances, etc.) they own, which not only minimizes the purchase expense, but also the amount of cleaning and maintenance required.
- Only going on a vacation every other year—and those vacations tend to be cheap (but fun) camping trips.

- Driving ten-year-old cars, one of which Chris and her husband bought used, and the other of which a relative gave them.
- Not replacing their old furniture and appliances until absolutely necessary. Their home is "shabby but comfortable."
- Giving homemade birthday and holiday gifts, instead of store-bought.

Chris and her husband are, in fact, living a life very similar to that recommended in *The Millionaire Next Door*. The authors of that book analyzed the behavior of typical American millionaires and discovered that, contrary to the stereotype, they weren't all hot-shot entrepreneurs. Many were people with ordinary jobs (for instance, teachers) who chose to live as simply and inexpensively as possible, and to save and invest as much of their money as possible.

Chris and her husband are also raising their children to take a lot of responsibility around the house: for instance, the kids get themselves ready for school each day, keep their rooms clean, and dust and vacuum the living room and other common areas. Although the kids sometimes balk at all the chores, they understand that by helping out around the house, they are also helping to create more time for fun family activities.

Chris and her husband splurge in two ways:

- They use an Internet-based grocery service to do the bulk of their grocery shopping. Chris only spends five minutes each week renewing her order on the Web, and the groceries are delivered the next day right to her kitchen.
- They order three takeout dinners per week.

These two "splurges" save Chris and her husband at least six hours a week in shopping and food preparation. At first, they seemed like extravagances, but when Chris added up the marginal cost of these services—i.e., their cost over what the family would have to pay anyway for the groceries and for the ingredients for the three dinners—they turned out to be a bargain. Chris and her husband, in fact, pay fifty extra dollars each week for these services, which works out to $8.34 per hour saved. That's a great deal, especially as neither she nor her husband particularly likes grocery shopping!

All of this means that Chris has a three-day weekend each week, with much less housework and many fewer chores to do than Alyssa has during her two-day weekend. Chris spends one evening a week and Sunday afternoons doing activist work. The rest of her free time (four weekday evenings, plus all day Friday and Saturday, and Sunday mornings) she devotes to having fun with her family, relaxing and doing housework and chores. Because Chris is not overscheduled, she can easily handle all of her responsibilities, plus emergencies and other interruptions; and because her whole family gets adequate sleep each night, everyone is usually rested, relaxed and productive at work (or school) and at home.

Moreover, Chris has involved her family in her activist work. This means that some of her activist hours are also family time—and that she's helping to educate her children to become happy and effective lifelong activists.

The main difference between Alyssa and Chris is that Alyssa has let others determine her lifestyle and schedule, while Chris has been aggressive in building her lifestyle and schedule around her values. Because of this, Chris is thriving, and so are her kids, her marriage and her activism.

Chris and her family occasionally take guff for their choices—"I wouldn't be caught dead driving that thing," says Chris's brother of Chris's beat-up old car. (Of course, the brother works a twelve-hour workday and is perpetually stressed.) Chris and her family can ignore these kinds of comments, however, because they have the peace, confidence and satisfaction that comes from living a life derived from their values. They also serve as an inspiration to those around them who seek to lead a self-actualized life.

CHAPTER 3

Do You Suffer From the AACL?

Alyssa, in the previous chapter, is a classic example of someone who suffers from what I call the Average American Consumerist Lifestyle (AACL).

Everyone has the same twenty-four hours a day, seven days a week. The question is: how will you spend that time?

There are plenty of people—including not just your family, friends, neighbors and coworkers, but also "news" reporters, politicians and corporations—who will be happy to tell you how. Mostly, they'll say to:

- Work a grueling job with long hours
- Spend every cent you make on "stuff"
- Spend most of your "non-work" time maintaining that stuff
- Spend whatever money and time you have left over on mindless entertainment

In other words, the AACL. Most people adopt it unthinkingly, having been brainwashed into it practically from birth. Many people aren't even aware that the AACL is a choice they are making; they think it's the natural way to live.

Pro-AACL propaganda influences most of our major decisions: to follow a certain educational and career path, get married, have children, buy a home, move to the suburbs, etc. I'm not saying that these choices aren't right for some people; only that many people, including, unfortunately, many activists, tend to make them unconsciously or semiconsciously, without a clear sense of the alternatives—or even that there are alternatives.

Sometimes, it's not the materialism of the AACL that controls people, but the psychological and spiritual emptiness it engenders. In her book *The Time Bind*, sociologist Arlie Russell Hochschild recalls seeing numerous instances of people working overtime at a company she studied when they had no obvious financial or other need for doing so. Here's one example:

> What worried Joann about her overwork . . . was that she didn't quite know why she was doing it. None of her explanations satisfied her. "The money's nice; but it's not worth it when you live at work," she concluded. But at the same time, she wasn't changing her hours. . . .

> Examples such as Joann, Hochschild said, caused her to wonder, " . . . how many other people were driving around their own 'country roads' at midnight, asking themselves why their lives are the way they are, never quite grasping the link between their desire for escape and a company's desire for profit."

Prevalent as it is, the AACL is, indisputably, the wrong choice for many people. Many people fail at it, while others "succeed," in the purely financial/materialistic sense, but are nevertheless unhappy.

And there are other problems that afflict even happy AACL people. They tend to be stressed, to eat badly and to get too little exercise and too little sleep. They tend to short-change their personal relationships. And they tend to feel guilty a lot of the time because they don't feel they are meeting their obligations either at home or at work. To use the clichéd term, their lives lack balance.

The AACL versus Your Activist (and Other) Dreams

The biggest problem with the AACL is that it acts against your Mission. The AACL pretty much demands that you take a high-paying day job; and that job, when combined with the overall busyness and stress of the AACL, will leave you little or no time and energy to do your activism. In fact, people who have bought into the AACL tend to view non-money-making activities such as activism with deep skepticism.

Why would an activist wind up on the AACL treadmill? As mentioned earlier, many people get brainwashed into the AACL from earliest childhood. They grow up not being aware that humans can, and should, create their own journey, and that that journey can take many fabulous and fantastic forms.

Often, people try to live a non-AACL life when they are young but get sucked into the AACL as they get older. Many activists are told that activism is a phase of "youthful idealism" that they are supposed to outgrow. But one can be a devoted and effective activist at any age; and as a middle-aged person myself, I can assure you that activism is a terrific preventative of, and cure for, a midlife crisis.

Another reason people get sucked into the AACL is that it tends to get people into debt, and once you are in debt, you pretty much need to keep living the AACL to pay off that debt—if, indeed, you ever do. Credit card bills, car loans and mortgage payments have probably shut down more activist careers than all the disapproving parents and failed campaigns combined. The lesson here is to avoid spending money and, when you must spend, to avoid taking on unreasonable debt. This is not radical, anti-capitalistic advice; your parents and other financial advisers will tell you the same thing.

Activists should at all costs avoid an unthinking slide into the AACL. Note that I am not saying that you can't have an "ordinary" lifestyle with kids, a house, etc. What I'm saying is that you should make your choices consciously and in accordance with your own values, not because you've unthinkingly caved in to family pressure or consumerist propaganda. You can have your kids, house, etc., but you will probably have a smaller house, with shabbier furnishings, than your siblings or friends who have fully bought into the AACL. That's OK, because you will own the greatest luxury of all: the ability to spend more of your time on activities that feed your soul.

If you are already living an AACL life, don't despair; like Chris in the previous chapter you can take steps to undo it. It will be hard if you're struggling under a mountain of debt, but it is doable, and people do it all the time. Consult a financial mentor or counselor, and the money-related books in the Bibliography.

CHAPTER 4

Lifestyles Inimical to Success

"Inimical" means "hostile," so the title of this chapter means "lifestyles hostile to your success." If you are living one of the following lifestyles, in other words, you are seriously reducing your chances of building a sustainable activist career and a happy life.

The AACL, not surprisingly, lies at the root of many of these inimical lifestyles. If, for example, you spend your whole day working at a stressful day job so that you can buy lots of stuff, it's not surprising that you don't feel like doing much of anything when you get home. Many people spend their evenings vegging in front of the tube not because that is how they want to live their lives, but because they are too exhausted to do anything else. If you are in this situation, you might want to do what Chris did and switch to a job that is, (a) easier, (b) requires a shorter commute or (c) both! Once you've made that important change, you will then have the time and energy you need to ponder, and then effect, additional changes.

If changing your job seems like too big a step right now, then work on a smaller problem, such as reducing your housework burden. The important thing to remember is that restructuring your life to fit your values takes time: often years or even decades. Some changes may come quickly and easily, while others may be more difficult. Just keep working at it.

Below and in Chapter 5 are some of the inimical lifestyles you must discard if you are going to succeed. Chapter 6 describes the lifestyle you should replace them with. And Chapters 7 through 17 describe the process for doing the replacement.

A TV or Other "Soft" Addiction

There's nothing wrong with watching a small amount of television each day, particularly if you record the shows and watch them after you've finished your work and met your other obligations. The problem is when you watch television indiscriminately and for many hours a day.

Television is almost always a waste of time. There are some exceptions, such as quality news shows, dramas or documentaries. But no matter how you rationalize it, most television is worse than useless; worse because it tries to brainwash you into the AACL. Unless you're a media activist, and perhaps not even then, the rule of thumb is: the less television, the better.

Psychologist Judith Wright characterizes compulsive television-watching as a "soft addiction" in her book, *There Must Be More Than This: Finding More Life, Love, and Meaning by Overcoming Your Soft Addictions* (see Bibliography). Ditto for compulsive Web surfing, video games, e-mail-checking, shopping, napping, fantasizing and about forty other activities. You know you are in the thrall of a soft addiction when you don't do the activity because you enjoy it or because it's important, but merely out of habit, boredom or to escape. Or, you do it instead of something more important that you should be doing.

Breaking a soft addiction takes time and is usually best accomplished gradually. If you are currently watching three hours of television a day, try cutting back to 2.5 hours, and only when you're comfortable at that level of television-watching should you try to cut back further.

Same for your other soft addictions: tackle them gradually.

Never berate or criticize yourself for your soft addictions, or for any other problems you may be having. As you will learn in Part III, blaming and shaming and criticizing yourself is usually counterproductive. Practice being a compassionate observer of your own flaws, since a compassionate attitude is key to helping oneself and others.

A soft addiction isn't as debilitating as a "hard" addiction such as alcoholism, of course. But it can still sabotage your success. So, if you have one, deal with it. If necessary, talk to a therapist or other professional.

A "Hard" Addiction

Hard addictions—to drugs, alcohol, gambling, etc.—are a whole different story. Unlike most soft addictions, a hard addiction can ruin your health and destroy your life.

Generally speaking, you should only work on one major life problem at a time, and if you have a hard addiction, that is unquestionably the problem you should be working on. Everything, including your activism, should take a back seat to your recovery and health. If, while you are recovering, you are able to do some activism, that's terrific. If not—if the activism stresses or depresses you to the point where you are tempted to break your abstinence—then you have to forego your activism at least temporarily. Eventually, perhaps, you may reach a point where you can integrate your activism into your recovery.

If you are addicted, don't be ashamed; many wonderful and talented people share your problem. Many experts, in fact, consider the AACL as a catalyst of addiction, due to its stressfulness, emphasis on immediate gratification and isolating tendencies.

Don't try to handle your recovery yourself; seek professional help from a therapist, doctor or Twelve-Step Program. Don't rush your recovery and don't feel like the time you spend on recovery is wasted. Recovery is growth: an increased ability to handle the world in all its rawness, pain and confusion. It is one of life's toughest challenges, and the ability and strength one gains from it are excellent qualities for anyone to possess.

Go-To Person or Doormat

Do you spend a lot of time doing things you don't want to do, but that other people want you to do?

Do you spend a lot of time feeling resentful or angry about it?

Do you often feel like someone is using or exploiting you?

If your answer to any of these questions is "Yes," then you have lots of company. Many people spend a lot of time doing things that are important to others, but not to themselves, and also a lot of time resenting it.

Typically, the problem manifests itself in two ways:

Doormats are people who are reluctant, or afraid, to say "No." They may seethe inside, but they swallow their anger and do whatever it is they've been asked. Or, they may not even be conscious of seething.

Go-To People are people who like saying "Yes." While some "Yesses" obviously spring from heartfelt generosity, Go-To People often say "Yes" because doing so makes them feel powerful and important. They like being the person others turn to for help, the one who's in charge.

From the standpoint of managing your time, it doesn't really matter whether you are a Doormat or a Go-To Person. Either way, you need to learn to say "No." Chapter 15 offers some techniques for doing so.

To be clear, I'm *not* arguing that you should never help anyone. I'm saying that you should create, and follow, a reasonable schedule that allows you to help the people whom it is important for you to help, as well as the occasional random stranger. Constantly subordinating your goals or agenda to other people's, however, is not being nice or noble: it's self-sabotage.

Activists Face Hard Choices . . .

Here, again, activists have it harder than most other people, since much of what we get asked to do is truly urgent or life-saving. (For example, interventions in cases of human or animal suffering.) The problem is that you can easily spend your entire life doing these urgent things without making progress on other important goals.

Not helping someone in dire need is obviously not an option. The best solution, therefore, if you get many emergency requests, is to find or create a group to back you up so that you're not handling everything yourself. You will not only be able to alleviate more suffering that way, but you will also be much less likely to ignore your other priorities or burn out.

Please don't forget that burnout, among frontline rescuers, is sometimes due to Compassion Fatigue, a psychological trauma condition for which you should seek professional help.

Drama King/Queen

Drama can take many forms. Perhaps your relationships, living situation, income or health are constantly in flux. Or perhaps you are constantly screwing up at home or at work. Or perhaps you're constantly getting into fights with friends, family members or colleagues. Or perhaps you are constantly zinging from one late-night or all-night party to the next, or one unfinished project to the next.

Many people, and particularly many young people, lead lives of great drama. Often that drama is painful, and yet it can also be exciting and escapist, and so sometimes we get hooked on it. The problem is that excessive drama depletes our time and energy and fosters a lack of emotional self-control. These conditions are inimical to professional and personal success.

That's why many successful people lead lives that, on the outside at least, seem static or even kind of boring. They tend to create stable relationships, stable incomes and stable living situations, and it's that very stability that allows them to focus on their Mission and succeed. Note the word "create": stable relationships, etc., don't just happen; you have to make them happen. As Gustave Flaubert put it, "Be regular and orderly in your life like a bourgeois, so that you may be violent and original in your work."

In his excellent book *The War of Art* (see Bibliography), Steven Pressfield says, "The working artist will not tolerate trouble in her life because she knows trouble prevents her from doing her work. The working artist banishes from her world all sources of trouble. She harnesses the urge for trouble and transforms it in her work." Same for activists.

Work, therefore, to create a life for yourself that is rich (in the nonmaterial sense) and interesting, but relatively free from drama. Even your activism should be as undramatic as possible. While activism is undeniably a drama-laden vocation, filled with emotional happenings and emotional people, you probably have more control over the level of drama you experience than you recognize. Acknowledge that *any* superfluous drama is probably detracting from your effectiveness as an activist, and strive to minimize it in your life and work.

Workaholism

I talked about workaholism in Part I, but the topic is worth revisiting. Workaholism fits neatly into the AACL, since people who work a lot tend to have more money with which to buy stuff. Workaholism also fits in with Puritanism, the "Protestant work ethic," and other self-denying strains in American culture. All of these reasons may be why so many people see workaholism not as the serious problem that it is, but a benign dysfunction or even an admirable character trait. Many workaholics, in fact, joke or even brag about their condition.

It doesn't help that, in the activist world, workaholism is often considered noble. Sometimes it is even demanded by the organizations we work for, or by other activists. But workaholism is incompatible with long-term success because workaholics tend to become miserable and burn out. That is particularly true if you're working long hours while living in poverty, or not seeing a result you feel is commensurate with your efforts and sacrifice.

If you are currently living a workaholic lifestyle, you should go back to Managing Your Mission, and strive to get your life and priorities back in balance.

CHAPTER 5

Another Inimical Lifestyle

I'm about to tell you something extremely subversive: a lot of people do too much housework.

Yup—the idea that it's possible to do too much housework is subversive. I know this because when I teach my eight-week class on entrepreneurship, out of the 600-plus slides I use, it's always the one on "perfectionist housekeeping" that elicits the biggest response from my students. When I start talking about how a lot of the housework people do does not really need to be done and should, in fact, be avoided by anyone with an ambitious goal, the whole room starts whooping and hollering.

Yes, most of us want a clean, well-organized living space—and the AACL fairly insists on it. Someone, after all, has to buy all that fancy-schmancy cleaning gear and chemicals that the corporations are trying to sell. But how clean a house do you really need?

Is it really necessary for you to mop the floors every week? The answer, for many of us, is no.

Is it a terrible thing to leave the sheets on the bed for an extra few days before laundering them? No.

Is it a sin to serve your family a take-out meal or to bring store-bought treats to a pot-luck dinner? No.

Or, for any suburbanites who happen to be reading this, is it necessary to keep your lawn constantly trimmed to golf-course neatness? Of course not—and golf-course lawns, which consume lots of water and are heavily dosed with chemicals, are terrible for the environment anyway.

I am not saying, I hope you understand, that you should live in a dirty house. What I am saying is that the AACL promotes an unrealistic idea of what a clean house should look like. It's even a dangerous idea if you count all the toxic chemicals one is supposed to use to achieve that state of hyper-cleanliness. Don't fall for it.

Everyone's situation varies, of course. A high-density household, whether it consists of lots of activist roommates or a family with young kids, generally requires more cleaning than a low-density one, and a household with companion animals generally requires more cleaning than one without. Or, if you happen to be a highly visual or highly organized person, you may require an exceptionally well-maintained home. Or, you may actually enjoy lavishing time on some housekeeping or gardening task. All of these are fine reasons to do more than the minimum level of housework, but just make sure you are not over-doing it or doing it at the expense of more important activities. In general, if the only reason you are doing a household task is because, (a) you think you're supposed to, or (b) "what will people say?" then get over it and start living your life according to your own values. Live comfortably and guilt-free in your "casually maintained" home.

If you want to minimize your housework burden without living in a messy home, here's the solution:

1. **Live simply, and don't buy too much stuff.** That way, you will have less to clean and maintain.

2. **Organize your space.** A well-organized home with adequate storage space for everything, and where everything is stored close to where it is used, takes much less time to clean than a disorganized home.

3. **Organize your time.** Treat your housekeeping not as an unending stream of random chores, but as a project you need to get done within a fixed period of time. Prioritize it so that the essential tasks, at least, get done—and consider forgetting about those tasks that aren't a priority.

4. **Invest in good tools.** Invest in quality cleaning supplies, and lots of them. Buy a good vacuum cleaner that gets all the dirt on the first pass. Buy several brooms, mops, etc., and leave one conveniently in each room that sees heavy traffic. Buy lots of biodegradable, cruelty-free cleaning products.[4] And any time you see a cleaning gadget you think will save you time, or make an unpleasant task easier, buy it. Buying good cleaning supplies is not about succumbing to the AACL, by the way. If you live simply, you will have relatively few cleaning tasks and need relatively little in the way of supplies. But do buy the supplies you need to do the job quickly and easily.

5. **Delegate.** Everyone in the house should be helping in a meaningful way with the housework. If you're living in a dorm or roommate situation, that means all the roommates. If you're partnered, that means the spouse and the kids (their future spouses will thank you!).

6. **Pay someone.** If you've got the money, then by all means hire a cleaning service or laundry service. If you feel guilty about it, then tip the workers lavishly; I guarantee you they won't mind. Don't think that only rich or decadent people pay someone to help with household chores; plenty of "ordinary" people do as well, including plenty with impeccable progressive *bona fides*. They tend to be ambitious people who properly value their time, and so if they can pay someone a few bucks to gain a few extra hours of precious time each week, they are happy to do so.

OK, now you know some lifestyles that are inimical to success. Here is the one lifestyle that supports success . . .

CHAPTER 6

Success Is Not a Hobby: The One Lifestyle That Will Support Your Success

So, now you know several lifestyles that are inimical to your success. But which lifestyle isn't? Which one is most likely to get you where you want to go?

That's easy: a lifestyle centered on achieving your Mission. In other words, one in which every major decision you make supports, or at least does not impede, your major goals.

Another way of saying this is that *success is not a hobby*. Meaning: it's not something you work on part-time or whenever you feel like it. It is not even a full-time job that you work on from nine to five and then forget about. Success is something you work on *all the time*, both in your professional and personal life.

Chris is a good example. All of her major choices, from taking a lower-paying job near to her house, to taking infrequent vacations, to driving an old car, were made to support her Mission. In making these choices, she actually restructured her life and made very conscious decisions about the way she uses her time, money and other resources.

Chris was able to make these choices because she:

- Is aware of what her values are. (She knows she values her family, her activism, and a non-AACL life.)
- Has determined what tradeoffs she is willing to make. (She has decided that her time is more valuable than new possessions.)
- Has the information she needs to make the right decisions. (She obviously knows about Mission Management and Time Management, and also, probably, about Fear Management and Relationship Management.)

- Uses the information she knows. (She obviously *did* her Mission Management and Time Management.)
- Works creatively to come up with solutions to tough problems. (She has organized her house to minimize cleaning hassles, and solved at least part of her shopping/cooking problem.)
- Is an independent thinker. (Despite society's constant pressure to live the AACL, she has crafted a simple, inexpensive, low-maintenance life for herself and her family.)
- Has the courage of her convictions. (She does what she knows is right, even in the face of disapproval from family and friends.)
- Can engage others to help her with her goals. (She has her husband and kids helping with the housework *and* her activism.)

And last but not least:
- Has chosen the right spouse, a supportive one.

That last point might sound silly, in a time-management context, but it is probably the most important decision Chris has made. **Nothing is more sabotaging of success than choosing the wrong mate—and nothing is more catalyzing of success than choosing the right one.** If Chris's husband were unsupportive—if he completely bought into the AACL, or refused to help with any of the housework or childcare—then she probably would have eventually faced the painful choice of either leaving him or abandoning her activism.

The right partner, in contrast, brings many irreplaceable benefits, including not just love and companionship, but inspiration, and the opportunity to work together as a team to help each other achieve a higher level of success and self-actualization than might otherwise be possible. Speaking more generally, and as discussed in Part I, you want to surround yourself as much as possible with supportive, successful people who will inspire and encourage you, especially during the inevitable hard times. This is such a crucial topic that I will be discussing it again and again throughout the remainder of *The Lifelong Activist*.

Strive to create a life for yourself that is focused on achieving your Mission. That doesn't mean you can't goof off once in a while, or take on a project on a lark just because you feel like it. Just make sure that, overall, your choices reflect your true values and needs.

CHAPTER 7

The Time Management Process

Now that you have a Mission, and a general idea of the kind of lifestyle that can make that Mission happen, let's work to make that lifestyle a reality. This means getting down to the nuts and bolts of Time Management, which is a process consisting of these six steps:

1. **Budget** your time based on the goals listed in your Mission.
2. **Schedule** your week based on the Budget.
3. **Follow** the Schedule and **Track** your time usage.
4. **Tally** your actual time use at the end of the week, and then **Review** your progress.
5. **Reflect** on what you did right and wrong. If necessary, **Refine** the Budget and Schedule. Then, **Repeat** steps 3 through 5 the next week, and **Do It** all over again.
6. **Watch** yourself get more productive!

No, it's not rocket science. Like Mission Management, Time Management is actually quite simple to understand. It's also easy to do. The key, as for every technique I recommend in *The Lifelong Activist*, is to take things slow and easy, and to aim for only a small amount of positive change at a time. That way, the process itself remains unthreatening, and so you'll be less likely to abandon it.

The following chapters discuss each of the above steps individually.

CHAPTER 8

Time Management Step #1: Create a Time Budget

In Part I, you created a Personal Mission Statement consisting of a set of specific and achievable goals for every important area of your life, including:

- Activism
- Health & Fitness
- Relationships
- Money
- Whole Person

Step #1 of the Time Management process is to budget your available time around these goals.

At the end of this chapter is a sample Time Budget table for a typical young activist who has allocated his waking hours among: a full-time non-activist job, activism, health and fitness, an active social life and a low-maintenance household. Following that is a blank Time Budget table that you can fill in to reflect your own situation.[5] Assuming that you sleep eight hours per night, that leaves 112 hours per week of "awake" hours that you can allocate. (168 total hours per week – 56 sleeping hours = 112 hours.)

So go ahead and try it. Take every goal you listed under the Activism, Health & Fitness, Relationships, Money and Whole Person sections of your Personal Mission Statement and allocate some time to it.

Some goals, such as earning your living, are probably going to require a lot of time each week, while others will probably require much less. **It's important to allocate time to *all* of your goals since if you omit a goal you may wind up never achieving it. Far better to allocate thirty or even fifteen minutes a week to a goal than to ignore it completely. Believe it or not, those fifteen minutes will add up over time, and you will wind up making much faster progress than you would have ever imagined.**

Sometimes we omit a goal because we have no idea how to get started on it. If that's the case for one of your goals, then use that fifteen or thirty minutes a week to research the problem. Read a book, talk to a mentor or just sit down and make up a list of the possibilities. That will probably be enough to break the logjam and get you started.

Budgeting is harder than it looks, by the way. Just as a "large" weekly salary starts to look frighteningly small when you start allocating it to rent, food, clothes and other expenses, your 112 hours a week is probably also going to look frighteningly small once you start allocating it to your goals. You are probably going to have to make some difficult choices and tradeoffs along the lines of: "Should I use my Sunday afternoons to do an extra three hours of activism each week, or should I use that time to socialize, visit my parents, get in a third exercise session (two per week isn't really enough!) or take that class I've been dying to take?" It's the very difficulty of the budgeting process that makes it worthwhile, however. Budgeting forces you to face the fact that you only have a limited number of hours each week, and it also forces you to make conscious choices about how you will spend that time. You'll have to prioritize your goals and determine how much time you want to budget, or allocate, to each.

Most people don't budget their time: they let others dictate their schedule and priorities for them. When you see how hard it is to budget, and how hard it is to "defend" your schedule against the sundry "time thieves" and "time nibblers" out there (see Chapter 15), you'll understand why so many people forego this difficult but essential task.

Some tips for budgeting:

- **Begin by allocating the "non-negotiables."** These are the commitments you cannot break, such as work or parenting duties. Please also consider all tasks related to your physical and emotional health non-negotiable. After you've finished allocating time to all of these, you can then move on to the "negotiables."
- **Be realistic.** If it takes you an hour each morning to get showered, dressed and ready for work, don't budget 45 minutes. On the other hand, think about why it takes an hour, and how you might be able to get everything done more quickly. If, for instance, you water your plants before leaving for work, try changing your routine so that you do that in the evening while dinner is cooking.
- **Don't cut back on sleep.** Numerous studies have shown that cut-

ting back on sleep to gain more time is almost always a false economy: the time you think you are saving at night is lost in reduced focus and productivity during the day. So, try to stick to eight hours of sleep a night, or however many hours you truly need.

- **Budget "all or nothing."** Your aim should be to devote a generous amount of time to each of your essential professional and personal priorities—i.e., the most important sub-goal in each area of your Mission—and as close to zero time as possible to everything else. This "all-or-nothing" approach is key to getting all the things you need to get done done within a reasonable amount of time.

- **Budget in fifteen-minute (1/4 hour) increments.** Why? Because you'll probably need to use every minute of your week productively to finish everything you need to get done. You may, for instance, need to trim your lunch "hour" down to forty-five or thirty minutes so that you can leave work early and have time to fit in an exercise class at the end of the day. Utilizing every minute well may sound like a recipe for stress, but by combining this rule with the "all or nothing" rule discussed just above, it's not. By utilizing every minute well, you'll be able to allocate a leisurely amount of time to your small number of priority tasks: this means that you won't be hopping frenetically from one activity to the next, and so should experience minimum stress. Fifteen minutes may sound like an insignificant amount of time, but it's really not. Most people who take time management seriously come to see it as a lot of time. If you do allocate generous amounts of time to your essential tasks, you may frequently find yourself with fifteen-minute chunks of open time between commitments. Oh happy problem! Don't waste that time, but use it to make a necessary call, send a necessary e-mail or do a bit of necessary reading. That single small change in your habits could make a huge difference in your overall productivity and success.

- **When you are finished with your Time Budget, show it to your mentors and get their feedback.** This is a very important step, as your mentors are your "reality check." Ask them whether they think you are allocating your time in a way that will help you achieve your Mission. If they say "No," ask them for suggestions on what to change.

The sample (filled-in) Time Budget table and blank Time Budget table follow.

TIME BUDGET

(Sample-for activist with full-time, non-activist job and an active social
life living in a low-maintenance apartment or house)

Category or Goal	Task (On a separate sheet break each task into as many "tasklets" or sub-tasks as possible.)	Hours per Week (include prep time, travel, etc.)	Notes
ACTIVISM			
Primary Movement	**Demos or Meeting**	3	
"	**Research, Letter Writing & Calls**	2	
"	**Misc.**	.5	Always allocate time for miscellaneous important activities that come up. You can also use this time as a buffer in case you run over on one goal or task—but if that happens repeatedly, you should go back and adjust your budget to reflect reality.
Secondary Movement	**Attend biweekly meeting**	2	Important to attend meetings so you become a part of the ally community. 1 3-hour biweekly meeting + 1 hour travel time = 2 hours allocated each week.
"	**Research, Letter Writing & Calls**	1	
Misc.		.25	
TOTAL		**8.75**	

HEALTH & FITNESS / SELF-CARE			
Exercise	Yoga; running	7.5	5 days per week. Includes travel, changing clothes, etc.
Personal Growth	Time Management / Journaling / Meditation / Relaxation	3	
"	Therapy, massage or other health appointment	1.5	Includes travel time
Self-care	Morning grooming and breakfast	5.25	Be efficient!
"	Dinners	5	Includes preparation and cleanup for 5 meals; does NOT include 2 dinners out with partner and friends, which are listed under Relationships
"	Evening grooming (before bedtime)	3.5	
Household shopping and chores	Cleaning Shopping Laundry Maintenance	6.5	Allocate specific time for each task. Try to multitask—i.e., do some activism while doing laundry.
Personal finance/pay bills		.5	This increases when you have more assets to manage (e.g., mortgage, investments, etc.)
Misc.		1	Could include additional health appointment, clothes shopping, etc.
TOTAL		33.75	

RELATIONSHIPS			
Spouse / Partner / Boyfriend / Girlfriend	1 date night plus lots of phone calls	9.25	.75 hour calls per day + 1 4-hour date. The partner can also participate in dinners and the friends' night out (see below), or hang out while you do some activism or other work, so you can get to see him or her more than one night a week. If you do want more than one "date night" a week, you're going to have to cut back on hours for something else.
Companion Animals	Care and play	5.25	
Friends	1 night out plus phone calls	9.25	.75 hour calls per day + 1 4-hour night out
Parents	Several calls/week plus 1 visit per month	1.75	.5 allocated to calls, and 1.25 to the biweekly or monthly visit. Could get more time here by eating with your folks and taking some time out of the Self-care/Dinners category.
Misc.		.25	
TOTAL		**25.75**	

MONEY/MATERIAL NEEDS			
Money	Job	40	
	Commute (45 mins per day)	3.75	Separate commuting time out so you are aware of the true "time cost" of your job.
	"Homework" brought home from work	0	Keep to 0 if possible, unless your job is your vocation!
TOTAL		**43.75**	

WHOLE PERSON			
Art, Music, Gardening, Spiritual Practice, etc.		0	
TOTAL		**0**	

TOTAL		
Activism	8.75	
Health & Fitness/Self-Care	33.75	
Relationships	25.75	
Money	43.75	
Whole Person	0	
TOTAL	**112**	

Notes:

- This time budget is intended as an example only. Every activist needs to create his or her own budget based on his or her Mission and life circumstances. Yours may or may not resemble this one.
- Yes, it seems as if this busy activist is not actually doing that much activism each week. The activist also isn't doing any Whole Person activities. But this was the best he or she could come up with, given the full-time job and busy social life. Because we only have a limited amount of time to allocate, time management is almost always going to involve painful compromise.
- Not all of the activities have to happen every week. I've budgeted half an hour for paying bills and personal finance tasks each week, but the activist may choose to spend an hour on it every two weeks.
- Notice how any unscheduled activity or time-wasting will occur at the expense of important goals. If this activist spends an extra quarter-hour on the phone with friends, an extra hour at her day job, or three hours playing video games, she has got that much less time to devote to her activism and other goals.

TIME BUDGET

(Blank for you to fill in—editable forms may be downloaded at
www.lifelongactivist.com)

Category or Goal	Task (On a separate sheet break each task into as many "tasklets" or sub-tasks as possible.)	Hours per Week (include prep time, travel, etc.)	Notes
ACTIVISM			
Primary Movement			
"			
"			
Secondary Movement			
"			
Misc.			
TOTAL			

HEALTH & FITNESS / SELF-CARE			
Exercise	???		
Personal Growth	Time Management / Journaling / Meditation / Relaxation		
"	Therapy, massage or other health appointment		
Self-care	Morning grooming and breakfast		
"	Dinners		
"	Evening grooming (before bedtime)		
Household shopping and chores	Cleaning Shopping Laundry Maintenance		
Personal finance/pay bills			
Misc.			
TOTAL			

RELATIONSHIPS*			
Spouse / Partner / Boyfriend / Girlfriend			
Companion Animals			
Friends			
Parents			
Misc			
TOTAL			

*   Activists with children or other significant personal relationships should amend this table to reflect those relationships.

MONEY/MATERIAL NEEDS			
Money	Job		
	Commute (45 mins per day)		
	"Homework" brought home from work		
TOTAL			

WHOLE PERSON			
Art, Music, Gardening, Spiritual Practice, etc.			
TOTAL			

MONEY/MATERIAL NEEDS		
Activism		
Health & Fitness/Self-Care		
Relationships		
Money		
Whole Person		
TOTAL	**112**	

CHAPTER 9

Time Management Step #2: Create a Weekly Schedule

Once you've done your Time Budget, take a break and congratulate your-self. Budgeting is hard work; the hardest in the entire Time Management process.

Creating a Weekly Schedule from the Time Budget is the next step and it's much easier. All you need to do is take the time allocations you commit-ted to in your Time Budget and fit them into a weekly schedule.

The form you'll do this on is called (surprise!) a Weekly Schedule. At the end of this chapter, you'll see a Sample Weekly Schedule based on the Sample Time Budget from the last chapter, and, after that, a blank Weekly Schedule that you can fill in based on your own Time Budget. (Reminder: you can download blank time management forms at www.lifelongactivist.com.)

Here are a couple of tips for filling in your Weekly Schedule:

- As with the Time Budget, fill in the non-negotiables first and then the negotiables.
- Try, whenever possible, to schedule the same activities at the same times on the same days each week. In other words, set up **routines** that help eliminate guesswork around your schedule, and also help you gear up, physically and mentally, for the scheduled activity. (More on the benefit of routines in Part III, Chapter 9.) If you reg-ularly exercise at 1 p.m., for example, your mind and body will gradually become accustomed to doing so at that time. You will thus be less likely to forget or skip a session.

SAMPLE WEEKLY SCHEDULE

(Example derived from previous chapter's Time Budget)

	Sunday	Monday	Tuesday	Wednesday	Thursday	Friday	Saturday
7:00 a.m.	Wake up	Wake up	Wake up	Wake up	Wake up	Wake up	Wake up
7:00	Grooming/ Breakfast/ Dog Walk	Grooming/ Breakfast/ Dog Walk	Grooming/ Breakfast/ Dog Walk	Grooming/ Breakfast/ Dog Walk	Grooming/ Breakfast/ Dog Walk	Grooming/ Breakfast/ Dog Walk	Grooming/ Breakfast/ Dog Walk
8:00							
8:30	Exercise	Commute	Commute	Commute	Commute	Commute	Exercise
9:00		Job	Job	Job	Job	Job	
10:00							
11:00	Household/ Lunch						Time Mgmt, etc./Lunch
Noon							
1:00 p.m.		Lunch & Phone Calls	Lunch & Phone Calls	Lunch & Phone Calls	Lunch & Phone Calls	Lunch & Phone Calls	
2:00							Activism
3:00	Phone Calls						
4:00							
5:00							
6:00		Exercise	Commute	Exercise	Commute	Exercise	
7:00	Dinner		Dinner		Dinner		
7:30							Friends
8:00	Activism	Commute	Activism	Commute	Household	Date	
8:30		Dinner		Dinner			
9:00		Household		Bills			
9:30							
10:00	Grooming/ Dog Walk	Grooming/ Dog Walk	Grooming/ Dog Walk	Grooming/ Dog Walk	Grooming/ Dog Walk	Grooming/ Dog Walk	Grooming/ Dog Walk
11:00	Bed	Bed	Bed	Bed	Bed	Bed	Bed
12:00 mid.							
1:00 a.m.							
2:00							
3:00							
4:00							
5:00							
6:00							

WEEKLY SCHEDULE

(Blank form for you to fill in from your Time Budget—editable forms
may be downloaded at www.lifelongactivist.com)

	Sunday	Monday	Tuesday	Wednesday	Thursday	Friday	Saturday
7:00 a.m.							
8:00							
9:00							
10:00							
11:00							
Noon							
1:00 p.m.							
2:00							
3:00							
4:00							
5:00							
6:00							
7:00							
8:00							
9:00							
10:00							
11:00							
12:00 mid.							
1:00 a.m.							
2:00							
3:00							
4:00							
5:00							
6:00							

CHAPTER 10

Time Management Step #3:
FOLLOW the Schedule and TRACK Your Time Use

You've created a Time Budget, and a Weekly Schedule based on that Time Budget. Now, you need to try to follow that Weekly Schedule for a week. While you're doing that, you should track your time use so that you can tell, at the end of the week, how closely you came to sticking to the schedule.

The way I track my time use is with the Time Tracking Form on the next page. Every time I work on a goal or task for a specific length of time—which I'll share with you in a moment—I put a checkmark in the box next to that goal or task. Alternately, I simply record the amount of time spent on the goal. At the end of the week, I tally the checkmarks and times in the various boxes so that I can tell how much time I actually spent on each goal or task.

Once, I was describing this system to a class and a woman raised her hand and asked, in a highly skeptical voice, "Are you telling us to interrupt our work every hour to record our time use?" Clearly, she thought that was asking too much.

"No," I said. "I want you to interrupt your work and record your time use *every fifteen minutes.*"

This caught everyone off-guard, but I went on to explain my reasons:

- Most busy people, believe it or not, have trouble remembering everything they did in the past hour. (Try it.) However, most people can remember everything they did in the past fifteen minutes. Since it's essential to keep an accurate record of how you spend your time, it's worth interrupting your work for a few seconds every fifteen minutes to keep an accurate log of what you've been doing.

- Recording every fifteen minutes helps keep you on track. Every time you record, you'll feel either a little bit of pride that you spent the past fifteen minutes doing what you were supposed to be doing, or a little bit of regret that you didn't—and that pride or regret might help you utilize the next fifteen minutes according to your plan.
- Recording time in fifteen-minute intervals encourages you to value small amounts of time. As discussed in Chapter 8, people who are bad at time management tend to see fifteen minutes as a short amount of time that might as well be wasted, whereas people who are good at time management tend to see it as a lot of time that can be put to good use. Recording your time usage every fifteen minutes helps reinforce the latter view.

Tracking your time may seem like a pain at first, but keep doing it and soon you'll be able to do it automatically, almost without thinking. If you do a lot of your work on a computer, as I do, you can do it in a spreadsheet. (I also downloaded a shareware (try first, pay later) stopwatch program to help me track my time.) If you're frequently away from your computer, you can do it with an ordinary notebook, pen and "real" stopwatch.

Two more tips:

- You will note that the Time Tracking Form offers a space where you can record the time you wake up and the time you go to sleep each day. This is very useful information to track. For maximum productivity, you want to wake up and go to bed at about the same time most days.
- As you will see from the Time Tracking Form, it is important to not just record the time you spend on your Mission's goals and tasks, but the time you spend on non-Mission activities, including (especially) television, video games and other forms of time wasting. You need to know precisely how much time you are spending on these activities so that you will be motivated to cut back, if necessary.

On the next page is a Sample Time Tracking Form based on the Sample Time Budget from Chapter 8. After that is a blank Time Tracking Form you can fill in based on your own Time Budget.

Lots of Notes on this one:

- This tracking is based on Chapter 8's Time Budget and Chapter 9's Weekly Schedule, but the actual time spent often doesn't correspond to the time allocated. (Our activist skipped her Sunday exercise, for instance, and she also did a bit of activism on Sunday that she hadn't scheduled.) That's because the activist isn't sticking to her schedule! As she continues to do her time management, she'll probably get better at this.

- Time is recorded either in checkmarks (each one representing 15 minutes) or hours (not minutes). "4" = 4 hours, and ".75" doesn't equal 75 minutes but 3/4 of an hour, or 45 minutes.

- Note that the activist records her awake and asleep time—this is very valuable information. If you get up two hours late, like she did on Saturday, this will obviously affect your productivity for that day. The solution, if the situation continues, is to either get up on time or adjust the Time Budget and Weekly Schedule to reflect the reality that she gets up at 9 on Saturdays.

- The form tallies not just the time spent each day on each area of her Mission, but also the time spent each week. The weekly tally, in particular, helps ensure that she makes at least a little progress in each area every week. When I track my time, I get very nervous, toward the end of the week, if I see some Goals and Sub-Goals that I haven't worked on at all. The little "0's" in the far-right column are a strong incentive for me to do at least a little work on those goals before the week closes!

- At the bottom of each column is the total hours she recorded for the entire day. If the activist gets 8 hours of sleep, that number should always be 16. It's often lower, however, because sometimes we get distracted and forget to record all our time. It could also be higher, if we're not getting enough sleep.

- The big Miscellaneous section down toward the bottom of the form (television, Web surfing, etc.) is really about time wasting, and she should work to bring those numbers down as close as possible to "0." If there are important television shows or websites she needs to follow, then she should build that time into one of her Mission areas.

SAMPLE TIME TRACKING FORM

(Partially Filled In. Every check mark equals 15 minutes)

			Sat	Sun	Mon	Tues	Wed	Thurs	Fri	TOTAL
	Awake Time:		9am	8:30 am	7am	7:15am	etc.			
Goals and Tasks		Budgeted (hrs.)								
Activism										
Primary Movement										
	Demos & Meetings	3	4							4
	Research, etc.	2								
	Misc.	.5								
Secondary Movement										
	Meeting	2								
	Research, etc.	1		✓✓						.5
Misc.		.25								
TOTAL		8.75	4	.5						4.5
Health & Fitness/Self-Care										
Exercise		7.5		1.5						1.5
Time Management etc.		3	3.5							3.5
Therapy etc.		1.5								
Morning grooming		5.25	.75	.75	.75					2.25
Dinners		5	.5	.5	.5					1.5
Evening grooming		3.5	.5	.5	.5					1.5
Household Chores		6.5		2						2
Personal Finance		.5								
Misc.		1								
TOTAL		33.75	5.25	5.25	1.75					12.25
Relationships										
Spouse/Partner		9.25	4							4
Companion Animals		5.25	1.25	1.25	1.25					3.75
Friends		9.25	✓✓✓	6.5						7.25
Parents		1.75								
Misc.		.25								
TOTAL		25.75	6.0	7.75	1.25					15.0

		Budgeted	Sat	Sun	Mon	Tues	Wed	Thurs	Fri	TOTAL
Money										
Job		40			8.5					8.5
Commute		3.75			.75					.75
TOTAL		43.75			9.25					9.25
Whole Person										
Art, etc.		0								
TOTAL		0								
Misc.										
	TV	0	1	1	2.5					4.5
	Video Games	0								
	Web surfing	0	1	1	.5					2.5
	Other	0								
	TOTAL	0	2	2.0	3					7.0
WEEKLY TOTAL		112	17.25	15.50	15.25					
Time Gone to Bed:			1am	12:00	10:30					

TIME TRACKING FORM

(Fill in Goals and Tasks and Budgeted Times based on your Time Budget.
Editable forms may be downloaded at www.lifelongactivist.com)

			Sat	Sun	Mon	Tues	Wed	Thurs	Fri	TOTAL
	Awake Time:									
Goals and Tasks		Budgeted (hrs.)								
Activism										
Primary Movement										
TOTAL										

Health & Fitness/Self-Care										
TOTAL										

Relationships										
TOTAL										

Money										
TOTAL										

Whole Person										
TOTAL										

Misc.										
	TOTAL									

WEEKLY TOTAL										
Time Gone to Bed:										

CHAPTER 11

Time Management Step #4:
TALLY Your Time and REVIEW your Weekly Progress

Now things are going to get interesting.

At the end of the week, take your filled-in Tracking Form, and figure out: (1) how much time you spent on your various goals and tasks, and (2) how close those numbers came to your Time Budget.

This is probably going to be an enlightening process, and it might also be humbling. Let me offer an example from my own life:

Several years ago, I was trying to get a business off the ground. I've always had workaholic tendencies, but at that time, I was spending almost all of my waking hours on the business. I was the business owner, so there was no shortage of things for me to be doing: writing business plans, talking to investors, supervising employees and contractors, and, of course, sales and marketing.

For all of my efforts, however, the business wasn't doing very well. Important things weren't getting done, and we weren't making much money.

I consulted a mentor, who suggested that I do the time management system I've outlined for you in this book. I was a little skeptical, but I gave it a try. I did the whole BUDGETING and SCHEDULING endeavor, then spent a week FOLLOWING the schedule and TRACKING my time.

Saturday morning, when the week was over, I sat down and TALLIED my time and REVIEWED how well I had done.

The result, to put it mildly, was surprising. It turned out that, while I *thought* I was working seventy or more hours a week, I was actually working far less. I learned, in fact, that, even though I might have been sitting at my desk for seventy hours, I was actually spending huge amounts of that time on personal calls, Web surfing, video games, coffee breaks and other non-work activity. In fact, out of the seventy hours I thought I was "working" I was actually only accomplishing around twenty-five hours of actual work.

I remember feeling shocked when I learned this, and even a little humiliated. What I had just learned was completely at odds with my self-image as an ambitious person and a dynamo. I learned that I was a person who might be ambitious, but who was also capable of wasting huge amounts of time.

That was one of the most painful lessons I ever learned, but it was worth it—as you'll learn in Chapter 13.

My only tip for Tallying and Reviewing is to do it at the same time each week, so that it becomes a routine. I did it first thing Saturday mornings; the whole process took less than half an hour, and was fun and interesting as well as enlightening.

CHAPTER 12

Time Management Step #5:
REFLECT and REFINE, Then REPEAT

Spend a few minutes REFLECTING on how successful you were at managing your time over the past week. Be sure to note the things you did right as well as the things you did wrong. Think about whether there's anything you can do in the upcoming week to improve.

Sometimes, your Weekly Review reveals a problem with your Time Budget or Weekly Schedule. Maybe you allotted one hour for your daily commute, but it really takes only forty minutes. Or maybe you allotted ninety minutes for your yoga session, but it really takes you two hours by the time you finish showering and changing clothes.

If you notice any discrepancies such as these, go back and readjust (REFINE) your Time Budget, Weekly Schedule and Tracking Form to reflect reality.

Whether you had to change anything or not, you should then create a new blank Tracking Form for the upcoming week, and repeat steps 3 (Following and Tracking) and 4 (Tallying and Reviewing) all over again!

CHAPTER 13

Time Management Step #6:
WATCH Yourself Get More Productive!

Let me finish my discussion of the Time Management process by telling you the rest of my own time management story:

> As you will recall, after tracking my time usage for a week and tallying and reviewing the result, I was left with the humbling realization that I was wasting lots of time. I thought I was working around seventy hours a week, but I was only accomplishing around twenty-five hours of actual productive work during that period. The rest of the time was going to personal phone calls, Web surfing and other time-wasters.
>
> The next week, I didn't make any conscious changes or resolutions, except to "do a little better." Amazingly, I wound up working only sixty hours, with thirty of those hours being productive.
>
> The following week, keeping the same modest goal, I worked fifty-five hours, with around forty of them being productive.

I kept at it, constantly raising the ratio of productive to unproductive hours, until I eventually settled into a routine where I was working around forty-five hours a week, with around forty of those hours being productive. What a difference that made in both my professional and my personal life! Let's just say I was a much more productive and happy person all around.

That's the way it typically works for my students, too. Tracking and Reviewing, it turns out, is tremendously empowering. By providing you with accurate information on how exactly you are using (and misusing) your time, it allows you to make the kinds of conscious choices and changes that can not only radically increase your productivity, but improve your quality of life and overall level of happiness. Moreover, this process of improvement often happens pretty much automatically once Tracking and Reviewing lets us see, finally, the scope and outlines of the problem.

CHAPTER 14

Objections

I run into three main objections when I teach my time management system:

- "I'm too busy to do all this!"
- "This system seems very regimented and robotic."
- "Do I have to keep doing this *forever*?"

Let's take them one at a time.

"I'm too busy to do all this!"

The more rushed you are, and the less time you think you have available to do time management, the more you need to do it. Trust me: it will help. It can't be much fun to be constantly rushing around trying to do twenty things at once, meanwhile missing deadlines, being late for appointments and doing a mediocre job at many tasks simply because you don't have the time to do any better. Time management will help you get past all that.

Besides, time management isn't as much work as it seems. It will probably take a day or two, at most, to create your Time Budget, Weekly Schedule and Time Tracking Form. After that, Tracking takes perhaps half an hour a day at most. You keep your Time Tracking Form next to you, and interrupt your work every fifteen minutes to put a checkmark in the appropriate box. This takes only a few seconds, and after a while you will hardly notice it. In fact, it's a mildly pleasant task, like giving yourself a gold star.

If you spend ten seconds recording your time after each fifteen-minute chunk of work, you will have spent a grand total of 640 seconds, or just over ten minutes, tracking your time over an sixteen-hour day. So, your daily Time Management won't take up that much time at all.

The end-of-week activities—Tallying, Reviewing and Planning for the next week—take an hour or less. Many people find these tasks enjoyable:

it's interesting to go back and review *precisely* how you spent your week, and whether and why you were more or less productive than the previous week.

To summarize: time management is probably going to take around an hour a week once you set up your system. That hour is probably the best investment you will ever make, as it will help you make much more rapid progress on all of your important goals than you might have ever thought possible.

"This system seems very regimented. I'm not a robot."

All of this budgeting, scheduling and tracking strikes some of my students as being too regimented. ("Fascistic" is a word that pops up every once in a while.) My answer to that is:

1. It *is* regimented—because that is what most people need. Some of my students have tried less regimented time management systems and they haven't worked. This one does, and it does *because* of its regimentation.

2. You are probably exaggerating the amount of regimentation. Most successful people exercise some control over their schedules, and many budget and track their time in just the way I've shown you. They don't consider it a big deal. If you have never managed your time, all of this work may look excessive, but it's really not. It's normal for people who hope to succeed at an ambitious Mission.

3. The system is similar to other systems people use to effect difficult personal change. We create a money budget to manage our finances and a calorie budget to manage our weight. Why shouldn't we create a time budget to manage our time? You need a plan to use any kind of limited and precious resource well, and time is the most limited and precious resource of all.

4. Often, when students complain about the system being "regimented," what they really mean is, "it's too much work." It isn't, as discussed above.

5. I would never say that this is the only time management system, or the best one. This is simply the one that works best for me and many of my students. There are other systems out there, some less regimented, some more. I urge you to try this one and see if it works for you. If it doesn't, try one of the others. The important thing is to do some form of time management.

Do I Have to Keep Doing This Forever?

"Forever" is a scary word, and I can understand how the thought that you might have to track your time forever would scare you. But don't worry: you probably won't have to.

The way time management works for me (and my students) is this: I use the system I've described for two or three months to establish new and better habits of using time. Once these habits are established, I am able to automatically manage my time without the formal process I've been describing.

If I start to backslide, or go through a difficult period where I'm having trouble being productive, I return to doing formal time management until I get back on track. Sometimes this only takes a day or two; sometimes it takes longer. And if my priorities or life situation changes, or I'm ready to boost my productivity or take on a new goal, I set up a new Time Budget and start formally managing my time all over again until the new habits take hold.

You can think of formal time management as the "training wheels" for the bicycle of your professional and personal life. It helps you make the transition to a more productive schedule, just as actual training wheels helped you make the transition from a three- to a two-wheeler. Once you're comfortable with your new schedule, you can set the training wheels aside.

Some people, you may be surprised to learn, keep doing their formal time management not because they need to, but because they like to. Like most organizational tools, it helps you maintain order and keep calm even in the center of a storm. As I mentioned earlier, it can actually be fun and meditative to spend a peaceful hour at the end of the week going over how you spent your time.

So, the answer is *no*, you don't have to do your time management "forever"—but you may want to.

CHAPTER 15

Three Crucial Skills for Staying on Schedule

In Chapter 8, I discussed how you should aim for "all or nothing" time management: devoting a lot of time to the things that are important, and as close to "0" time as possible to everything that's not. Or, looked at from a slightly different angle, you should come as close as possible to only spending your time working on things that advance your Mission.

One of the toughest challenges you will face, as you work toward that goal, is eliminating tasks you don't want to do or shouldn't be doing. There are three main techniques for doing so—**Discard**, **Delegate** and **Say "No"**—which I discuss individually below. They work well even when used in the absence of a formal time management system such as the one described in the previous chapters, but they work even better when used with one.

Discard

Personally, I could never understand time management systems where everything is ranked A . . . B . . . C . . . 1 . . . 2 . . . 3. . . . In my mind, I rank everything into two categories: Important and Unimportant. And then I *immediately* discard everything Unimportant and try not to think of it again.

Is this method flawless? No; sometimes, in my rush to Discard, I throw out something valuable. I'm speaking figuratively, but I also sometimes do this literally: throwing out an important envelope with a pile of junk mail, or losing track of an important article someone leaves on my desk. None of these errors has been "fatal," however. (If an envelope or article is truly important, someone will usually get in touch with you about it.)

You don't want this kind of thing to happen too often, of course. But far better to occasionally Discard something important than to spend your whole life doing stuff you shouldn't because you don't Discard assiduously enough.

Delegate

We tend to think of delegation as a hierarchical activity—something bosses do *to* subordinates. I see delegation as non-hierarchical, however: it's about asking for help and reciprocating with your own help when and where appropriate. It's also about sharing responsibility with others, often in a way that provides a learning or growth experience not only for those with whom you share, but for yourself.

Delegation, in short, builds community. It also implies responsibility and a relationship. You need to generously support those persons you delegate to with whatever information, training and other resources they need to get the job done.

You can, and should, delegate to all kinds of people in your personal as well as professional life, including (judiciously) those "above" and "lateral" to you in whatever hierarchies you happen to find yourself in. Delegation is ultimately a way of leveraging your time, talents and energies with those of other people; it's something that anyone in a position of leadership or influence, or with an ambitious Mission, must learn to do.

Many people say they "can't delegate." What most of them really mean is that they are reluctant or afraid to try. Delegation isn't difficult, although there are some tricks to it that I explain below. But there are lots of people out there who are afraid or unwilling to ask others for help.

Other non-delegators often use one or more of the following excuses:

- "It's easier for me to just do the thing myself."
- "No one can do as good a job as I can."
- "It will take less time to do it myself than to explain to someone else how to do it."

And my favorite:
- "I don't have time to delegate."

These excuses almost always fail to hold water. Most time-management experts agree that if you have to do a "delegate-able" task or project more than once, you should, in fact, delegate it. They also agree that you should delegate most tasks outside of your core competence. In other words, you should be spending most of your time doing the one or two things you do best, whether it's managing organizations, organizing demos or creating Web communities; and you should delegate as many of the other tasks as possible to activists who excel at *them*. (See the related discussion on "focus" in Part I, Chapter 8.)

Sometimes people fail to delegate because they underestimate the amount of time it will take to complete a task. A task that might have looked trivial before you started it can sometimes quickly expand to take up much more time than planned. Better to delegate from the outset.

Non-delegators also commonly use the excuse, "If I delegate, the task won't be done the way I would do it, or as well as I could do it." The first part of that statement is certainly true—the task won't be done in exactly the same way you would do it—and the second part may well be true, since often a "delegatee" does not do as good a job as a "delegator." Sometimes, it's because the delegatee doesn't know as much as the delegator, and sometimes it's because he or she doesn't care as much.

You know what? It doesn't matter. You have to delegate anyway—being careful, of course, to choose the right delegatee so that even if the task isn't done to your high standard, it's done adequately.

If you have trouble delegating, the solution is to practice: on colleagues, coworkers, classmates, volunteers, roommates, neighbors and family. Delegate, even, to the dog or cat—he or she may not obey, but the important point is that you will have tried! (Not all the humans you try delegating to will cooperate, either. . . .) If you can't bring yourself to delegate the big, important tasks, then practice delegating the small, trivial ones. ("Would you mind doing the dishes?" "Can you pick up the mail?") Eventually, you'll get more comfortable delegating and be able to move up to the big stuff.

Years ago, I attended a leadership workshop at which one of the participants claimed she couldn't delegate. During the afternoon exercises, the facilitator literally tied her to a chair so that she had to ask others to do every single thing she wanted done. By the end of the afternoon she was an expert delegator. So, practice does work.

Here are some other tips to help you become a good delegator:

When to Delegate: If you have an ambitious Mission, you should be delegating constantly. Again, the goal is to delegate as much as possible that's not related to your Mission or that's outside your core competence.

Whom to Delegate to: As many people as possible.

Professionally: not just your colleagues, employees and volunteers, but people in allied organizations. Members of your target audience. Members of the media. Even members of the opposition, if you're particularly clever. If someone asks you to mail them some documents, tell them that you'd like to e-mail them instead. That way, you will have delegated the printing and collating chores to them, and eliminated the mailing chore altogether.

At home and in your personal life: spouse or partner, parents, friends and kids. Neighbors. People you hire to help with the housework.

Many people who are bad at delegating look around them and don't see anyone they can delegate to. "This person" is too busy; "that person" doesn't know enough; and "the third person" has some other stuff going on. Expert delegators, in contrast, view many of the people they come in contact with as potential delegatees. When in doubt, they at least try asking for help—and if the person they ask turns them down, they ask someone else. And someone else.

How to Reciprocate: Say you delegate a big project to a colleague, employee or volunteer, and they do a good job. You reciprocate by being there for them when they need help. They may need it in the form of advice, a letter of recommendation or assistance with a project. If the assistance they need is not within your core competence, you should try to help them find someone else to do it.

In other words, reciprocation doesn't mean an exact exchange of services or time. It means an exchange of *value*. Someone may do ten hours of volunteer work for you, and then you might make a phone call that gets them a good job. Even though your call only lasted a few minutes, the recipient of your services will probably feel that she received a service of equal or even higher value for her ten hours.

Conversely, there are probably people for whom you would gladly work ten hours in exchange for them making a single phone call on your behalf. So it all cancels out.

A good rule of thumb is to always seek to give a bit more value than you receive in any exchange of services. If you do this, besides accumulating good karma, people will be anxious to work with you, and you'll always have lots of people to delegate to.

Say "No"

You can Manage Your Mission and Manage Your Time perfectly. You can be great at Discarding and Delegating. But it still isn't enough. Sometimes, you just have to say "No." As discussed in Chapter 4, this is hard for many people to do, and harder still for many activists, because the things people ask us to do often tend to be urgent, if not life-or-death. But you're still going to have to say "No" if you hope to achieve your Mission.

Successful people have lots of ways of saying "No" without actually saying "No." They will:

- **Postpone.** "I can't do that now; maybe in a few months?"
- **Swap.** "I'm really busy, right now, but if you could help me with my project, I could help you with yours."
- **Delegate.** "You know, I would love to help you out, but this kind of work really isn't my strong point. Have you asked Susan Jones? She's really good at it."
- **Punt.** "I can't do the whole project for you, but I would be happy to make a few calls."

But sometimes you just have to say "No."

As with Delegation, the solution, if you have trouble saying "No," is to practice. The more you do it, the easier it gets. Practice saying "No" to everyone around you, in big and small ways. (Tell them what you're doing ahead of time, so they're not caught off-guard.) Remember, the goal is not just to say "No," but to do so in a way that doesn't damage the relationship. As demonstrated in the examples above, there are plenty of ways to say "No" that respect the other person and offer him or her alternatives.

If saying "No" seems selfish to you, then talk to a mentor or just watch one. Successful people in any field are very good at saying "No"; they say "No" all the time, and in a myriad of ways.

Practice the three skills outlined in this chapter—Discard, Delegate and say "No"—and you'll quickly notice several positive changes in your life:

- Your schedule will start to clear.
- You'll have more time to do the things you need to do for your Mission.
- You'll rush around less.
- Your stress level will drop.

All from three simple skills!

Chapter 16 offers a few more skills and pointers that will also help you Manage your Time.

CHAPTER 16

Seven Time Management Tips

Like the three skills discussed in the previous chapter, you could use the tips below in the absence of a formal time management system and they would still help you be more productive. But they are best used as part of a system such as the one described earlier.

1. **Strive First for Effectiveness; Then Efficiency**

Effectiveness means doing the right things and doing them well; efficiency means doing whatever you are doing fast. Obviously, if you do the wrong things well, or the wrong things fast, it's not going to advance your Mission.

So focus first on doing the right things. Then on doing them well. And then, finally, on doing them fast.

If you have trouble figuring out what the right things are—and it's often trickier than it might at first appear—ask your mentors. Ditto for figuring out how to do those right things well. As for doing them fast, the key is often to set a *reasonable* deadline for yourself. There's nothing like a deadline for focusing the mind on the task at hand.

2. **Develop an Intolerance of Wasting Time**

Successful people often develop an intolerance of wasting time. That's because they are incredibly focused on achieving their goals, and incredibly cognizant of how little time they have to do so. Knowing how little time they really have, they'll be darned if they are going to spend any of it playing a video game or in a worthless meeting.

You should emulate that attitude. That means, mostly, aggressively Discarding, Delegating and saying "No." It also means reflexively making choices that save time; for example, not traveling to someone's office for a meeting when you can talk over the phone, and not talking over the phone when you can send a quick e-mail.

It also means setting time limits on common activities; for example, thirty minutes for meetings and five minutes for phone calls. You won't always be able to enforce these limits, but you will be surprised at how often you can. (Often, the other people involved will thank you for helping save *their* time!) Most meetings and phone calls go on way too long.

One of the best things you can do to save time is to start timing everything you do. Buy a phone with a timer and also buy a kitchen timer (or a watch with a stopwatch feature) and use them to time your phone calls and other activities. Just the simple act of timing yourself is often enough to help you reduce the amount of time you spend on an activity.

3. **Defend Your Schedule against "Time Thieves" and "Time Nibblers"**
As discussed way back in Chapter 3, there are many people out there who are happy to tell you how you should use your time, or to annex a piece of your schedule for their own use. Sometimes it's coworkers, sometimes it's other activists, sometimes it's your family or friends, and sometimes it is total strangers, including strangers who work for "news" shows and corporations. You need to defend your schedule against these "Time Thieves" and "Time Nibblers."

Time Thieves typically demand a large chunk of your time—say, half an hour or more. Time Nibblers, in contrast, only want a few minutes. In some ways, it's harder to deal with Time Nibblers, since there are a lot more of them out there and it's often harder to say "No" to a seemingly minor request. But, as I hope you now recognize, even a fifteen-minute chunk of your time is precious. If you wouldn't give someone $25 just because they asked, then don't give them fifteen minutes. And if you can't say "No" entirely, at least try to limit your donation to five minutes.

4. **Make Sure Your Computer is Working With, and Not Against, You**
A computer can either be your best productivity tool or worst time-sink: it depends on how well it's been set up and how well you've been trained to use it.

For many activists, unfortunately, their computer is a time-sink. They're using old (often donated), badly maintained equipment, or lack the proper applications to really be efficient. Or else, they have a good computer setup but haven't been trained to use it well.

If you are stuck using a sub-standard computer, or don't know how to use your programs well, then one of the very best actions you can take to boost your productivity and effectiveness not just in the short term, but the long term, is to improve your computer situation and literacy.

Even if you work for an organization that provides computer support, therefore, try to take personal responsibility for your computer system and computer productivity. That means making sure your computer works well and is equipped with the right programs, and that you're well trained in using it. You don't have to become a computer guru, but you should find a computer guru to help you out. If your workplace won't or can't provide such a guru, ask a friend or colleague to provide at least informal advice or help. Or, consult one of the many organizations out there that provide free or cheap computers and/or computer training to nonprofit and activist organizations. Some are local computer or software clubs (often called User Groups), others are corporations (call the Community Relations or Public Relations office), and still others are nonprofits themselves. Check around, and just make sure that whoever is helping you is truly an expert and not simply well-intentioned. One way to do this is to give him a highly specific list of what you're trying to accomplish with your computer, so that he can determine whether he does have the appropriate skills, time and tools. If not, he can probably point you to someone who does.

And don't forget automation. Many e-mail programs and websites can be set up to automatically send group e-mails or to reply automatically to certain types of incoming e-mails, such as requests for information. Other programs can be set up to automate database work or budgeting. And antiviral and backup programs are routinely automated so that they will work in the background with little input from the user. (You should always use up-to-date antiviral and backup programs. Few things kill productivity more than a computer virus.)

5. **Manage Your Personal Time as Well as Your Professional Time**
    Sorry, but it's true: you'll need to manage both your professional and your personal time. This is not just to ensure you meet your personal goals, but also because, if you neglect to manage your personal time, your personal life and commitments are likely to impinge on your professional time. An obvious example of this is the devoted partier who keeps oversleeping, but non-partiers whose personal lives are merely over-booked will also have trouble sticking to their weekly schedule.

    So, for the sake of your cause and your own emotional health, make sure your personal goals and priorities are included in your time management.

6. **Organize Your Physical Environment**

I've noticed a fascinating difference between productive and unproductive people: productive people tend to shape their physical environment to suit their needs, whereas unproductive people tend to passively accept whatever physical environment they find themselves in.

Back in that leadership workshop I mentioned earlier, we participated in an exercise that involved, among other things, putting together jigsaw puzzles. When the exercise began, the participants were working on tables in poorly lit areas of the room. Some people, however, quickly moved their tables to places in the room where the lighting was better, and—guess what?—they got much more done than the people who stayed in the poorly lit locations.

So, take a fresh look at your workspace and living space and . . . go bananas! Re-organize them so that they are more comfortable, efficient and otherwise conducive to productivity and happiness. Lack of money might be a barrier to doing this, but creativity and enthusiasm will often more than compensate for that lack.

7. **Make Quick Decisions**

Indecisiveness didn't work for Hamlet and it's not going to work for you. Successful people tend to make quick decisions, and you should learn how to do so, too.

The trick, of course, is to make them quickly but not *too* quickly. Gather all the information you need, including, if at all possible, input from a diverse range of people directly knowledgeable on, and affected by, the topic. Then, make your decision.

If you're stuck, try writing out the issues and then *promptly* go out and talk to a mentor.

Recognize that indecisiveness is not helping you make better decisions; it's just procrastination, pure and simple. Also acknowledge that some of the decisions you will make in your career and life, including some important ones, will inevitably be wrong. Far better to make a few wrong decisions than to lose lots of time and opportunities due to chronic indecision.

If you are having a lot of trouble making decisions, try practicing being decisive in small areas; for example, what to have for dinner or which movie to see. With enough practice, you'll get comfortable enough to start making bigger decisions.

CHAPTER 17

How Others May React to Your Time Management

You'll know you're doing your time management correctly when you start annoying or disappointing people. If you're not annoying or disappointing others, the odds are you're still letting them have too much control over your schedule.

Once you do take charge of your schedule, you'll probably be telling people "No" a lot more often. People generally don't like being told "No," especially by people they're used to hearing "Yes" from. They may initially react to your "No's" with disbelief or even resistance, but stick to your guns and they'll eventually get the message.

Some of the people you say "No" to may call you "selfish" or "self-centered." You aren't: you are being "self-directed." You may never convince them on the point, but make sure you yourself understand it and don't feel guilty for taking appropriate charge of your time.

Hearing you say "No" more often isn't the only behavioral change others will see in you as you start managing your time more effectively. They may also see you:

- Do more and different things. For example, get more serious about your activism, or finally take that class you've been talking about for years.
- Speed up: walk, talk and work more quickly, and end conversations sooner. ("Abrupt" is how they might perceive it.)
- Have less stress and more leisure time. (As mentioned earlier, by clearing out all the extraneous stuff from your schedule, you will leave more time for the important stuff AND for relaxation.)
- Have *less* leisure time (if you have been previously spending too much time relaxing and socializing, relative to your other priorities).

- Acquire new colleagues and friends.
- Use a different, more professional vocabulary.
- Become more confident, sharper and focused.
- Become more self-controlled and less impulsive.

And, because success in one area of life often empowers you for success in others, they may even see you:

- Dressing better and looking better all around.
- Maintaining a pleasanter and more organized household.
- Having more fun.
- Enjoying more fulfilling relationships.

These new attitudes and behaviors may inspire those around you, or they may confuse or psychologically threaten them. Those last reactions often happen when your success throws an uncomfortable spotlight on someone else's "failures," or her inability to make progress on her own goals. Such circumstances can easily engender significant bad feelings and resentment.

Have compassion for those who react negatively to your time management and other achievements. Society pushes down on us all, trying to get us to conform and be passive. You may possess unusual vision, courage or other qualities that have helped you make progress, but others are no doubt limited by circumstances that don't affect you, and they probably also have positive qualities that you, or they, don't recognize. Rather than blaming or shaming them, or allowing them to blame or shame themselves, remind them that everyone faces different sets of obstacles, and that you are there to support them as they make progress *in their own way and at their own pace*. Be humble, in other words; be a good, and generous, winner.

If people are receptive, share with them your goals and the reasons you are doing what you are doing. Ask for their help and advice; that will not only "disarm" any skepticism, but also help them access their own strengths. (Plus, they probably do have something to teach you.) Eventually, perhaps, you'll be able to work with them to help them develop their own Mission and to recognize and utilize the qualities they possess that will help them get there.

Have compassion—but if someone is relentlessly hostile or tries to undermine you, then remove yourself from that person as quickly as possible. By "remove yourself," I mean emotionally and, if necessary, physically. It's a profoundly sad thing to have to leave your family and friends behind, but it is something that ambitious people have done throughout the ages. Never forget that the people you surround yourself with will be a key determinant of your eventual success or failure. They will either lift you up or pull you down, so make the decision to be lifted up.

Here, again, is how successful activists view and manage their time. They . . .

- Value it properly, recognizing that it is their most precious resource.
- Manage it, using the system described herein or another one.
- Take active charge of their schedules, not letting others set their schedule for them.
- Discard, Delegate and Say "No."
- Use the other tips I discussed to defend their schedules and be more effective and efficient.
- Stand up to peer pressure telling them not to change.

Another thing they do is to recognize when, despite their best efforts, they are not sticking to their schedule. In other words, when they are procrastinating. Which brings us to . . .

PART III. MANAGING YOUR FEARS

PART III

MANAGING YOUR FEARS

PART III. MANAGING YOUR FEARS

CHAPTER 1

How YOU May React to Your Time Management

It would be wonderful if, once you got started with your time management, you continued to do it effortlessly; if it became second nature to you, and you just kept getting better and better at it, and better and better at your work.

It *would* be wonderful, but that's usually not what happens. Here's what does: you stick to your Time Management system for a few days or even a few weeks, then start to backslide. First, you stop Tracking your time, then you stop doing your weekly Tally and Review, and then you lose track of your Weekly Schedule entirely.

Eventually, you're back at square one—not managing your time at all—only now you feel worse than before because, in addition to not doing your work, you're also not doing your Time Management.

Clear one hurdle on the path to success and self-actualization, and you're likely to encounter another. Having established a realistic Mission and a reasonable Schedule, you're now faced with the challenge of sticking to that Schedule. If you're unable to do so, don't be ashamed or discouraged; in this section of *The Lifelong Activist*, I will tell you exactly how to conquer procrastination, which is probably the biggest hurdle you face and a leading cause of activist frustration, failure and burnout. It is usually rooted in fear, so the key to beating it is to learn how to Manage your Fears.

In Chapters 2 through 6, I provide an overview of what procrastination is, how it feels, who suffers from it, and the exact nature of the problem.

In Chapters 7 through 10, I offer a simple behavioral solution to procrastination that may work for you, if your procrastination problem is not rooted in too high a level of fear.

In Chapters 11 through 19, I discuss the kinds of fears that can cause more severe procrastination problems.

In Chapters 20 through 26, I offer a plan for defeating fear-based procrastination.

Because fear is a frightening topic in itself, I want to offer a word of encouragement up front: fear-based procrastination is a solvable problem, and can be solved much more quickly than you might imagine. So, stay brave!

CHAPTER 2

What Procrastination Is

Do a Web search on the word procrastination and you're likely to come up with a lot of complex, fancy definitions.

Here's how I define procrastination:

> **Procrastination is when you get bumped off the "path" you set for yourself for the day.**

Meaning, you start the day with a plan, but somehow, by the time bedtime rolls around, you haven't accomplished some, or any, of what you had intended. Graphically, here's what procrastination looks like:

Figure 1. Procrastination means you get "bumped" off the path you intended to take . . .

I like my definition because it reflects the notion that, at every moment of the day, you're making a choice that either keeps you on your path or bumps you off it.

Let's say you are a grassroots activist who works a part-time job four days a week, with the remaining three days being devoted to your activism. You have a good plan for those three days: wake up at 7:00 a.m.; take two hours to shower, dress, eat, and feed the cat; and then start your work at 9:00 a.m. Then, put in four hours of activism before spending your lunch hour at the gym. Afterwards, eat a healthy, low-calorie lunch on the run between meetings, and then put in five more productive hours before ending the workday at 7:00 p.m. You have a leisurely dinner with your partner, and then at 9:00 p.m. put in a couple more hours of work, followed by an hour relaxing with a good book. Then, to bed at midnight.

A great schedule—well, *not* such a great schedule, since it's a bit crowded. I'd like it better if you had allotted some more time to leisure, relationships or self-care, and maybe not eaten lunch on the run. Anyhow, let's ignore those concerns for now. The immediate problem with the schedule is that, on the day in question, you didn't follow it. Instead, you:

- Woke up late.
- Felt groggy, so you ran down to the corner store to pick up some coffee.
- Drank the coffee while reading a newspaper and checking out some blogs.
- Called your parents to see how they were doing.
- Started work at around 11:15 a.m.; returned some phone calls and did some miscellaneous small tasks.
- At 1:00 p.m., got an "emergency" call from another activist asking you to look over some documents he was planning to present at a meeting that evening. Even though this would interfere with your own work plans, it was an important meeting, so you agreed to help.
- Went out for lunch at 1:30 p.m.
- Didn't exercise; ate a gigantic meal.
- Returned to your home-office at 2:45 p.m. Started looking at the other activist's documents. Saw that they needed a lot of work. You were already feeling sluggish and unmotivated and angry with yourself for not having followed your schedule. Now you felt even angrier for having taken on a bigger task than you wanted. So the work went slowly. You stopped frequently to sip your coffee and check your e-mail and voicemail. You also did some online shopping.
- Received a personal call at 4:00 p.m. that you spent 40 minutes on.

- At 5:30 p.m., finally got the other activist's project done.
- At 8:00 p.m., finally got some, though not all, of your own work done.
- At 9:00 p.m., ate a grumpy, late dinner with your partner.
- Spent the rest of the evening vegging out in front of the television.

Two things to notice about the above, all-too-typical scenario:

1. There are *many* things that can bump you off your path.
2. Some of these bumps may seem "good" or "worthwhile" (for example, helping another activist), while others may seem "bad" or "unworthy" (for example, Web surfing or a personal call). But they all interfere with your ability to stay on your path.

From the standpoint of procrastination, it doesn't matter which reasons are good or bad. **Procrastination is when you get knocked off your path for *any* reason except an emergency.**

Which brings us to the question, "What is an 'emergency?' "

What is an "Emergency"?

Good question—and not as easily answered as you might guess. Here are some guidelines:

If the answer to the question **"Can this task be possibly handled later?"** is "Yes," then you're not dealing with an emergency. This category of "things that can be handled later" is vast, and includes many even seemingly "urgent" telephone calls and other activities that mysteriously pop up right at the moment you're supposed to be doing other work.

If the answer to the question **"Does this work have to be done at all?"** is "No," then you're not dealing with an emergency. Many even urgent-seeming projects and tasks turn out to be, in the end, unnecessary, and therefore not just a non-emergency, but a waste of time.

If the answer to the question, **"Is there a serious penalty *to me* for not doing this task?"** is "No," then you're probably not dealing with an emergency . . . for you. As discussed in Part II, we often spend time on tasks that are important to other people, but not to us. If that is the case with a particular task, then let the person to whom that task is important take responsibility for getting it done. As discussed in Part II, successful people learn to say "No."

And, finally, if you do have an authentic emergency to deal with, then deal with it, and later ask yourself this question: "**Could this emergency have been prevented by better planning or some preventative measures?**" If the answer to that question is "Yes," then, while you may have been dealing with an authentic emergency, it is one that you yourself are at least partly responsible for creating. This is beyond procrastination; it is self-sabotage. As you become better at not procrastinating, this kind of self-created emergency should happen less and less often.

What about personal, as opposed to activist or work, emergencies? The same rules apply. If the task can be postponed, it is not an emergency. If it doesn't need to be done, it's not an emergency. If it is important to others but not to you, it is not an emergency for you. If it could have been prevented by good planning or other measures, it is self-sabotage.

Obviously, life is complicated, and things can get tricky, especially when you're dealing with loved ones. I'm not saying that you should ignore them, or stint them in any way. I'm also not saying you should ignore your civic duties, or needy strangers. What I am saying is that, **if you hope to succeed at an ambitious goal such as activism, you need to make conscious decisions about how you spend your time, and not let others, or random circumstance, decide for you.** Your schedule can probably accommodate some interruptions each week, but not too many.

Conversely, if a particular person or project does interrupt you frequently, and he or it is something you must attend to, then that reality should be acknowledged by incorporating that person or project into your Mission and Time Management.

To sum up: Whatever pulls you away from your path and is not an *un*preventable emergency, is procrastination.

CHAPTER 3

How Procrastination Feels

How does procrastination feel? In a word: rotten.

Most procrastinators blame themselves for their procrastination. They tell themselves things like *I'm lazy. I'm undisciplined. I have no willpower or self-control.* And that's often just the beginning. Many of them then move on to more generalized types of self-abuse, such as *I'm a failure. I'm hopeless. I'll never succeed at anything.*

And many activists take it yet a step further, framing their procrastination as a fundamental moral flaw. *Why can't I motivate myself to work on this important cause? I must be a selfish, uncommitted person.*

Many procrastinators lead a double life, pretending on the outside to be happy and productive, but ashamed and terrified on the inside. They walk around with a happy face, boasting about how they work best under pressure, and bemoaning, in a joking way, their huge workloads and constant need to pull all-nighters. Underneath, however, they are desperate; and when things get too hot—when they are about to miss a serious deadline, thereby revealing their true "shameful" nature—they often cut and run: abandoning a project, dropping a course, leaving a job or organization or ending a relationship.

Procrastination feels miserable. Sometimes it is so overwhelming that you become depressed almost immediately upon waking up, because you know you are destined to fail at the day's tasks. Procrastination can also feel very confusing. At bedtime, you look back on the day and don't have a clue as to where your time went. You remember reading the headlines, drinking a cup of coffee with your officemate, watching some television and surfing the Web, but you are convinced that those random activities could not possibly have added up to the long hours of wasted time that day. But, of course, they did. That's what Charles Dickens meant, in *David Copperfield*, when he had Mr. Macawber call procrastination "the thief of time." To a procrastinator, it really does feel as if his or her time were somehow stolen.

If a procrastination problem is serious enough, and lasts long enough, it is often called a "block," as in "writer's block." It's not just writers who get it, although that's the example we're most familiar with. Anyone can be blocked, and many people, perhaps most, are. Sometimes, blocks last for days or weeks, but often, tragically, they last for years, decades or even entire lifetimes. Being blocked is one of the worst feelings in the world; it drives some people to absolute despair.

Wait! There's Good News!

But wait—there's no need to feel ashamed or despairing! When one of my students confesses to a procrastination problem, even a block, I congratulate her. Yes, congratulate. Here's why:

- Procrastination is an affliction of ambitious people. If you don't believe me, do a Web search on procrastination; you'll get links to hundreds of pages advising you on how not to procrastinate when (a) writing your novel or thesis; (b) pursuing a fitness program; or (c) looking for a new job. These are all ambitious endeavors, and people who pursue them should be admired even if they do procrastinate.

- All procrastinators, no matter how thwarted, can boast at least one spectacular achievement: they haven't given up on their dream. If they had, they wouldn't be worried about procrastinating on it. To hold onto an ambitious dream despite one's fears, and also despite (frequent) discouragement from those around us and the larger society, shows true vision, dedication and courage.

These qualities—ambition, vision, dedication and courage—are things to be proud of. So instead of seeing your procrastination problem as a shameful flaw, try seeing it instead as a symbol of something great within you. Yeah, you've got some work to do to realize your true potential—who hasn't?—but at least you keep showing up and fighting the good fight.

Another reason not to feel bad about your procrastination problem is that, as you'll learn in the next chapter, *everyone* procrastinates. . . .

CHAPTER 4

Who Procrastinates

Who procrastinates? Everyone—or at least everyone I've spoken with on the topic.

Ever since I became interested in procrastination a few years back, I've made a point of asking many of the people I talk with whether they procrastinate. I've asked very successful people and people who were less successful, people with long-established careers and those who were just starting out.

And guess what? Everyone procrastinates. Everyone has days when they get bumped off their path. Everyone has goals—often, the goals nearest and dearest to their hearts—that they have trouble making progress on. It's true that the successful people tend to procrastinate much less than the unsuccessful ones—that is, I believe, the very thing that makes them successful—but sometimes they do it, too.

So, again, don't feel bad that you procrastinate. It's a universal problem, and it's solvable. The word *procrastination*, by the way, dates from 1588, according to the Oxford English Dictionary, so you know that people have been procrastinating a very long time.

What About Activists?

I don't think activists procrastinate more than other people, but I do think that activism provides more than its fair share of opportunities for the kinds of fears, doubts, anxieties and confusions that, for many people, lead straight to the P word. For example:

- Activists are highly committed people who tend to fight big, important battles against powerful enemies. It's easy to get **overwhelmed**.
- Activism is psychologically challenging. It takes guts to take a public stand, especially an unpopular one; and even the simplest

activist activities, such as handing out fliers on a street corner or calling up strangers and asking them to vote, can inspire **fear**.

- Activists tend not to make much money. This means we often either have to live in poverty, take a day job, or both. This inevitably leaves us **stressed**.

- Many activist organizations are—how do I put this nicely?—not very well run. Many see high levels of employee and volunteer turnover due to their poor working conditions and low pay. These types of work environments are also often chaotic, and the chaos, combined with all of the other dysfunctions, often leads to **anger**, **bitterness**, **confusion** and **despair**. And, finally,

- Many activists are sensitive and compassionate people who have chosen, through their activism, to constantly look suffering in the face and to confront the seemingly unvanquishable powers that cause it. Many activists are also exposed, day after day, to some of the worst aspects of human nature. Make no mistake; this is a **traumatizing situation** in the psychological sense. Psychiatrists even have a name for the secondary trauma stress disorder that activists and others who work with traumatized individuals are at risk for: Compassion Fatigue. See Part I, Endnote 1, for more information on this important topic.

You may not be able to do much about the inherent stressfulness of the activist vocation, but you can learn to control—or, more specifically, to moderate—your own response to that stress. This is an essential skill that every ambitious activist needs to master, and the remainder of Part III of *The Lifelong Activist* is devoted to it.

CHAPTER 5

The Problem You *Think* You're Solving

Look, you're a smart person. An ambitious person. A creative person. A dedicated person. I'm pretty sure about all of that, or you wouldn't be an activist, or reading this book.

So, how come such a smart, ambitious, creative and dedicated person can't solve a little procrastination problem? A problem, I might add, that is entirely under your control. . . .

If you're like many of my students, that is a question that has haunted you for years. The frustrating thing about procrastination is that it seems like it would be the easiest thing in the world to solve—"Just work harder, Sally!"—when, in reality, it is one of the hardest.

Actually, that's not quite true. Any problem is hard to solve, if you're not really solving it.

Huh?

I mean it—the only way to solve a problem is to solve it. If you try to solve a problem using actions designed to solve some other problem, or actions designed not to solve any problem at all, but instead to maintain the status quo, then you are bound to fail.[1]

Makes sense, doesn't it? And here's how it applies to your procrastination problem.

You probably think the root problem causing your procrastination is laziness, lack of discipline, immaturity, lack of willpower, lack of commitment or some similar character flaw.

But guess what? It's none of those.

First of all, most procrastinators are not—I repeat, NOT—lazy, undisciplined, etc. In fact, they tend to be dynamos, at least in areas other than the one they are procrastinating in. One of the peculiar tortures of procrastination is that we are often productive in all areas *except* the one that is closest to our heart.

Secondly—and you will hear me say this repeatedly because it's such a vital point—applying negative labels such as "lazy" or "undisciplined" to yourself is, from a problem-solving standpoint, worse than useless. Not only do those labels misidentify the problem and fail to motivate you into action, they actually make the situation worse by undermining your self-confidence and predisposing you to failure. Parents, teachers, coaches and other mentors all know this: **criticism, shame and blame do not inspire positive behavioral change. What *does* work, rather, are encouragement and praise for *any* small step taken.** And that's not just true for kids; it's true for everyone, at any age. Within even the most worldly and mature activist, there's a little kid who craves, and responds enthusiastically to, praise and encouragement—and who grows resentful and contrary when subjected to criticism, shame and blame. I'll have more to say about this in Chapter 16.

There's also another problem: labeling. As I discussed in Part I, Chapter 11, the psychology of expectations means that people often live up or down to the labels others stick on them; so if someone repeatedly calls you, or you repeatedly call yourself, lazy or uncommitted, you are likely to one day fulfill that "prophecy." I'll have a lot more to say about labels in Chapter 17, but in the meantime—stop labeling yourself!

The Myth of Laziness

Think of yourself as a lazy or uncommitted person? In a book entitled *The Myth of Laziness* (see Bibliography), pediatrician Mel Levine, M.D., discusses how many cases of "laziness"—or, as he calls it, "output failure"—can often be traced to undiagnosed or untreated learning disabilities, teaching failures, environmental problems or distractions such as a chaotic family life. Once these causes are diagnosed and addressed, a person's supposed "laziness" often evaporates.

His approach highlights just how important characterizing your procrastination problem properly is to solving it, as described in the next chapter.

CHAPTER 6

The Problem You *Should* Be Solving

> More often than not, solving, or resolving, a problem is a rather trivial exercise—once we know what the problem is.
>
> —**Gause and Weinberg**, *Are Your Lights On? How to Figure Out What the Problem REALLY Is* (see Bibliography.)

Treating procrastination as a symptom of laziness or lack of discipline doesn't work because those are not the causes of procrastination. Rather, they are symptoms, just like procrastination itself is a symptom, of a deeper problem. That problem is usually either:

1. You were never taught the habits of productive work.
2. Fear: of change, success, failure, etc.

Often, it's some combination of the two.

Fear-based procrastination is a complex subject and I discuss it, and the solution to it, in Chapters 11 through 28. Most of us experience some level of fear relative to the goals that mean most to us. Let's begin, however, with problem number 1: procrastination as a behavioral issue. It may be that the behavioral "fix" described in this and the following chapters will be enough to help you solve your procrastination problem.

Productive work begins, as you now know, with Mission Management and Time Management. Once those are accomplished and you have a schedule in keeping with your core values, your next challenge is to be able to stick to that schedule. This can be reduced to three simple Productivity Behaviors:

1. Showing up to work exactly when you are supposed to.
2. Instantly starting the work you are supposed to be doing.
3. Staying focused on the work for an hour or more.

These Behaviors—showing up, getting right to work and keeping at it—are the essence of productive work. They are also the points at which procrastination happens, and, consequently, the points at which it can be attacked.

EXERCISE

Being a Compassionate Self-Observer

Note: This is an important exercise, so take your time with it.

Find a quiet place to think and write (writing is optional). Now, review your school/work/activism personal histories, and think about the role procrastination has played in them. In particular, think about the role procrastination played in preventing you from reaching your goals or finishing important projects.

If procrastination did interfere with your success, answer these questions:

- Did you work as hard as you wanted to on the goal or project? If not, why not? (Hint: the answer is probably not that you were lazy.) Think of other projects you've been involved in, in which you were energetic. How did they differ from this one?
- Did you really care deeply about the project? If not, why not? (Hint: the answer is probably not that you were uncommitted.) Think of other projects you've been involved in, to which you were deeply committed. How did they differ from this one?
- Did you follow through on all the details? If not, why not? (Hint: the answer is probably not that you were undisciplined.) Think of other projects you've been involved in, in which you were focused and organized. How did they differ from this one?
- Look beyond the project to your other projects, and your personal life. Were there things going on beyond the project that could have interfered with your ability to work hard on it, or work in a committed and disciplined fashion?

Answer these questions truthfully but without self-blame or shame. In doing so, you will probably see that there were understandable and forgivable reasons for your disappointing performance. You might even see that not all of the reasons were your fault. In the case of a failure at work, for example, your boss might not have given you all the resources and support you needed to succeed.

Even if you think you screwed up, however, do not be hard on yourself. Like everyone else, you're not perfect, and are bound to screw up in big and small ways. In the future, whenever you feel you've failed at something, your response should be one of compassionate understanding: "Too bad, but I did my best under difficult circumstances. Let's think about how I can do better next time."

Of course, this equally applies when you witness others struggling. If appropriate, remind them that they did their best under difficult circumstances and help them figure out how to do better next time.

Remember: kindness and compassion, to self and others, not only heal— they empower.

CHAPTER 7

The Three Productivity Behaviors

Here, again, are the three Productivity Behaviors, with some important words italicized:

THE THREE PRODUCTIVITY BEHAVIORS

1. Showing up to work *exactly* when you are supposed to.
2. *Instantly* starting *the work you are supposed to be doing*.
3. Staying *focused* on the work for *an hour or more*.

These important words all amount to the same thing: NO CHEATING.

Showing up late for work is cheating. Not doing the stuff you're supposed to be doing is cheating. And not sticking with it for an hour or more is also cheating.

Let's get more precise:

In *Behavior #1*, the word "exactly" means on the dot. 8:00 a.m., not 8:01, 8:05 or even 8:00:10. You need to train yourself to be exactly where you are supposed to be—not thinking about it, not en route, not pouring a cup of coffee—at the exact moment you are supposed to be there.

In *Behavior #2*, the word "instantly" means that, about a second after your butt hits the chair (or your feet, the picket line, etc.), you begin your work.

"The work you are supposed to be doing" is self-explanatory, but I would like to add this: no exceptions. Impromptu "urgent" phone calls, coffee sipping, newspaper reading and Web surfing are all procrastination, pure and simple. So is doing other work—even important, virtuous-feeling work—that wasn't scheduled for this time period. You can spend your whole career immersed in these activities, and make little or no progress on your Mission.

In *Behavior #3*, the word "focused" means that you are thinking about your work, and only your work. In other words, you are NOT thinking about other work you could be doing, or your worries regarding your work, or philosophical issues related to your work.[2] And, of course, you're not thinking about your personal life, last night's television show or the birdies cheeping enticingly outside your window.

"An hour or more." The amount of time one can, or should, stay focused on work varies from person to person. Most people, however, can train themselves to work in a focused manner for at least an hour before having to get up and take a break. If you're a very ambitious person, you'll want to push this limit to ninety minutes, two hours or even longer, because every break is a major distraction and disruption when you're working in a deeply focused way. Many professional "thinkers," such as writers, programmers, artists and scientists, max out at between four and six hours of intense creative work per day, usually with a *quick* break or two in the middle. So that may be a natural limit for most people. That doesn't mean you stop working after six hours, by the way: it means you move on to easier stuff, like paperwork, reading and routine meetings and phone calls.

Now that you understand the Three Productivity Behaviors more fully, you can begin teaching yourself to use them. The next chapter tells you how.

CHAPTER 8

Adopting the Three Productivity Behaviors:
A Process for Creating Behavioral Change

The seven steps for creating desired behavioral change are:

1. Educate yourself.
2. Marshal needed resources and support.
3. Break the change down into a series of modest and attainable goals; then tackle those goals one at a time.
4. Maximize your positive response to any "success."
5. Minimize your negative response to any "failure."
6. Anticipate, and cope with, plateaus and backsliding.
7. Keep at it!

The overall process is one of empowering yourself to take continuous small steps toward the behavior you wish to adopt.

Here's how to do it:

1. **Educate yourself.** To solve a problem, you first need to understand it as fully as possible. You also need to understand the process of problem-solving itself. Jumping into a solution feet-first, without prior study, reflection and strategizing, rarely works; just ask the millions of people who fail at their New Year's resolutions every year. By reading *The Lifelong Activist*, you're fulfilling this educational requirement relative to your procrastination problem. Good job!

2. **Marshal needed resources and support.** The next step is to gather everything you need to beat your procrastination problem and have those resources readily available. This ranges from time and money (say, for therapy or a workshop), to a supportive communi-

ty (see Chapter 25), to mundane office supplies. Although it's best to have everything you need ready at the outset of the process, if there's something you can't get, don't let that stop you. Creatively brainstorm around the problem and see what you can come up with. Activists who need but can't afford a therapist, for instance, may be able to do group therapy, which is cheaper, or join a support group at a nonprofit agency, which is often free. A spiritual advisor, if you are so inclined, may be another good alternative. At the very least, you can borrow some relevant books from the library, starting with those listed in the Bibliography. Fortunately, you don't need much in the way of resources to solve your procrastination problem: just this book, a quiet place to work, and a stopwatch or kitchen timer to time yourself for Productivity Behavior #3.

3. **Break the change down into a series of modest and attainable goals; then tackle those goals one at a time.** This step is key because setting over-ambitious goals is classic self-sabotage. Someone whose New Year's resolution is to lose ten pounds in a month is likely to fail, for example, whereas someone whose more sensible resolution is to lose a pound a week for ten weeks is much more likely to succeed.

    Here's what I mean by "modest and attainable":

    •   You practice the Three Productivity Behaviors on only one or two tasks at a time.
    •   You practice on simple, low-stress tasks, not big, scary ones.
    •   You aim to make many tiny improvements in your current work habits, instead of a few big ones.
    •   You set very lenient deadlines for achieving those tiny improvements.

    Only after you are successfully "not-procrastinating" (i.e., employing the Three Productivity Behaviors) on a couple of tiny tasks—and give it a week or two to be sure—should you move on to practicing on two new tasks. And only after you've mastered those tasks should you move on to two others. It's simply a process of learning how not to procrastinate on an ever-widening range of tasks until, eventually, you are hardly procrastinating at all. If you are having trouble achieving your modest goals, then you should set even more modest ones. If, for instance, you want to build your work endurance beyond your current level of five minutes, then set your kitchen timer for six minutes. If you can't handle that, set it to five and a half minutes. As that example indicates, if the goals you are setting seem trivially, even embarrassingly, small, then you are doing it exactly right. And if you are worried that setting such tiny goals means that it will take forever to solve your procrastination problem—don't! The beauty of this process is that it accelerates: your first few improvements may take a while, but the more you practice the Three Productivity Behaviors, the better you will get at them and the faster you will make progress. Haste and pressure are your enemies, as they almost always result in fear and backsliding.

4. **Maximize your positive response to any "success."** When you succeed in even the tiniest way, celebrate it! Pat yourself on the back, indulge in a treat, and generally make a fuss over yourself. As mentioned earlier, this kind of positive reinforcement is key to behavioral change; not only does it boost your confidence, it helps imprint your achievement in your memory so that you can call on it when needed—so that, for instance, when you one day find yourself about to procrastinate, you can suddenly think, "I'm feeling tired and anxious and I *really* want to ditch my work. But—wait a minute!—I felt exactly the same way last week, and managed to get past it and have a productive afternoon. If I did it then, maybe I can do it now."

5. **Minimize your negative response to any "failure."** If you fail to meet a goal, DON'T criticize yourself or put yourself down. As discussed earlier, this depletes your self-esteem, undermines your self-confidence, and only makes the problem worse. Instead, be a compassionate observer and analyst of your situation, and come up with a plan to try to do better in the future. For example: "Gee, I didn't get much work done today. What happened? Oh yeah, I was upset after that lunchtime phone call with my parents. Well, it *was* an upsetting call. OK, so I won't blame myself—but next time, I won't call my parents until after I've finished the day's work."

6. **Anticipate, and cope with, plateaus and backsliding.** A plateau is when you remain stuck at a level of achievement despite repeated efforts to move ahead. Backsliding is when you actually lose ground. Both are discouraging, and yet both are an inevitable part of any personal growth process. If you have an off day, or an off week or month or year, don't criticize or shame yourself, just simply accept it for what it is, and hope to do better soon.

   Plateaus and backsliding often indicate that you are setting too-ambitious goals. If that is indeed the case, the solution is to go back to a prior level of accomplishment you're comfortable with, and stay there for a while until you regain your confidence. (See the Case Study at the end of this chapter for an example.) Then, remember to set more modest and attainable goals in the future. Plateaus and backsliding can also mean that you are experiencing personal or other problems that are interfering with your ability to work on your procrastination problem. **Most of us can tackle only one major problem at a time and, let's face it, many problems, including illness (your own, or a loved one's) or a financial crisis, trump procrastination.** Narrow your focus down to your most urgent problem and put the bulk of your time, energy and other resources into dealing with it decisively. (This is yet another variation on Peter Drucker's dictum, to "do first things first and . . . do one thing at a time.") Eventually, you will be able to return to dealing with your procrastination.

7. **Keep at it!** What can I say? The people who succeed are *always* those who persevere. Sometimes, they have to temporarily put their dream aside while they work on other priorities. But they always come back to it. They never give up—and neither should you.

The next chapter offers seven tips that will aid your success in using the Behavioral Change Process to adopt the Three Productivity Behaviors. First, however, here's a little story from my own experience that shows how the process works in real life.

CASE STUDY:

Getting Past a Plateau

While writing this book, I went through a period of several weeks when, due to personal issues, I was getting little done.

I was frustrated, but knew to keep self-criticism to a minimum. I kept reminding myself: "This procrastination problem is a problem I need to solve, not a reflection of who I intrinsically am. The situation will improve when I'm ready for it to improve." The lack of shame, blame and negative self-labeling meant that I was able to maintain my self-confidence, which aided me in solving the problem sooner rather than later.

After a few weeks of struggle, I eventually had the presence of mind to do what I just told you to do in case of backsliding: return to a prior level of productivity. I dug deep into my computer hard drive and resurrected a program I hadn't needed in a couple of years—my software stopwatch. I set it for five-minute intervals and, during those intervals, committed to focusing on my work. (In between those intervals, I could be as distracted as I wished for as long as I wished.) This is the third Productivity Behavior—sustained focus. At the same time, I also practiced the other two behaviors: starting work exactly on time, and working on exactly what I was supposed to be working on.

Having to use the stopwatch again was a little humiliating—like putting training wheels back on my bike—and having to set it at mere five-minute intervals was more so. But guess what? The strategy worked, and worked quickly and spectacularly! In fact, it took *only a few hours* of stopwatch-practice for me to return to my normal level of productivity.

The strategy worked primarily because the five-minute time limit I selected was so small that success was more or less inevitable—and my tiny successes motivated me enough so that I was able to get past my block and keep going with the process.

There's one more important lesson to be learned from my story—the difference between solving a problem and dithering over it. I discuss that in Chapter 10. But first, some tips to aid you as you go through the Behavioral Change Process. . . .

CHAPTER 9

Seven Success Tips

1. **It All Begins with a Mission . . . and a Schedule**

   Always begin your day with a schedule.

   It's important to be thoroughly scheduled and clear about your plans for your workday because, to a procrastinator, even a slight amount of confusion is like that first sip of beer to a recovering alcoholic: it opens the door to more trouble. Or, in this case, to being bumped off your path.

   Ideally, you will have gone through the Mission Management and Time Management processes outlined in Parts I and II. If not, at least come up with a simple two-column schedule that says *specifically* what you are going to be doing at various times throughout the day:

MONDAY, SEPTEMBER 14	
7:45	Wake up
8:00–9:00	Shower, dress, eat, feed cat
9:00–9:30	Emails, IMs, & calls
9:30–10:00	Commute to school
10:00–3:00	Classes (with half-hour break for lunch)
3:00–4:30	Gym (including shower)
4:30–6:00	Schoolwork
6:00–7:30	Dinner with friends
7:30–10:30	Schoolwork
10:30–11:00	Commute home
11:00–12:00 midnight	Emails, IMs, & calls
12:00 midnight	Bed

Note that this is a "school day" for this particular activist, dedicated mainly to classes and homework. Other days, he'd focus more on activism or relationships. Transitioning between important goals or tasks is often hard, so allocating your time so that you spend entire days focusing on one particular Mission area is often a good idea. But don't overdo it or get overly rigid—this activist does fit in some fitness and relationship time.

Always create your schedule the night before, so that the act of scheduling itself does not itself become a form of procrastination.

2. Be Prepared

The Boy Scouts got this one right. For the same reason as #1, above—to avoid confusion that can bump you off your path—you need to begin your day with all the information, tools and materials needed to accomplish your work right out there in front of you.

That means *everything*: books, paper files, computer files, telephone numbers, writing implements, even paper clips. It should all be available, organized and in perfect working order. (Cell phone charged? Pencils sharpened?)

Note: If, despite repeated attempts, you are unable to show up for work scheduled and prepared, that may be a sign that, fighting as hard as you are to solve your procrastination problem, on some level you're fighting harder *not* to solve it—in other words, to remain at your current level of productivity. I'll discuss why this may be the case in Chapter 11.

3. Approach Your Work Without Hesitation

Remember that Productivity Behavior #1 is showing up to work on time, and Productivity Behavior #2 is getting right to work on the right stuff. While practicing these behaviors, the goal is not to hesitate.

Hesitation is the enemy because, once you do it, you open the door to procrastination. Hesitation gives your thoughts time to wander, and they will often wander directly away from your work. (Now you understand the meaning of the proverb: *he who hesitates is lost*.)

Practice gliding over to your desk and starting work without any hesitation.

4. **Stay Calm**

   Strong emotions, as you will learn in Chapter 13, can be obstacles that bump you off your path. They also make it harder for you to stay focused on the present so that you can practice the Three Productivity Behaviors.

   Work, therefore, to remain calm as the clock ticks toward your start-time. Try not to let yourself experience even a moment of fear, anxiety or doubt. If necessary, put yourself in a little "trance" just long enough for you to glide over to your desk and start working. One model to emulate is that of a Zen warrior: alert and receptive, but calm.

5. **Don't Make Your Work More Difficult Than It Is**

   Don't fall into the trap of assuming that procrastination is inevitable. Popular culture likes to portray activists and other creators as tormented because it makes good drama, but that's the wrong model to follow.

   The right model is this: you should approach your work with a light touch. Your work should be like play—safe, easy and fun.

   This idea of work-as-play may be alien to us as serious activists. But **your work *should* be play. Even your hardest work. Even your most serious activism.** Play can, in fact, be an antidote to despair and burnout. To repeat Julia Butterfly Hill's wonderful quote, "Activism is so much more than just a response to something that is wrong. Activism is a celebration of life itself. It is a manifestation of the miracle of being alive. And isn't that something to celebrate!"

   In his book, *Letters to a Young Activist*, Todd Gitlin says, "When you act politically, act playfully, too."

   Usually, when our work isn't fun, it is because we are being blocked by stress, or a negative emotion such as fear, sadness or guilt. (These may be related to our activism, or to some other area or areas of our life.) If none of those are afflicting you and your work still isn't fun, that could be a sign that you're following the wrong vocation. Return to Part I of this book and work on Managing your Mission.

6. **Focus on the Tasklet**

   Often, we procrastinate because we're overwhelmed by the project we're working on. If the scope of your project intimidates you, then try ignoring the big picture and focusing instead on the next small task that needs to be done. If that's scary, break the task down into tasklets and focus on one of those. And, if *that's* scary, break the tasklet down even further, and focus on a mini-tasklet.

Accomplish a mini-tasklet and you will be empowered to accomplish a tasklet. Accomplish a tasklet and you will be empowered to accomplish a task. Accomplish enough tasks and you will be able to finish even the biggest, scariest project.

Again, if your tasklet seems embarrassingly trivial, then you're doing this exactly right. Solve your procrastination problem for little tasklets, and you're well on your way to solving it for big tasks, and even bigger projects.

7. **Practice the Three Productivity Behaviors in Your Non-Work Life**
Don't just practice your Productivity Behaviors while you're working—practice them at other times, too. If you procrastinate around doing the dishes, paying the bills or exercising, then practice doing those activities on time and without hesitation. (Don't do them for long periods, however—just however long is necessary!) After dinner, don't dwell on how much you hate doing the dishes: just get up from the table and glide calmly over to the sink and get started.

The more you practice the Three Productivity Behaviors *in any context,* the better you'll get at them.

EXERCISE

Identify two small tasks, either from your professional or personal life, that you would like to stop procrastinating on. The simpler the better—in fact, doing the dishes or doing the laundry are ideal choices because we usually don't bring any psychological "baggage" to them. In other words, they may be boring and tedious, but they are usually not stressful or anxiety-provoking.

Use the Behavioral Change Process and the tips described in this chapter to practice the Three Productivity Behaviors on these tasks until you stop procrastinating on them. Then, after you've succeeded, practice on two new tasks.

If you can't stop procrastinating, it probably means you've chosen too difficult a task or are setting too ambitious a goal. Chose one really easy task that you can approach without fear or stress and try again.

If you absolutely cannot stop procrastinating, don't worry—the rest of this section of *The Lifelong Activist* will help you.

CHAPTER 10

Solving v. Dithering

Solving a problem means taking specific actions, such as observing its symptoms or manifestations; precisely defining it; researching it and its possible solutions; developing a strategy for solving it; testing the strategy; implementing the strategy if it tests well; and evaluating success or failure.

Dithering includes *all the other things* you do about your problems, including worrying; feeling guilty; beating yourself up; complaining to family and friends; and feeling sorry for yourself.

Dithering is pernicious. It gives you the illusion that you are solving your problem, so that you don't have to feel guilty for ignoring it. It also gives you the illusion that you are making progress, so that you don't have to feel like you've given up hope. But dithering doesn't really solve your problem. **The hallmark of dithering is that, no matter how long or seriously you do it, the problem never gets solved.** Sadly, this is true even in cases where a person dithers for decades, or his or her whole life.

How do you know when you're dithering versus solving? Easy: **if you've been working to solve your problem, but making no progress, you're probably dithering.** Even the toughest problem is solvable, at least to some degree—and, as I'll discuss later, it often takes only a small amount of actual solving to make noticeable progress. If, therefore, you are making no progress, then you are almost certainly dithering.

Another difference between dithering and solving is that **dithering tends to focus on the problem, while solving focuses on the solution.** That isn't an absolute rule, because part of what you do to solve a problem is characterize and analyze it. But if all you are doing is thinking about the problem and how miserable it's making you, and you're not devoting any time to designing and implementing a solution, then you are dithering.

Another difference is that **dithering tends to occur in isolation.** You do it yourself, in the privacy of your own room, or at least in the privacy of your own thoughts. Even when you confide in friends and others, you use those conversations more to vent, or to see your own ideas and emotions echoed back at you, than to observe, define, etc. Maybe you don't even listen very closely to what the people you are talking to are saying, or you ignore their advice.

Solving, on the other hand, usually involves other people—not just your friends, but professionals such as a doctor, therapist, spiritual advisor, twelve-step sponsor, teacher or mentor—often, more than one of those. And instead of using these people as an echo-chamber to reflect your own thoughts and feelings back at you, you listen closely to what they are saying and do your best to follow their advice.

Because many procrastinators tend to be ashamed and insecure, they have a natural inclination toward isolation. But most of life's toughest problems, including procrastination, can only be solved with the help of a community.

Why would anyone waste time dithering when they could be solving their problem? In some cases, it may be because they don't know that what they are doing is, in fact, dithering—they think they are solving. (Now that YOU know the difference between the two behaviors, try going back and implementing the Three Productivity Behaviors.) But it could also be that they don't really want to solve their procrastination problem: that, despite their feverish desire for self-improvement, they nevertheless feel a stronger desire to maintain the status quo. The next chapter explains why someone might feel that way.

CHAPTER 11

Fear

Our bravest organizers . . . plunged into darkness not because it was stylish or because they were proud possessors of a theory that assured them that they were destined to win, but because *they decided to overcome fear*, period.

—**Todd Gitlin**, *Letters to a Young Activist*

You had to not be afraid.

—**Aleksandr Podrabinek**, Soviet dissident

Fear, in itself, is not a bad thing—it can help keep us out of trouble. Just as it was in our remote ancestors' interest to be scared of terrain likely to harbor predators, it is in our interest to be scared of certain risky situations.

The problem is when our fears are excessive, irrational or otherwise an impediment to our growth and success. Fear is one of the strongest, most primitive emotions; scientists believe that there is even a kind of early warning system in the amygdala (the part of the brain that governs emotion) that allows us to experience fear before we've consciously become aware of the thing we are afraid of. If a leopard is threatening to eat you, it's a good idea to feel fear and react to that fear, as quickly as possible.

This early warning system may be one reason fear is such a difficult problem to overcome, and why it can be so disabling. It's hard to do anything when you're feeling afraid, other than try to escape the thing that is frightening you.

If you have tried repeatedly and without success to break your procrastination habit, or to adopt the Three Productivity Behaviors, then there is a good chance that fear lies at the heart of your failure. Furthermore, you are unlikely to make much progress unless you first deal with your fear. The good news is that, once you do that, progress can happen very quickly!

Below, I examine the three most common fears at the heart of procrastination: fear of change, fear of failure and fear of success.

Fear of Change

A key difference between successful and unsuccessful people is that *successful people initiate and control more of the changes in their lives.* They decide where they want to be today, this week, this month, next year, ten years from now, and thirty years from now, and take actions designed to achieve that result. Unsuccessful people tend to be more passive: they take what life or other people throw at them, and as a result often lead constricted, embittered lives that don't reflect their authentic values and needs.

Of course, someone who is afraid of change is going to have a harder time initiating and controlling it. That person may be a super-cautious or even pessimistic "devil you know is better than the devil you don't," "don't fix it if it ain't broke," "leave well enough alone," "let sleeping dogs lie" kind of person. Moreover, he may have perfectly good reasons for that mindset. (People from troubled or deprived backgrounds often learn these lessons.) But it is not a mindset likely to lead to success in any ambitious endeavor.

As activists, we must work on our fear of change even more than most people, because our vocation is all about creating change. That often necessitates, to quote Gandhi, that we "become the change we want to see." Confucius agrees: "To put the world in order, we must first put the nation in order; to put the nation in order, we must first put the family in order; to put the family in order, we must first cultivate our personal life; and to cultivate our personal life, we must first set our hearts right."

To be an activist, you must overcome your fear of change.

Fear of Failure

If an action we take brings us the result we desired, or an even better one, we call it a "success." If not, we call it a "failure." The trouble comes when we over-identify with our projects, conflating their success or failure with our own as human beings. Unfortunately, many people, and especially many procrastinators, do this all the time.

So, when our projects succeed, we don't just tell ourselves, "Wow, I did that so well!" No—we say, "*I* succeeded. *I'm* fabulous, brilliant, queen of the world!" And we *do* frequently feel like queen of the world, at least for a little while.

Now, I don't have much problem with that. Most people spend way too much time criticizing themselves, not to mention being criticized by others, and could use some extra self-praise. The more, the merrier, as far as I'm concerned—just keep it to yourself so you don't alienate others.

No, the problem isn't when our projects succeed—it's when they fail. Then the reverse happens, and we don't just tell ourselves, "Bummer. I guess I'll have to do better next time," but, "*I* failed. *I'm* stupid, uncommitted, a loser." Such negative thoughts, as you now know, are undermining.

As Steven Pressfield puts it in *The War of Art*, "Resistance [Pressfield's word for a phenomenon similar to procrastination] knows that the amateur composer will never write his symphony because he is overly invested in its success and over-terrified of its failure. The amateur takes it so seriously it paralyzes him."

Many procrastinators, in fact, have it even worse: they are comfortable taking credit for their failures, but not their successes. So, success is due to luck or some other external factor, while failure is due to the activist's own limitations or ineptness. Can you imagine a more disabling attitude?[3]

Interestingly, most young children don't have this problem. A child whose tower of building blocks falls down will cry, "It fell down!" not, "I failed!" She is not likely to transform *the* failure into *her* failure—at least, not until she becomes older and learns some of society's destructive lessons. If anything, she is likely to blame other people or even the blocks themselves, which is why her disappointment is likely to be only temporary, and she can return happily and confidently to block-building the next day.

At some point, we all have to learn to take responsibility for our failures and look objectively at our personal limitations. Children raised with kindness and insight become resilient adults who can do this without judging themselves harshly. Many of us, however, were not so well raised, and as a result are unable to refrain from harsh self-criticism. This makes us terrified at even the possibility of failure, and thus unable to take appropriate risks. And so we remain frozen:

- We don't leave a bad job in hopes of finding a better one.
- We don't leave a bad relationship in hopes of finding a better one.
- We don't take on ambitious projects.
- We don't move to a new, more interesting and invigorating place.
- We don't deviate from our ingrained habits in even small ways.
- We don't try to beat our procrastination problem.

In short, we remain stuck in our ruts.

And we usually don't tell ourselves we're in a rut, by the way. On the contrary, we usually tell ourselves that *we really are trying very hard* to leave the job, the relationship, etc. We just don't do a very good job of it or we never get around to trying.

All of this goes double for procrastinators, who, as you will soon learn, have perfectionist, negativist, hypersensitive and panicky tendencies that lead them to (1) define failure extremely broadly, and (2) experience it extremely harshly. Many procrastinators, in fact, stack their emotional deck so that it's almost impossible for them not to fail, and not to be devastated when they do.

Fear of Success

Fear of failure is an intuitive concept—no one likes to fail. But what about fear of success? How could anyone be afraid of success?

Consider this: failure, at least, usually has the virtue of leaving us in exactly the same place where we started out. Success, by contrast, always takes us to someplace new and unknown. And that is scary.

Moreover, the new place is likely to be busier, trickier, more difficult, more confusing and less comfortable than the place we left behind.

- Succeed at running a campaign and you'll wind up with a whole new set of obligations, including new people to interact with. Moreover, while some of these people might be wonderful, others might be needy or exploitative.
- Succeed at landing a new job and you'll have to master a whole new set of relationships, information and skills.
- Succeed at finding a new relationship and you put your heart on the line.

Success also always comes coupled with a new possibility of failure. There's no guarantee, after all, that you'll prevail at your new challenges, and you could fall flat on your face. As Saul Alinsky writes in *Rules for Radicals*, "In the world as it is, the solution of each problem inevitably creates a new one."

Success also puts you in the line of fire. Run a great campaign, attract a lot of positive press and raise your cause's profile in the community, and your opposition will surely come gunning for you. Even though the attacks will be a clear sign of your success, the experience probably won't be pleasant.

Finally, and perhaps hardest to take, is the phenomenon I discussed in Part II, Chapter 17: that your success may spark resentment and even hostility from family and friends who don't support your goals, or remain stuck in their ruts. Don't underestimate this—alienation from loved ones is a common, and often very hurtful, consequence of success.

Success, in other words, is stressful, and sometimes greatly so. Children raised with kindness and insight become resilient adults who can manage this stress, but many of us were not, and cannot. And so, we don't even attempt to succeed.

If success is so risky and stressful, why even bother going for it? In *On Becoming a Novelist*, John Gardner says: "Nothing is harder than being a true novelist, unless that is all one wants to be, in which case, though becoming a true novelist is hard, everything else is harder." Same for activists, and for any other type of ambitious dreamer.

On a more prosaic level, success also brings its own rewards. Not just monetary rewards, although these tend to be slight for activists, but also social and spiritual ones. Sure, your new successful life will be busier and more stressful than your old one, but it will also be richer (at least in the non-monetary sense), more interesting and more fulfilling. Your new friends and colleagues will not only support you through the stressful times, but encourage you along to even greater heights of success and self-actualization.

No Such Thing as Pure Failure or Success

A few years ago, during the high-tech boom of the late 1990s, I started a high-tech business into which, over three years, I sank every penny I had saved. This represented an enormous financial hit for my family. But the business never took off and, looking back, I can see that it never took off because of mistakes I made.

Was the business a failure?

At the time it certainly felt that way. When the money ran out and I had to take a job, I was hugely depressed—and who could blame me? After all, a few months earlier I had been visualizing myself as a titan of the new economy. Now I was scraping by as a business coach at a nonprofit agency.

But guess what? My coaching job turned out to be one of the best experiences of my life, and in fact it changed my life in every way for the better.

I turned out to be better at coaching than at most of the other things I had done to earn a living; and through my coaching I also wound up meeting some of the most amazing and inspirational people I've ever been privileged to know. Also, as a result of helping people work through their problems and blocks on a daily basis, I found myself undergoing a period of rapid personal growth and learning. And finally—the icing on the cake—in my classes, just as in this section of *The Lifelong Activist*, I was able to transform my business "failure," along with prior business "successes," into something useful for me and for my students.

Eventually, my coaching experience led me to get the contract for this, my first book, thus fulfilling a lifelong dream.

So, was my business a failure? Only in the narrowest sense.

Steven Pressfield tells a wonderful story about "failure" in *The War of Art*. After seventeen years of trying to break into the movie business, he finally had a screenplay produced for a movie called *King Kong Lives*. (If you haven't heard of it, you can probably guess the rest of the story. . . .) "We were certain it was a blockbuster," he tells us, and he and his colleagues arranged for a fancy party after the premiere.

Well, no one came to the premiere *or* the party, and the next day, the reviews were scathing. Pressfield writes: "I was crushed. Here I was, forty-two years old, divorced, childless, having given up all normal human pursuits to chase the dream of being a writer . . .I'm a loser, a phony; my life is worthless, and so am I." (Sound familiar?) However, he was quickly set right by a wise friend, who said, "Be happy. You're where you wanted to be, aren't you? So you're taking a few blows. That's the price for being in the arena and not on the sidelines. Stop complaining and be grateful."

The moral of Pressfield's story, and of my own, is that there is no such thing as pure success or pure failure—and sometimes, we can't even tell the difference between the two! Every experience, including my business and *King Kong Lives*, is a mixed bag. (Now you know why I frequently put the words "failure" and "success" in quotes throughout this book.) Of course, success is better than failure, but most successes contain some element of compromise or failure, and most failures contain some element of success, even if that element may not be immediately apparent. So the line between the two is not nearly as clear as many people think.

No Regrets

In my coaching, I constantly run into people who feel a deep shame for some, or many, of their past actions. Sometimes, the "sin" was dropping out of college, while other times it was remaining in an abusive relationship, spending one's twenties drunk or stoned, or having committed a crime (or crimes). Often, the sin was something most onlookers would consider relatively minor, or not even a sin at all—like my student who had to stop doing volunteer work at her church when her child became ill. (Believe it or not, she was deeply ashamed of this.) Many people are filled with shame for things they did back when they were teenagers or even younger, or for things that *other* people did *to* them.

Most of these people shared one thing in common: their shame and regret were keeping them frozen and unable to make progress on their goals.

Shame and regret are toxic—and useless—emotions. **The *only* proper response to your mistakes is to learn from them, work to ensure that you do not repeat them, make whatever amends you can to people you have hurt, and move on.** Anything else—any regret, remorse or shame—won't accomplish anything, and can, in fact, lead to a pernicious form of procrastination. Sure, I could choose to dwell on the many mistakes I made in my business, not to mention all the money I lost and the opportunities I thereby deprived my family of. But what exactly would that accomplish? (A non-rhetorical question; think about it.) Once the relevant lessons are learned, and you've made amends as best as you can, it's time to move on.

Failure and success are red herrings. Enjoy success when it happens, learn from failure when *it* happens, and always try to locate the element of success in any failure. But in each case, whether you succeed or fail, your job is to keep your eye on your Mission and move quickly on to the next step.

EXERCISE

Finding the Success in Failure

Re-examine some of your worst, most shameful "failures," and see if you can locate the successes hidden within. (Hint: Even the worst "failure" is useful as a learning experience.) Give yourself credit for those successes—you earned them the hard way. And stop dwelling over the failures—you've probably done that enough, already, to last a lifetime.

CHAPTER 12

One More Point About Fear

In my experience, many people, and especially many men, are ashamed of their fears. They see them as disgraceful and as a sign of weakness.

I disagree. As humans, we are subject to death, disease, disappointment, injury, loss, heartbreak, natural disaster and human-made disaster, among many other afflictions. Fear, in my view, is an entirely reasonable and understandable response to this reality.

Then there are the many hardships, risks and rejections of the activist life. These give you even more reason, in my view, to be afraid.

In other words, to paraphrase the old activist quip about outrage, "If you're not afraid, then you haven't been paying attention."

So stop blaming yourself for your fears and start asking yourself this question instead: *How should I respond to my fears?*

Steven Pressfield tells how the actor Henry Fonda suffered from extreme stage fright throughout his long career. In fact, he got so nervous before every stage performance and film shoot that he threw up. That's *forty years* of throwing up.

And after every episode of throwing up, he proceeded to give his performance.

The proper response to fear is not to let it paralyze you, and not to waste time blaming yourself for it, but to **keep moving forward**, no matter how slowly.

EXERCISE

Experiencing Fear Without Shame

Take three tasks you have been procrastinating on, and for each one, write a list of the negative consequences of accomplishing it. If, for example, you've been procrastinating on visiting a doctor, your list could include "It will cost $100," "She'll give me a shot," and "She might discover something seriously wrong."

Take your time with this exercise, and you will probably come up with a long list of negatives for each task. Two things might then happen:

- You might find yourself becoming more understanding about, and forgiving of, your procrastination. ("No wonder I keep putting this off!") This is a much better response than criticizing or blaming yourself.
- By writing down the negatives, you may defuse them, so that they seem less scary. You may even feel motivated to go ahead and do the task. (If that's the case, go for it!) But don't feel bad if you don't experience that motivation, or if it quickly goes away and you're back to feeling stuck again.

Whatever you do, do not put yourself down for having fears and anxieties. Everyone has them, including highly successful people, who often consciously or unconsciously develop skills and strategies for coping with them. That's what you'll learn to do in the remainder of this part of *The Lifelong Activist*.

CHAPTER 13

Fear Creates Obstacles to Success

Relatively few people, when they procrastinate, think, "Hold on, there! I am procrastinating as a symptom of my fear of failure," or "I am procrastinating as a symptom of my fear of success." That's because our fears tend to remain buried beneath our consciousness, where they work by impelling us toward "protective" behaviors that take us physically or mentally away from the situation that is scaring us. So . . .

- Someone who is afraid of intimacy might keep starting fights with her boyfriend, until the relationship ends and she no longer has to worry about getting too close.
- Someone who is afraid of the challenge that new information and ideas may present to his way of thinking may close himself off to new sources of information, thereby ensuring that his preconceptions are never challenged. And,
- Someone who is afraid of failure or success might keep procrastinating or otherwise screwing up her work, so that there is no question of her making progress.

I call the fear-based behaviors that bump you off your daily path, causing procrastination, "obstacles." They fall into three categories:

1. The Big Three are the fear-based obstacles **Perfectionism**, **Negativity** and **Hypersensitivity**. These are extremely common among procrastinators, and I discuss them individually in Chapters 15 through 18.

2. Additionally, there are **Logistical Obstacles**, which may have some

component of fear to them, but which are also often caused by simple ignorance or bad habits. For example:

- Lack of a clearly defined Mission
- Lack of Time Management
- Lack of preparation, skills and/or facilities
- Lack of mentors or other support

Logistical Obstacles without a large fear component can usually be easily addressed. Common solutions include: doing Mission Management and Time Management, organizing your office, taking a class on a subject you need to master, and setting up regular consultations with mentors.

If, however, you have trouble adopting the solution to your Logistical Obstacle—if you seem to lack the willpower to solve it, no matter how hard you try—then your procrastination problem probably does have an underlying component of fear. You'll need to deal with that first, using the techniques described in the remainder of this part of *The Lifelong Activist*, before you can move on to the more superficial "fix."

3. Finally, we have what I call **Situational Obstacles**, which involve other people or circumstances outside your full control. A tough day job and an unsupportive spouse are Situational Obstacles. So is a disability or serious health problem. Situational Obstacles are often the toughest to overcome. Most do have a strong component of fear, which must be addressed before any more superficial aspects of the obstacle can be addressed. But once you get past that, you are still left having to deal with some very tough circumstances.

Besides these three categories of obstacles, we also have **Panic**: not an obstacle in itself, but an obstacle-amplifier that can turn small bumps in the road into giant mountains. I discuss it in Chapter 19.

CHAPTER 14

The Most Important Thing
You Need to Know About Your Obstacles

The most important thing you need to know about your obstacles is that all *of them can be overcome.*

Get it? Not some or most of them: *all* of them.

It doesn't matter who you are, how you were raised, what race or nationality or sex you are or how much money you have. All of your obstacles can be overcome.

Overcoming an obstacle may not be easy. It may not be fun. It may take months, years or even decades. It may take more money than you can easily put together. But it can be done.

Your Perfectionism, Negativity and Hypersensitivity can be overcome.

Your Logistical Obstacles—lack of preparation, information, support—can be overcome.

Your Situational Obstacles—bad job, bad relationships, disability or chronic illness—can be overcome, at least in part.

I'll say it again: ALL of your obstacles can be overcome.

By "overcome," I mean eliminated, minimized or compensated for. You may have a disability that you must live with, or have experienced a terrible loss from which the hurt will never entirely go away. But you can still work to at least minimize the negative effect of your misfortune on your future success. One of my heroes in this regard is Christopher Reeve, the late actor who was paralyzed from the neck down in a horseback-riding accident. Suicidal immediately after the accident, and later unable even to breathe without the help of a mechanical respirator, he rallied to become a celebrated activist and author who provided hope and inspiration to millions around the globe.

True, Reeve was a movie star, so he had certain advantages. How about Victor Frankl, an ordinary, non-celebrity doctor who was imprisoned in Auschwitz and other concentration camps during World War II? He wrote a best-selling book about his experiences, *Man's Search for Meaning*, in which he reported that, even in the concentration camps, "It was possible for spiritual life to deepen. . . . The intensification of inner life helped the prisoner find a refuge from the emptiness, desolation, and spiritual poverty of his existence." In one incredible scene, Frankl describes how, in the midst of a terrifying nighttime forced march, he called up the memory of his wife, whom he hadn't seen in years, and how her memory brought him peace.

> I understood how a man who has nothing left in this world still may know bliss, be it only for a brief moment, in the contemplation of his beloved. In a position of utter desolation, when man cannot express himself in positive action, when his only achievement may consist of enduring his sufferings in the right way—an honorable way—in such a position man can, through loving contemplation of the image he carries of his beloved, achieve fulfillment.[4]

Frankl may or may not have been an extraordinary man, but we can all learn this from his experience: that, regardless of external circumstance, we can still maintain a large degree of control over our thoughts and move them in a positive direction—and that, once you do this, even the most horrific barriers to success (or, to life itself, in Frankl's case) become much more manageable.

Did I say that all of your obstacles can be overcome? What I really meant to say is this: All of your obstacles *must* be overcome. Because what other choice, really, do you have? Failure to overcome your obstacles leads to a life of bitterness and wasted potential.

The process of overcoming your obstacles is the very essence of the human journey. If you've been procrastinating a long time, you are probably demoralized and have lost sight of your strengths, talents and virtues. Once you stop running from your obstacles and start working to overcome them, you will reclaim those positive qualities and also probably discover some new ones. This process of reclamation and growth—which, incidentally, often goes pretty quickly once you stop dithering and really start working to solve the problem—is one of life's most awesome and joyful experiences.

Remember: all of your obstacles *must* be overcome.

Non-Obstacles

Often, my students raise points such as these to explain their inability to succeed:

- A person who wants to pursue activism full-time says she can't because she doesn't have enough ***money***.
- Someone else says he can't because he doesn't have ***transportation***.
- Finally, someone else says she's so busy running her household and watching her kids that she doesn't have the ***time***.

Guess what: not having something you need to succeed, such as money, transportation or time, is not an obstacle; it's a problem, a *solvable* problem.

So start solving it.

When pressed, my student "without" money comes up with a plan for minimizing her living expenses so that she can live off an activist's salary. . . .

My student "without" transportation recalls that there is public transportation that can cover his route, a friend who can lend him a car or that he can take the occasional taxi without breaking the bank. . . .

And my student "without" time . . . well, she should read Parts I and II of this book.

Two things to note, from these examples:

1. The solutions are quite simple. Solutions usually are, once you stop dithering and start solving. Remember: focus on the solution, not the problem.
2. Many of the solutions are, as my technical friends say, "suboptimal." Few people like having to cut back on their lifestyle or commit to a long bus ride every day. But what's the alternative? You can sit around hoping that you'll win the lottery or that grandma will give you her Mustang, but as the saying goes, hope is not a strategy.

The above compromises and sacrifices are, in fact, highly typical of those that ambitious people of all kinds make to achieve their goals. All around you, people are making them, and without that much of a fuss, in the hopes of one day living a more self-actualized life. ***A key difference between successful and unsuccessful people is that the former often view*** *barriers to success as petty inconveniences or exciting challenges, while the latter often view those same barriers as huge and insurmountable.*

How you view your own barriers and limitations will go a long way toward determining how successful you will be. It's glib, but true: your attitude really does determine your altitude.

Myths that Promote and Excuse Failure

Another set of barriers that activists face are the many condescending and undermining myths out there that promote and excuse their dysfunction and unhappiness. (Only artists are more condescended to and undermined.) For instance:

- "Activists should be serious and work-focused at all times."
- "You must cut all ties with your bourgeois roots to succeed."
- "Any time and energy that doesn't go to the cause is wasted."
- "If I'm not sacrificing my all for my cause, I'm a bad activist."
- "If I'm happy, I must be a shallow person or a bad activist."

If you believe one or more of these myths, your belief is probably standing in the way of both your success as an activist and your ability to lead a happy, self-actualized life. Try writing out your thoughts and feelings around the myth—you will probably discover that it doesn't survive the light of close scrutiny and objective, dispassionate analysis.

CHAPTER 15

Perfectionism

Fear, as you now know, lies at the heart of many a procrastination problem. That fear frequently manifests itself as one or more of the Big Three obstacles: Perfectionism, Negativity and Hypersensitivity. When I ask people in my classes to raise their hands if they are prone to any of these dysfunctional behaviors, nearly every hand goes up. Conversely, I have never met a procrastinator who wasn't prone to at least one.

Let's take them one at a time, beginning with Perfectionism.

Perfectionism is the feeling that the things we do or create are never quite good enough. Perfectionists hold themselves to an unreasonably high standard, and then, when they fail to meet that standard, judge themselves harshly. They also often inflict that same behavior on others, holding them to an unreasonably high standard and judging them harshly when they "fail."

Here is a list of specific mistakes perfectionists make in their thinking and behavior:

- They refuse to acknowledge the incremental nature of creation: that it happens in stages and that the early stages are likely to be rough and unsatisfying. In fact, they think their early efforts should be fabulous. They often don't think this consciously—it's a viewpoint, after all, that doesn't make sense—but unconsciously or semiconsciously, they are thinking, "The first draft of this press release ought to be fantastic."
- They underestimate the difficulty of their projects, e.g., "I'll just make a few calls and hang up a few flyers and that will fill the room for my event."
- They set ridiculously high or impossible goals, e.g., "I'm going to write a fifty-page grant proposal this weekend" despite the fact that

they've never written more than ten pages a day *and* have numerous other obligations.

- As mentioned above, when perfectionists fall short of their impossible goals, they are extremely hard on themselves and on others, e.g., "I'm a failure, and this community is stupid." (See, also, the discussion on Negativity in the next chapter.)

- They tend to see things in "black and white": total success or total failure. **They don't understand that doing half of a job—or even one-tenth of a job—is** *far* **better than doing none of it.** After all, even if you do just a tiny bit of a job every day, you will eventually finish it. But if you do none of a job every day, you never will. Emotionally, if not intellectually, perfectionists don't get the difference.

Perfectionists, above all, see work as a kind of epic struggle. They don't quite trust things when they come too easily. Because of that, they often do things that make their work harder, such as framing their projects in monumental terms, adding unnecessary tasks to projects, and over-reacting to good or bad events that occur throughout the workday (see Chapter 18, Hypersensitivity, for more on this topic). The result is that they frequently wind up fighting themselves every step of the way.

The truth is, activist work *is* often monumental and urgent. Failure to win a union vote or to get a factory to reduce its emissions can result in real suffering. This reality shouldn't be used as a rationale for perfectionism, however, since perfectionism will almost never spur you to a better outcome, but only stand in your way. In other words, the more urgent your task is, the more you need to work to avoid perfectionism and other dysfunctional attitudes and behaviors.

Activism is a serious business, but its seriousness does not exempt it from the "work should be play" rule discussed in Chapter 9. Strive to step freely and lightly around your activism, to plunge into it and back out of it at will, and enjoy taking risks around it, knowing that some of those risks will inevitably lead to failure. Yes, there will be stress—an activist career is perhaps the most stressful around—but it is essential that you not only learn to handle that stress gracefully, but recognize that, at any given moment, *you are making a choice* as to how stressed you feel.

The Solution

Perfectionism, you recall, is a dysfunctional response to fear, so the solution for it is to replace your dysfunctional thoughts and behaviors with functional ones. For example:

Replace this Perfectionist Response . . .	. . . with this More Functional One
"The first draft of this press release ought to be fantastic."	"This is a first draft, so I'm just going to focus on getting my thoughts down on paper. It doesn't matter how organized they are, or whether or not I use good spelling or grammar."
"I'll just make a few calls and hang up a few flyers and that will fill the room for my event."	"I probably shouldn't count on filling the room. Maybe I should aim to get just ten audience members instead."
"I'm going to write a fifty-page grant proposal this weekend."	"Given my writing speed and other obligations, I'm only going to aim to get ten pages done." (Extra credit: "Hey, maybe I'll call Jason and get him to write Section Three!")
"I'm a failure, and this community sucks."	"I wish things had turned out better, but I did my best. I'll learn from this episode and do better next time." And, "Who can blame people for not showing up, when the event was so poorly publicized?"
"I can't believe I only wrote five pages. What a total loser!"	"Well, I wanted to do ten pages this weekend, but I only got five done. Too bad. But still, five is way better than nothing."

How do you change your thoughts? There's no special technique—you just catch yourself thinking the old perfectionist drill and consciously replace those thoughts with their more functional equivalent. At first, this may seem foolish or contrived—and you'll probably keep forgetting to do it—but keep trying and eventually you'll see that:

- Replacing perfectionist with non-perfectionist thoughts feels good, and doesn't hurt anyone.
- The more you practice, the more automatic the process will become. (You'll forget less often.)

You can get started doing this right now. Don't set yourself an unreasonably high goal such as "I'm going to catch every perfectionist thought," and don't berate yourself harshly when you slip up. These are the very problems you're trying to solve! Just start out a little at a time, and whenever you successfully replace a perfectionist thought with a functional one, congratulate yourself. Soon, the replacements will happen so often, and so automatically, that you won't even notice them. And, eventually, your thoughts will generally become less perfectionist, so that you won't have to do much replacing at all.

CHAPTER 16

Negativity

EXERCISE

Name Your Strengths

Before reading this chapter, take a few minutes and do this preliminary exercise: On a sheet of paper, list the strengths, skills, talents and other positive qualities you bring to your activism. These could be anything from the mundane-seeming, but vastly underrated, "I'm punctual," to the pragmatic "I'm good with computers," to the more impressive-sounding "I'm a social visionary," or anything in between. Don't be shy or modest; come up with as long a list as you can. You don't need to show it to anyone. Keep the list near you while reading this chapter; I'll be discussing it soon.

Say you're a fair-trade activist who wants to hold a film-and-discussion event at your local library. You reserve a room, contact the newspapers, hang posters up all over town and call everyone you know.

The subject is so timely you're sure you're going to get a big crowd. When the event rolls around, however, only a handful of people show up: one being the projectionist, and two of the others, your roommates.

There are two basic ways you can react to this kind of disappointing situation. Here is one:

What a disaster. I'm such a dope, a complete loser. I always screw up. I don't even know why I bother to try. And this town—it's full of jerks. It was a dumb idea to try to teach them anything. They just don't get it. I feel like crap. I just can't stand it. I'm going to get a quart of ice cream and rent a bad movie and crawl into bed.

And here's the other:

Darn, this is so disappointing. I worked so hard on this, but I must have done something wrong. Oh, well—I lost some time, and I'm kind of embarrassed in front of the library staff and my roommates, but there's no real harm done. In fact, those two strangers who showed up at the very last minute were very well-informed and seemed motivated to do some future work with us! That's a great outcome.

Tonight, meanwhile, I'm going to take a break. Even though this event didn't turn out the way I had hoped, I did my best. I feel kind of low, so I'm going to do something nice for myself. I know! I'll call my buddy Sam, explain the situation, and ask him to go out to dinner and a movie. And tomorrow I'll call Karen, who ran that well-attended event over in the next town, and ask what she's doing that I'm not doing. If I do what she says, next month's event should be much better attended.

My guess is that, if you're a procrastinator, the first monologue seems much more familiar than the second. If so, you've got some ingrained negative thought habits.

Negativists, as shown in Figure 2, "skew to negative." That means they tend to see themselves, their accomplishments and everyone and everything around them, as less good, or much worse, than they actually are.

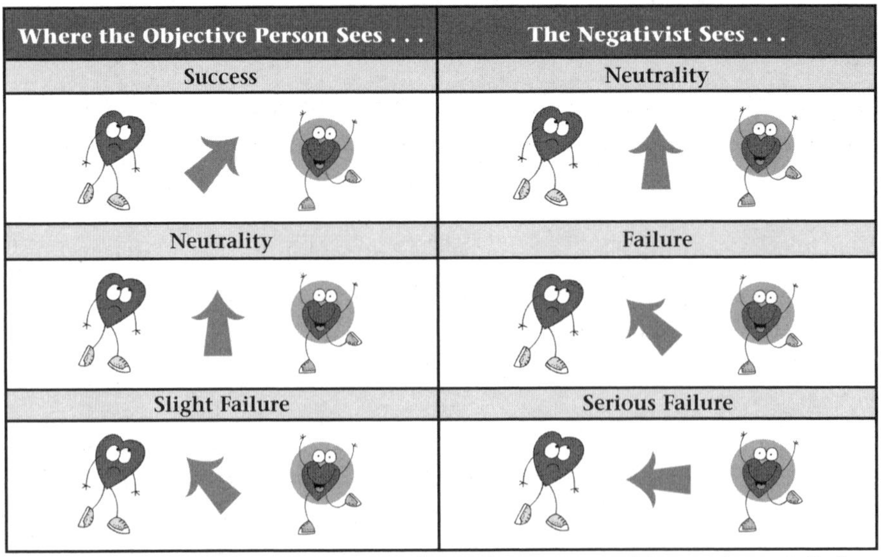

Figure 2. A negativist skews to negative: she tends to see everything, and especially herself and her achievements, as being less good than it actually is.

Negativity is a serious problem for anyone, but particularly for activists, for two reasons. First, activists regularly do confront the world's negative forces, and it's easy to exaggerate those, particularly when you're in the thick of the battle. Todd Gitlin warns against this tendency: "Just because you let the dark side of the world into your nervous system doesn't mean that you have to surrender to gloom, which in any case is never as justified as it thinks."

Secondly, negativity conflicts with your primary responsibility to view the world objectively so that you can act on it effectively. In *Ethics Into Action*, Peter Singer advises activists, "Above all, keep in touch with reality." And in *Rules for Radicals*, Saul Alinsky says that an activist's primary duty is to "see the world as it is."

Here are two specific mistakes negativists make in their thinking and behavior:

- The negativist is not looking at people and situations objectively. Therefore, she is bound to make erroneous assumptions, draw inaccurate conclusions and take inappropriate actions. The activist who plans an event based on erroneous assumptions is likely to fail. The one who thinks her event failed because she's a "complete loser" living in a community full of "jerks" is drawing inaccurate conclusions. And the activist who is blind to her movement's successes is likely to become unreasonably discouraged and to discourage others.
- Negativity is isolating. Negativists often believe they appear "realistic," "pragmatic," or "hard-headed," but colleagues and mentors with a healthy world-view recognize negativity for what it is—a sign of insecurity and a disabling force—and flee from it. When that happens, it often deepens the negativist's insecurities and reinforces her tendency toward negativity and isolation, so the problem compounds itself.

To be clear, I'm *not* talking about adopting a naïvely optimistic "this is the best of all possible worlds" attitude. I'm also not talking about disabling your critical faculties or setting low expectations for yourself. I'm talking about being an objective or, if you prefer, truthful observer and evaluator of yourself and your work, as well as of those around you and society in general.

The Negativist's View of Self

Negativists tend to be harshest on themselves.

As a coach, I get to witness this phenomenon at close range and it never ceases to amaze me. The most talented and impressive people often see themselves as failures, and drag a heavy burden of shame along with them wherever they go. Many of my students put themselves down in big and small ways as a matter of course. Their conversations are peppered with expressions that undervalue their achievements, such as, "It's not such a big deal," or "I didn't really do that much," or "Anyone could have done that." Even the ubiquitous, "I can't do math," usually turns out to be wrong, and is therefore an example of negativity.

Some students are so divorced from their strengths, skills, talents and accomplishments that I have to conduct the psychological equivalent of an archaeological dig to help them build a resume or personal history statement reflecting their skills and accomplishments. We'll sit for hours facing each other across a desk, with me interviewing them minutely on their past experiences and writing up all their positives—many of which they initially don't even recognize as such. Often, when we are done, they are astonished to see how much they have accomplished.

A truly adept negativist can turn even a stellar accomplishment into a failure. One day, I asked a student who had an MBA what school he had gotten it from, and he told me Northwestern University's Kellogg School of Management. That is a top school, so I congratulated him. His self-deprecating, negativist response amazed me: "Oh, it's only the third or fourth best school."

How big a negativist are YOU? Look at the Name Your Strengths list you created before starting this chapter. (If you didn't create it, set this book down and create it now, before you read on.)

If you listed twenty to thirty strengths, skills, talents and other positive qualities, you did pretty well.

If you listed ten to twenty strengths, skills and talents, you did okay.

If you listed five to ten strengths, skills and talents, you did average. When I do this exercise in classes, most students respond within this range.

If you listed zero to five strengths, skills and talents, you did poorly, but you've got lots of company. There are always a few people in every class who can think of few or no good things to say about themselves.[5]

My own Name Your Strengths list, which I keep on my computer and regularly print out, review and add to, currently includes more than eighty items. That is not because I'm some kind of prodigy or egomaniac, but simply because I work hard to recognize all my talents and strengths and am not embarrassed to admit them to myself. I often share my list with my students, who, by the way, are frequently amused to find "humility" listed among the dozens of other paeans to myself. They also see entries such as "loves animals" and "not a slave to fashion" along with the more standard fare such as "smart" and "good with computers." We typically define success too narrowly, for reasons I will explain in the next chapter, and that often leads us to ignore some of our more interesting and unique qualities. But why not include them? Who knows when they won't come in useful? The fact that I love animals seemed irrelevant for years, for instance—until I started doing animal activism.

Make no mistake: Name Your Strengths is an important exercise. If you do not recognize and "own" your strengths, skills and talents, how can you use them to build your success? And if you go around feeling devoid of talent, how are you going to have the confidence to set an ambitious agenda for yourself and then follow through on your plan?

Go back now and see what you can add to your list. Then, talk to friends and mentors and see what they would add to it. You will be amazed at all the good traits your friends see in you that you never suspected.

To help you out, here is a list of attributes I'm guessing you have just because you're an activist and reading this book:

Ambitious	Intelligent	Compassionate and caring
Passionate	Well-informed	Intellectually honest
An independent thinker	A risk taker	Values people, animals, the environment
A good observer	Not overly materialistic	A lifelong learner

See how easy! Even if not every one of these applies to you, I've probably just doubled or trebled your list. I could probably list twenty or thirty more, but I'll leave that work to you. . . .

Don't analyze your Strengths list and, for goodness sake, don't sit around and think about to what degree you are punctual, a great speller, etc. Just keep the list near you, review and add to it every so often, and (privately) celebrate your strengths. That small effort will go a long way toward helping you succeed.

EXERCISE

Create Your "Life Resume"

If you have trouble recognizing your talents and accomplishments, you can address that problem by creating a Life Resume. It resembles a normal, professional resume, but also includes experiences and accomplishments from outside your work life. A good way to write one is to begin with your professional resume and then start adding to it. Begin with your Activist experiences and accomplishments. Then, move on to the areas of Health and Fitness, Relationships and Whole Person (creativity, spirituality, etc.). Write down each experience or accomplishment in detail, and also write down the strengths, skills and talents you used for it. Needless to say, do not write down any of your perceived failures, flaws and weaknesses. You wouldn't do that on a normal resume, so why would you do it here?

In a Life Resume, none of your achievements is devalued or unworthy of note. If you've . . .

- created a pleasant and welcoming home
- been a wonderful friend/partner/parent/child/guardian
- enjoyed a passionate hobby such as cooking or gardening
- developed a distinctive personal style
- made terrific art or music
- worked hard to recover from childhood traumas and/or to reconcile with a parent or other estranged loved one
- helped a needy neighbor or stranger

. . . it all goes in your Life Resume.

Also, a project doesn't have to be finished or "perfect" to be included. Even if you haven't yet fully reconciled with your parent, your reconciliation work nevertheless counts as an achievement and should be listed.

A Life Resume usually turns out to be a much bigger project than we anticipate, because we've usually done many more wonderful things than we realize. Take your time and have fun creating your Life Resume, and when you're finished, go out and celebrate your many strengths, skills, talents and accomplishments!

CHAPTER 17

Negativity II: Why It's Not All Your Fault

Many people do badly on the Name Your Strengths exercise for reasons that are not their fault:

1. **Cultural Norms**

   To many people, the exercise feels like boasting, immodesty or blowing one's own horn: behaviors many of us were taught are rude.

   To those of you who consider this exercise a form of boasting, remember that I am only asking you to write your strengths down on a sheet of paper, not shout them from the rooftops. Also, to discuss them frequently with yourself, but only infrequently, if at all, with others.

   To see the importance of owning your strengths, seek out successful people and study how they behave. You will probably see that they are not rude or boastful, but neither are they self-effacing or falsely modest. They display proper objectivity about, and pride in, their strengths and achievements—and this is true of successful people from *any* culture.

   After witnessing how a misplaced sense of humility hobbles some people, I consider it a very fortunate thing that I somehow grew up unafraid to blow my own horn. I was born and raised in New York City, so you can draw your own conclusions. . . .

2. **Narrow Definition of Success**

   The capitalist system often promotes a very narrow, and very dysfunctional, view of success—namely, that if you've got a lot of money, you're a success, and if you don't, you're a failure. It doesn't matter how much of *non*-monetary value you've achieved, or what ethical lapses, if any, you committed to make your fortune.

   As an activist, you see the evil behind that definition. However, it's one thing to get a point intellectually, and another to embrace it on an emotional level. Many people who understand the limitations of the capitalist model of success nevertheless feel like failures because they don't live up to it. They can't escape their earlier conditioning or the ongoing pressure to conform.

If you suffer from this problem, my advice is to reread Parts I and II of *The Lifelong Activist* and do more work on your Mission Management and Time Management. Then, practice living your Mission without shame or regret. It's vital, in this effort, that you surround yourself with people who understand and support you, and remove yourself from people who don't.

3. Labels

The entrepreneurship program I used to run typically offered two kinds of classes: one for artists (any kind of creative professional), and another for non-artists (everyone else, including people who wanted to own cleaning services, computer consultancies, coffee shops or auto detailing shops). I would do the Name Your Strengths exercise in both, and it was interesting to compare the types of lists the two classes generated. Practically all the artists included the word "creative" high up on their lists, and practically none of the other entrepreneurs did. Most entrepreneurs are highly creative, however, so the question is, why didn't the non-artists see themselves that way?

The answer: labels.

From a young age, the artists were probably told they were creative. It was probably drummed into them all the time. They were probably encouraged to paint, sculpt or make music; urged toward art classes and artistic extracurricular activities; and praised for their accomplishments in these areas.

No wonder "creative" appeared high up on their list of strengths.

The non-artists, many of whom might have been just as creative as the artists, probably didn't get the same label attached to them. So, they didn't grow up thinking they were creative.

Labels, as any child development expert will tell you, are powerful. They influence us enormously and shape our self-images. They are also hard to shake. Many of my students were labeled negatively in their youth, and those labels continue to haunt them as adults. Maybe they were called "oversensitive" or "an impractical dreamer." Or maybe they were called "lazy" or "stupid" or "bad at math." Or maybe they were called worse. In many cases, they are still fighting, as adults, to free themselves from those childhood labels.

What labels are holding *you* back? Try to break free of all of your labels, and to see yourself and your achievements with fresh eyes. Friends and mentors can really help here; as discussed earlier, they will probably see strengths and talents in you that you never imagined.

By the way, although I sometimes use terms such as "perfectionist" and "negativist" in *The Lifelong Activist* for rhetorical convenience, I would never use these terms to label someone in real life. I might tell someone that they are acting perfectionistically or negatively, or that they have those tendencies—never that they *are* a perfectionist or negativist.

The Solution

As with perfectionism, the cure for negativity is to replace dysfunctional (negative) thoughts and behaviors with functional (objective) ones. For example:

Replace this Negativist Response . . .	. . . with this More Functional One
"I really blew that project."	"I did half of it well, and the other half not so well."
"I'm a terrible activist—I don't know why I even try!"	"I seem to be better at designing campaigns than managing them. Maybe I can find a good manager to help me with my next one."
""We only got 25 signatures on our petition."	"We got 25 signatures—not a bad start. Let's figure out how to do better next time."
"We only got five people to attend our last meeting. We're losers, and this whole community is full of losers."	"Those five people seemed very dedicated and well-informed, so it was great that they came. Let's get them involved in our campaign."

The process you'll go through is the same as described in Chapter 15 for perfectionism: practice, practice, practice. At first, it may be hard to remember to replace a negative thought with a functional one, but after some practice, it will seem more natural, and after still more practice, it will happen automatically. Eventually, you'll stop thinking so negatively.

As always, never berate yourself when you slip up.

CHAPTER 18

Hypersensitivity

Hypersensitivity is the tendency to overreact to life's ordinary stresses. It's a trait that procrastinators share with addicts, "blocked" artists and others who are having trouble coping.

Notice that I'm talking about "hypersensitivity," not "sensitivity." Sensitivity is a great personality trait. It means we're deeply and meaningfully aware of ourselves, our environment and the living beings around us. The world needs as many sensitive people as possible because they are often the ones who notice, and strive to fix, problems.

Hypersensitivity, however, goes overboard. If a minor irritation, disappointment or rejection ruins your day (or week or month or year), then you're hypersensitive. Conversely, if minor good news makes you gleeful or manic to the point where you can't function, that's also hypersensitivity.

Hypersensitivity is, in essence, a lack of emotional self-control. It's a very common problem, judging from the hundreds of books out there that purport to address the problem, and a particularly serious one for activists because:

- **The activist life is filled with emotional "triggers."** Most people, in their daily lives, experience a range of positive and negative emotions. Few people, other than artists, perhaps, actively court emotional highs and lows the way activists do. By working to change the status quo, activists pretty much guarantee that they will be exposed to frequent disapproval, rejection, frustration and even ridicule. "Go where you are least wanted, for there you are most needed," advised Abigail Kelley Foster, the nineteenth century abolitionist and pacifist. Excellent advice, but the inevitable rejection and negativity the activist will face when she follows it will make life extremely unpleasant if she has hypersensitive tendencies.

- **Hypersensitivity steals not just your time and energy, but your objectivity.** As discussed earlier, the primary requisite for doing activist work is an objective worldview. Hypersensitivity clouds your objectivity, thus making you less effective. Often, moreover, the clouding is negative, so that you see a situation as being worse than it actually is. This breeds the kinds of cynicism and hopelessness that presage so many cases of burnout. Even excessive optimism can be a problem, however. Here's Gitlin, again: "If you're giddy with expectations, like the revolutionists of the late sixties, your giddiness will work on you like a drug—until, if you're lucky, you crash, and if you're unlucky, something worse happens. This was the way of the Communists and their fellow travelers, who were always looking to explain (away) any criticisms of the Soviet Union as fabrications of the bourgeois press. . . . The equivalent rapture was the fate of too many hard-core activists of my generation, who mistook their dizzy desires for real revolutionary prospects."

- **Hypersensitivity leads to a tendency toward isolation.** Many hypersensitive people have trouble tolerating life's ordinary stresses. They react strongly to irritants such as a late train, a slow line at the grocery store or even bad weather. At the workplace, they simply can't abide cubicles, dress codes, fluorescent lights and nosy coworkers. One "solution" many hypersensitive people employ, either consciously or unconsciously, is to retreat from the world and its stresses. They spend more and more time alone in an environment that is as much under their control as possible. Professionally, they may try to work from home, or, if they can't manage that, take other actions to isolate themselves from their colleagues—for example, keeping their office door shut or avoiding the popular lunch hangout. After hours, they may retreat into a solitary couch potato or "Internet addict" existence. The problem with isolation is that, while it may feel good in the short term, it is almost always inimical to success. Lone Ranger–type myths aside, success in almost any important endeavor invariably requires a team effort. And even the Lone Ranger had Tonto and Silver. . . .

If you are hypersensitive, one of your primary challenges will be to learn to experience negative emotions such as rejection, frustration and disappointment, as well as positive ones such as pride and happiness, without being derailed by them. This may not be easy, but it will be an important part of your growth as an activist.

Hypersensitivity is also often linked to addiction. **If you are "hooked" on extreme emotional highs and lows that you are unable or unwilling to moderate—or that you may be attempting to moderate through drinking, drugs, overeating, oversleeping or through a "soft" addiction such as compulsive television-watching or video-game-playing—you're going to have to deal with that issue.** See a therapist, join a twelve-step program, or at least do some reading in the field of addiction and recovery. A good place to start is *Addictive Thinking: Understanding Self-Deception* by Abraham J. Twerski, M.D. (see Bibliography).

COMPASSION FATIGUE

Hypersensitivity can also be symptomatic of a serious psychological condition called Compassion Fatigue, which I discussed in Part I, Endnote 1. If you think you may be suffering from Compassion Fatigue, you should seek professional help.

The Solution

As with perfectionism and negativity, the cure for hypersensitivity is to replace dysfunctional thoughts and behaviors with functional (objective) ones. Hypersensitivity is a somewhat simpler problem to work on than the other two, however, because the functional thought pattern is always a variation on, "I'm going to calm down and do what I'm supposed to be doing." For example:

Replace this Hypersensitive Response . . .	. . . with this More Functional One
"I hate talking to the press! I was stupid to let Jane talk me into running the press conference! I'm going to call her and tell her I can't do it. It's the last minute, and she'll be ticked off, but she'll find someone else."	"I'm going to calm down and do what I agreed to do. I'll call Jane and see if she can provide backup, but I committed to doing this and so I'll do my best and see what happens."
"It's snowing out; do I really want to leave my warm apartment and attend the meeting? No way! I know I agreed to attend, but I really don't want to go . . . "	"I'm going to calm down, dress warmly, grab a cup of hot coffee, and go to the meeting. I know I'll feel better afterward if I meet my obligation."
"I can't believe that that jerk talked to me like that! He has some nerve! I'm so mad I just can't believe it. My whole afternoon is ruined!"	"I'm going to calm down—maybe do some yoga stretches—and then try to get back to work. If the stretches don't work, I'll try to deal with my anger by writing for a while in my journal." (See Chapter 23)
"Wow! I can't believe we landed a meeting with XYZ Foundation. That's great news! If we do a great presentation they could give us $300,000. With that money, we could move to better offices, hire five new people, start that new campaign, and replace all the office computers. Also, if XYZ Foundation gives us money, so will ABC Foundation. We could probably get $150,000 out of them and could use THAT money for. . . . Wow, this is good stuff! I'd better write it all down . . . and then I have a few people to call and share the good news with . . . and, oh, I need to get Bill's advice on how to handle this, so I'd better call him, too. . . . "	"That was a GREAT call with XYZ. I'm so happy we landed that meeting! It's not until next month, however, so I'm just going to jot down a few notes about XYZ and then try to calm down and get back to today's work. I can start preparing for the XYZ meeting next week."

The process you'll go through is the same as that for solving Perfectionism and Negativism: practice, practice, practice. At first, it may be hard to remember to replace a hypersensitive thought with a functional one, but after some practice it will seem more natural, and after still more practice it will happen automatically. Eventually, you'll stop reacting so hypersensitively.

As always, never berate yourself when you slip up.

CHAPTER 19

PANIC!: The Obstacle-Amplifier

> **IMPORTANT NOTE**
>
> The "panic" referred to throughout this chapter is the ordinary panic of everyday life. If you suffer from disabling anxiety or panic attacks, you should see a doctor or psychologist.

Remember the negativist response in Chapter 16?

What a disaster. I'm such a dope, a complete loser. I always screw up. I don't know why I even bother to try. And this town—it's full of jerks. It was a dumb idea to try to teach them anything. They just don't get it. I feel like crap. I just can't stand it. I'm going to get a quart of ice cream and rent a bad movie and crawl into bed.

What if, instead of that little speech, the activist had reacted this way, instead:

What a disaster. I'm such a dope . . . oh, well, I could keep dwelling on this, but why bother? There was no real harm done, and I really did try my best, so I shouldn't dump on myself for it . . . In the meantime, I've got other work to do. I'll spend a few minutes making some notes on the experience, and maybe call a friend for support, but after that I'll get started planning this weekend's demo.

Notice how, in the second speech, the activist consciously interrupts her negative thoughts and introduces a more functional line of thinking.

A key difference between the activist in the first example and the one in the second may be *panic*. Everyone experiences regular episodes of fear, anger and disappointment; and people in challenging professions such as activism probably experience those emotions several times a day. Non-procrastinators can usually experience those emotions briefly and then return to a positive, or at least neutral, mood and continue to do their work. Procrastinators cannot: they panic, and their panic amplifies their fear and anxiety until they can no longer function. Then they retreat into dysfunctional behaviors such as perfectionism, negativity and hypersensitivity.

The other thing panic does, besides amplify negative emotions, is disable your coping mechanisms. This could, in fact, be the definition of panic: the state of being unable to cope. Someone who is able to change a tire during practice runs in her driveway, but forgets how to do it when she has a flat on the side of a highway, is panicked. So is someone who knows a school subject well, but bombs the test; or who plans and practices for an important meeting, but screws it up.

Students frequently come to me with problems that they claim to have no idea how to solve. I ask them, "What advice would you give someone else with the same problem?" and they invariably rattle off a good solution without even stopping to think about it. They can do that because it's usually much easier to solve other people's problems than our own, mainly because we panic over our own.

"Stealth Panic"

We're all familiar with the type of high-energy panic where you feel frantic and out of control. But panic often happens much more quietly than that. What I call "stealth panic" may actually be a more common problem for procrastinators.

Stealth panic is what happens when you sit down to do your work at 9:00 a.m. and then get a sudden, irresistible urge to do something else, like get a cup of coffee. You don't feel panicked—it actually feels like a calm, even trivial decision—but *wham!* You've been bumped off your path. Sometimes this happens even before 9:00 a.m., so that you don't even make it to your desk.

Stealth panic often precipitates a kind of trance state that lets you keep procrastinating. First you get the cup of coffee, then you read the newspaper, then you make a personal call, and then you do some Internet shopping—and then, suddenly, it's time for lunch. All the while, you're semi-aware that you should be doing something else, but never quite aware enough, or focused enough, to actually stop what you're doing and get back to work.

The Solution

We now arrive at the true heart of fear-based procrastination. **Minimize or eliminate your panic, and you should be able to manage your emotions and continue with your work. Or, as my teacher Jerry Weinberg, says, "The problem is not the problem. The problem is your reaction to the problem."** This would seem to put a lot of pressure on you, but in reality it takes a lot of the pressure off. What it means is that, thanks to your panic, you are probably perceiving your problem as being much worse than it actually is. In Chapter 20, you'll see how, once you remove panic from the equation, even the worst-seeming situations can become much more manageable.

CHAPTER 20

A Process for Defeating Fear

By now, you know what fear-based procrastination is, what causes it, and how it manifests itself in your thoughts, emotions and behavior. Now we can discuss a solution. It basically involves your being aware of your fear as it occurs, and substituting a more functional response to it for your current dysfunctional one.

1. The **dysfunctional response** you're replacing is procrastination; more specifically, the obstacles that threaten to bump you off your path—including not just the Big Three (Perfectionism, Negativity and Hypersensitivity), but any Logistical or Situational obstacles you face. Also, of course, Panic.
2. The **functional response** you want to substitute for the dysfunctional one is to (1) recognize and acknowledge your fear; (2) not panic, or take steps to defuse your panic; (3) characterize the specific nature of, and solution to, your obstacle(s), using journaling and other tools; (4) overcome the obstacle(s); and (5) if possible, return to your path without having lost too much time.

This substitution usually takes practice to get right, although if you really work at it, improvement should happen fast.

In Chapter 7, you learned about the Three Productivity Behaviors: showing up on time, doing the work you're supposed to be doing, and doing it for an hour or more. And in Chapter 8, you learned the following seven-step Behavioral Change Process for incorporating those behaviors into your work and personal life:

1. Educate yourself.
2. Marshal needed resources and support.

3. Break the change down into a series of modest, attainable goals, then tackle those goals one at a time.
4. Maximize your positive response to any "success."
5. Minimize your negative response to any "failure."
6. Anticipate and cope with plateaus and backsliding.
7. Keep at it!

If you've been making good progress toward solving your procrastination problem using the Three Productivity Behaviors, then there probably isn't much fear underlying your procrastination, and you may not even need to use the Fear Defeating Process described in this chapter and the next. If, however, you can't manage to adopt the Three Productivity Behaviors no matter how hard you try, then you probably do have fears and/or a panic response you need to address. The Fear Defeating Process described below will help you do just that. It is basically an additional sequence of steps inserted into that Behavioral Change Process:

1. Educate yourself.
2. Marshal needed resources and support.
3. Break the change down into a series of modest, attainable goals, then tackle those goals one at a time. (Utilize the Fear Defeating Process if you're having trouble achieving your modest, attainable goals.)
4. Maximize your positive response to any "success."
5. Minimize your negative response to any "failure."
6. Anticipate and cope with plateaus and backsliding.
7. Keep at it!

Once you use the Fear Defeating Process to dissipate your fear and panic, you can usually stop procrastinating and return to both the Behavioral Change Process and your daily path.

The Fear Defeating Process consists of these nine steps:
1. Use Mission Management and Time Management to establish reasonable goals and a reasonable schedule.
2. Start your work: catch yourself procrastinating.
3. Don't criticize, berate or shame yourself!
4. Start journaling.
5a. Defuse your panic through journaling or other means. (5a, b and c

all happen simultaneously while you journal around the problem. I'll explain journaling in Chapter 23.)

5b. Characterize your obstacles.

5c. Design a solution for overcoming your obstacles.

6. Start to implement the solution and, if possible, return to your path.

7. Celebrate your victory.

8. Repeat when needed.

And . . .

9. Watch change happen!

I'll discuss each step individually in Chapter 22. First, however, you need to be aware of two basic requirements for this process to work, which I discuss in the next chapter.

CHAPTER 21

Defeating Your Fears: Requirements

The two main requirements you need for working on your fear-based pro-crastination problem are **time** and **honesty**.

First, **time**. You should expect to devote a few hours a week to working on your procrastination problem, at least in the beginning. This is time spent not just on the Fear Defeating Process, but also on Mission Management and Time Management, both of which, as you know, are essential to success. It can also include time spent journaling, or talking to a therapist or other helping professional.

The amount of time you will need to spend should lessen over time, as you become better able to cope with your fears and panic. While it may now take you a couple of hours of journaling to calm down after a disturbing or annoying event, it may eventually take only ten minutes or a few seconds. Eventually, your procrastination problem will mostly go away, and you'll become one of those in-control, effortlessly productive people you've always envied. But don't expect that result without putting in your time first.

Make no mistake: a few hours a week is *not* an unreasonable amount of time to devote to this process. In fact, it's one of the best possible uses of your time. (It is the frantic people who feel that they have absolutely no time to do this who probably need to do it most.) The time you devote to beating your procrastination problem, you'll get back many times over in the form of increased productivity over the rest of your career.

Next, **honesty**. You should be prepared to be completely honest with yourself, and with anyone helping you, about your thoughts, feelings, fears and insecurities concerning your work, life goals, current situation and pro-crastination problem. If you are used to censoring unpleasant or "unaccept-able" thoughts or feelings, it may take you a while to learn to un-censor yourself and own up to your truth—for instance, that you are sick and tired of activism and want to take a break. Or that, while you want to continue to do activism, it is also important for you to lead a "normal" life with a house, kids, yard and car. Or that you have doubts about the validity of your movement, the motives of the people in it or the tactics they are employing.

See Part I, Chapter 4, for more guidance on truth-telling in difficult circumstances, and remember that **anything less than total honesty sabotages the process, and may even make your procrastination problem worse.**

What about Money?

Do you need money to solve your procrastination problem? Not necessarily—although it helps.

In Chapter 24, I recommend that all my readers see a therapist, which of course takes money. If you don't have it, then creatively brainstorm around the problem. Group therapy sessions are cheaper than solo sessions, and support groups and twelve-step programs (if addiction is a problem) are cheap or free.

Want to take a self-improvement or leadership class or workshop but can't afford it? Ask if the school gives a discount for activists, perhaps in exchange for your helping out at the event.

At the very least, you can always borrow a library book on whatever topic you're interested in.

NEVER let a lack of money stop you from achieving your goals. Lack of money should always be an inconvenience, never a hard barrier.

CHAPTER 22

Defeating Your Fears: The Process in Detail

Let's look at each step of the Fear Defeating Process individually.

Step 1. Use Mission Management and Time Management to establish reasonable goals and a reasonable schedule.

By now, hopefully, you understand the importance of Mission Management and Time Management, and won't be tempted to skip those steps. I won't repeat the information in Parts I and II of this book—just remind you that setting reasonable goals and a reasonable schedule is the primary catalyst of success, while setting unreasonable goals and an unreasonable schedule, or no goals and no schedule, is the primary catalyst of failure.

Step 2. Start your work: catch yourself procrastinating.

To deal with your procrastination, you need to be able to catch yourself in the act of doing it. This step will either be very easy or very hard, depending on how deeply you "zone out" when you procrastinate.

As mentioned earlier, many people enter a kind of trance when they procrastinate—that trance is the whole *point* of the procrastination, really, as it allows you to avoid doing your work without experiencing pain or guilt. (Those come later, when you look back at your wasted day.) When you're in that trance, you're only dimly aware of what you are doing, and the hours just seem to melt away.

Some people don't enter too deeply into the trance. They can be in the middle of an unscheduled video game and think, "Oops! I'm procrastinating." If you can do that relatively quickly, then you've completed this step.

If, however, you are one of those people who really zones out, it may take some time and practice for you to reliably catch yourself early in the act of procrastinating. One thing that may help is to get into the habit of asking yourself, at fifteen- or thirty-minute intervals, "Am I doing what I'm supposed to be doing, or am I procrastinating?"

Keep working at it, and eventually you'll be able to quickly and reliably catch yourself in the act of procrastinating.

Step 3. Don't criticize or berate or shame yourself!

As I've said many times in *The Lifelong Activist*, self-criticism does nothing to solve your procrastination problem, and instead is likely to make it worse. Don't do it.

Instead of criticizing yourself, be an objective, compassionate observer and analyst of your own behavior. Tell yourself, "Oh, I'm procrastinating." Do not even add a mildly negative phrase such as, "Too bad."

Step 4. Start journaling.

You have caught yourself procrastinating: now's the time to figure out why. Your main tool for doing this is journaling, which will help you (a) defuse your panic, (b) characterize the precise nature of your obstacles, and (c) come up with solutions for overcoming those obstacles. Journaling isn't hard, but there are a few tricks to it that I'll share with you in Chapter 23. The important thing to note here is that the moment you catch yourself procrastinating, you should stop whatever you are doing and begin journaling.[6]

There are many ways of journaling, incidentally, but the one I want you I want you to do here is the uninhibited "stream of consciousness" type journaling that is also sometimes called "free writing." It basically "dumps" the content of your thoughts and feelings, in undiluted, uncensored format, onto the page (or screen). For this kind of journaling, spelling and grammar don't matter: just get everything down as honestly and as fast as you can.

If you are desperate to get some work done, you may be reluctant to stop and journal. Journaling may even seem like a waste of time. In reality, however, it is the very best use of your time, as it is your main tool for solving your procrastination problem. The thirty minutes or one or two hours you invest in journaling now will be returned to you a hundredfold, once you start to overcome your obstacles and work more productively.

NOTE: Steps 5a, 5b and 5c all happen simultaneously while you're journaling.

Step 5a. Defuse your panic.

As discussed in the Chapter 19, you can't solve problems while panicked. So your first step, before getting down and dirty with your procrastination problem, is to defuse any panic you may be experiencing.

Fortunately, journaling is a "miracle cure" for panic. The simple act of writing down your problem is often all it takes to relieve a lot of the anxiety and panic surrounding it. Psychologists have even discovered that the simple act of *naming* the problem, which you can also do as part of your journaling, is often enough to do the trick. After a journaling session, you should feel mentally and even physically more relaxed.

Journaling is, in fact, powerfully healing. It's a way of giving yourself the time, attention and respect most of us crave but never get enough of. It also provides a way for you to really focus in on your problems, which empowers you to solve them. It's no wonder that journaling is an accepted therapeutic tool for working with many types of distressed people, including cancer survivors, victims of violent crime, troubled teens and people in jail.

Journaling yourself to a calm, centered, reflective state of mind can take a few minutes or a few hours: the important thing is not to rush it. If you are journaling for a long time—with fear, confusion and other strong emotions pouring out of you and onto the page—it's because you need to. Don't be impatient: trust the process and understand that (1) this intensive-journaling phase is one that you probably have to go through; and (2) it won't last forever. In a few days or weeks, you will probably be generally less anxious or panicky, and have a better handle on your obstacles than you ever did before. You will probably also be able to calm yourself much more quickly than in the past, and use journaling mainly for its analytical and problem-solving benefits (5b and 5c).

IMPORTANT NOTE

Journaling sometimes uncovers memories that we have trouble handling, including memories of childhood abuse. It can also force issues to our attention that we have been in denial over, usually because they are painful. Either event can be traumatic. If journaling isn't helping you calm down but, rather, is making you more upset, or if it is raising issues that you are not sure you can handle, see a therapist or other professional. You may even wish to consult a therapist before you start journaling, if you are concerned about how the process will affect you.

Step 5b. Characterize your obstacles.

At the same time you've been calming down, you've also, in your journal, been creating a "snapshot" of your mental state. This snapshot is likely to tell you exactly why you're procrastinating—i.e., the precise nature of your obstacles.

It's important to characterize obstacles precisely, because the more precisely you characterize them, the more focused and effective a solution you can come up with. Trying to solve a problem you haven't accurately characterized is an exercise in futility—in fact, it's probably what you've been doing all these years when working on your "problems" of laziness, lack of discipline, etc. All of that effort, directed at the wrong targets, didn't solve your procrastination problem, did it?

Use your journal to create a list of the specific obstacles (thoughts and feelings) that are preventing you from continuing with your work at this moment. For instance, suppose you should have been writing a grant proposal, but spent the past hour doing all kinds of other stuff instead. In the course of your journaling, you discover that the reasons you haven't been writing are one or more of the following:

- You hate to write, and have never been confident of your writing skills.
- You are pretty sure you won't get the grant, so the whole project seems futile and a waste of time.
- You don't like the project the grant is funding, so if you do get the grant, you're going to be stuck doing something you don't want to do.
- The people who promised to help you have made themselves scarce, so you're stuck doing everything yourself.
- Fundraising isn't in your job description.
- Fundraising is, in fact, several grades above your pay level, and you're not getting paid to do it, so you feel exploited.
- Your work situation overall is not very happy, which interferes with your ability to motivate yourself for this project.
- You are worried about things in your personal life, and that worry interferes with your ability to focus on this project.
- You are in love, which interferes with your ability to focus on this project.
- You're not feeling well.
- Your computer keeps crashing.

These are all Logistical or Situational Obstacles, and several also hint at one or more Big Three Obstacles underneath. For instance, "hate to write" could be grounded in perfectionism or negativity. The fact that the solution to many of these Logistical or Situational obstacles is simple, or even trivial, I'll discuss below.

First, however, I want to be very clear that all of the above obstacles are not just reasonable, but understandable and forgivable. In other words, nothing to be ashamed of. This shouldn't be used as a license to procrastinate, however. To live a happy, successful life, you must learn to persevere even in the face of stress or misfortune. So . . .

Step 5c. Design a solution for overcoming your obstacles.

The solution to the Big Three obstacles is, as discussed in Chapters 15 through 18, to replace dysfunctional thoughts and behaviors with functional ones.

Once you do that, and once you defuse your panic, you may be able to easily overcome your Logistical and Situational Obstacles. What's amazing, actually, is how many even intractible-seeming obstacles turn out to be rather easily overcome, once they are exposed to the light of day via journaling. It's like in *The Wizard of Oz*, when Toto pulls back the curtain and reveals the Almighty Oz to be a flim-flam man. Pull away the "curtain" of your panic and dysfunctional thinking, and your toughest obstacles are often revealed to be small and easily solved.

To repeat Jerry Weinberg's wonderful quote: "The problem is not the problem. The problem is your reaction to the problem."

So:

- You hate to write, and have never been confident of your writing skills. SO, you ask a coworker or friend to edit your writing.
- You are pretty sure you won't get the grant, so the whole project seems a waste of time. SO, you check with your boss, and perhaps others, to see if your assumption is warranted. If it is, then you talk with your boss about canceling the project or reworking it so that it's more likely to succeed.
- You don't like the project the grant is funding. SO, you see if you can rework the project so it's more acceptable, or find someone else in your organization to manage it.
- You feel exploited. SO, you decide to either discuss this situation

with your boss, or to do the project but start looking for another job as soon as possible. If nothing else, the project will look good on your resume . . .

Your Situational Obstacles, as discussed earlier, tend to involve other people or circumstances not entirely within your control. As such, they tend to be harder to overcome than the Big Three or Logistical Obstacles. The steps you need to take, however, are often just as straightforward—it's the implementation, or "taking them," that can be painful. If, for instance, the Situational Obstacle is a health problem, you can plan to make an appointment with a medical specialist. (Expensive, time-consuming and scary.) If it's a troubled relationship, you can have a frank talk with your partner, or plan to consult a couples counselor. (Ditto.)

Go ahead and use your journal to design detailed solutions to your logistical and situational obstacles.

Step 6. Start to implement the solution and, if possible, return to your path.
Your goal here is to implement *just enough* of the solution you've designed so that you can calm down enough to return to your daily path—i.e. the work you are supposed to be doing. You don't want the solution itself to become a form of procrastination, after all.

Sometimes, just writing out the problem in detail in your journal is enough to get you back on your path . . .

Or, writing out the solution . . .

Or, making a phone call or two . . .

Or, taking a few more substantive and time-consuming steps . . .

Again, there's no wrong way to do this, and you should take as much time as you need to stop panicking and calm down, especially early on. Eventually, however, you should be able to return back to your path in less and less time.

Figure 3. Back on the path!

Step 7. Celebrate your victory.

It doesn't matter whether you've returned fully to your path or not, or even if you returned at all. If you've made it this far in the process, you are victorious. You are finally grappling with your procrastination problem in a meaningful way, perhaps after years of fear, confusion and dithering. That's a huge step, and you should give yourself huge amounts of credit for it.

If you don't believe me—if you think that only a "clear win" against your procrastination problem is worth celebrating—then please go back and reread Chapter 15, Perfectionism.

As I've mentioned repeatedly, it is important to celebrate every small achievement or victory in every area of your life, and *never* to bash yourself for any perceived "failures." Most of us grow up oppressed by too much negativity and criticism, and we continue to be oppressed by those in adulthood. It is up to us to counteract that negativity, both for ourselves and for those around us.

So, congratulate yourself—a lot. Call up a good friend and boast of your achievement. Treat yourself to a movie, CD, bubble bath or sinful dessert. Or all four! Make a fuss—if you don't, who will?

This is not merely an exercise in feeling good, although that itself is a worthwhile goal. It also helps you "own" your victory, and the skills that went into achieving it, so that you have that memory and those skills readily available the next time you do battle with your old nemesis, procrastination.

Step 8. Repeat as needed.

Even if, this time around, you score a spectacular success—meaning, you are able to quickly defuse your panic, overcome your obstacle(s) and return to your path—you shouldn't consider your procrastination problem licked. Procrastination is a wily, persistent enemy: it *will* return. So, be prepared to repeat this process as often as it takes—and occasionally, throughout your entire life. Rest assured, however, that by persisting you will get to . . .

Step 9. Watch change happen!

When I teach my students these techniques for defeating their fear-based procrastination, many begin to make amazingly fast progress at their goals. That's because, in contrast to their negative self-image of being lazy, undisciplined or uncommitted, they are actually *highly* energetic, *highly* disciplined and *highly* committed. The problem is, as discussed earlier, that they were trying to solve the wrong problem. Once they start trying to solve the right one—their fears, obstacles and panic—many shoot ahead like arrows toward their goals, often making more progress in a few weeks than they had in the previous few years. That's because **beating procrastination is an act of self-liberation**. Begin to conquer your procrastination problem, and you begin to redefine yourself and your possibilities.

Self-liberation is an exciting journey to make, and an inspirational one to witness. I have no doubt that many readers of *The Lifelong Activist* are poised to make that journey within a very short time. (If they weren't, they wouldn't have picked up the book to start with.) If you hunger for self-liberation, the key is to start following the advice in this book but not to expect too-quick progress: to set modest, attainable goals; focus on the journey, not the destination; and remember that the time to tackle fear is either immediately after you become aware that you are experiencing it, or, better yet, *before* you experience it, by empowering yourself (see Chapter 27).

Now, onto journaling and other tools for change . . .

CHAPTER 23

Tools for Change I: Journaling

There are four main tools you can use to help you defeat your fears and spur personal growth: Journaling, Therapy, Self-Care and a Created Community. I discuss these in this and the next two chapters.

Journaling would seem like the easiest thing in the world—and it is! Journaling is just the writing down of your thoughts and feelings at any given moment in as much detail, and with as little inhibition or censorship, as possible. The kind of journaling I mean is sometimes called "free writing," "automatic writing," or "stream-of-consciousness" writing. All of these terms are fine by me. What I *don't* mean by journaling is keeping a chronological calendar detailing the events in your life. In other words, I don't care about the events themselves, so much as your thoughts, and especially your feelings, surrounding them.

The Journaling Arc

You'll recall how, in the last chapter, I said that journaling calms you mentally and physically. That's definitely the way it is for me. When I start journaling, especially when I'm upset or angry, I tend to type like a demon, and my sentences are short, almost fragmentary, as in this hypothetical example:

Damn I'm upset! I can't stand it! I don't know what to do! I want to kill Frank. I hate him. I can't believe he stood me up for this meeting. What an asshole. What a jerk. And I guess I'm a jerk, too. . . .

My sentences are short because my anger and fear prevent me from holding a thought for very long. (Your journaling really is a window into your emotional state.) By the end of the half-hour, or hour, or three hours, of journaling, however, I'm feeling much more relaxed and in control, and it shows in my sentences:

Well, something obviously happened to Frank. As soon as I finish this, I'll give him a call to make sure he's OK. It's not like he's always unreliable—although, the truth be told, he's not the most dependable of guys. Still, it's not a sin to be a little unreliable, and in other ways, he's a terrific colleague. He really sticks up for me when Liz gets on my case, and he was really terrific during that project we worked on last summer. And I guess he's going through a difficult time with his girlfriend—he told me that. In fact, now that I think about it, he did ask me to cut him some slack. That's no excuse for being a no-show, of course—but maybe in the future, I'll call him to remind him of meetings ahead of time. . . .

Note not just the calmness and longer sentences, but the more contextualized, compassionate, accurate view of Frank and his situation.

I call the path one travels in one's journal—from fear, anger and blaming, to calmness, control and compassion—the "journaling arc." You will probably notice a similar arc in your own journal entries. Look for it, and use it to track your emotional growth during each journaling session, and throughout your activism career.

Tips for Effective Journaling

Here are some tips to help you journal:

1. **Speed is key.**

   The faster you write, the better, because fast writing leaves little time for self-censorship and rationalizations. Just get your feelings and thoughts down on paper, and don't stop to think or ponder for more than a few seconds. Don't worry about spelling or grammar, and, for goodness' sake, don't censor yourself. Listen for that little "heart" voice inside you that you may be habitually drowning out, and get it down on paper. Get *everything* down on paper. Honesty is the most important thing in journaling.

2. **Any medium and format are fine.**

   A computer, a sheet of paper, a dinner napkin—they're all OK. If you don't like to write, try talking into a tape recorder. Also, paragraphs, lists or any other format is also fine, so long as the format doesn't interfere with your primary goal of writing honestly and quickly.

3. **The more the merrier.**

   As discussed in the last chapter, you want to start journaling at the moment you catch yourself procrastinating, because that will help you characterize the precise problem. But you can journal at other times, as well. Some people journal first thing every morning, or last thing every night, as a form of meditation and reflection. Others journal at odd times whenever the mood strikes them, and still others set aside a few hours every week or month. Whatever works for you is fine.

4. **It's OK to become emotional.**

   Sometimes the process of journaling can cause you to uncover painful memories or tap into feelings of sadness, hurt or shame. These can be tough to experience, but it's great that you are doing so, as it is a step toward healing. Give yourself permission to experience these memories and emotions and, as mentioned earlier, if you are having trouble coping, see a therapist or other professional.

5. **Guys can journal, too.**

   In my classes, there are usually plenty of men receptive to the idea of journaling, but also plenty of others who think it's a sissy way to spend their time. If you are a guy (or gal, for that matter) with that prejudice, I urge you to get over it. Many of history's most famous male scholars, statesmen, scientists and activists, among others, saw keeping a journal or maintaining extensive self-reflective correspondence, as an essential part of their quest to lead a civilized and accomplished life. You should, too. Journaling may, in fact, be the single most efficient route to the Socratic goal mentioned at the beginning of *The Lifelong Activist*, to live an examined life.

6. **Don't show your journal to anyone.**

   To ensure that you tell the whole, unvarnished, often embarrassing and/or painful truth, make sure you keep your journal private.

7. **Don't rush it: when you're done, you're done.**

   Write until you're "written out" and can think of nothing further to say. This may take a few minutes, a few hours or an entire day or weekend. However long it takes, don't rush it: if you've got a lot to write, it means you've got a lot to say.

   That's it for journaling! Try it out!

CHAPTER 24

Tools for Change II: Therapy and Self-Care

"Go to therapy!" I tell my classes. Just like that: flat out.

The reaction I get is interesting. Most of the time, the students giggle in an embarrassed way. Sometimes, the class goes dead quiet, as if people are too embarrassed even to giggle.

Therapy remains very much a taboo subject. Many people are ashamed to admit that they are or have been in therapy.

Not me. I have been in therapy, on and off, for two decades, and I consider my therapy to be among the very best investments of time and money I ever made. They helped me get past the problems in my life much faster than I ever could have on my own.

Not surprisingly, I think therapy is wonderful. I think everyone should be in therapy. Seriously—*everyone*. We all carry around emotional baggage from our childhood, and we all live in difficult, stressful times. Also, as I've mentioned numerous times throughout this book, I think activists have it tougher than many other people because of the innate difficulty of our Mission, and the lack of societal and (often) familial support for it. These are all good reasons to see a therapist.

Some people think that seeing a therapist is a sign of weakness, but nothing could be further from the truth. Seeing a therapist is a sign that you have the strength to admit to, and work on, your problems. That's why so many successful people see a therapist and are quite unashamed of the fact. They see therapy as simply one more tool they are using to build their success.

Some people might prefer to consult a spiritual advisor or some other kind of professional. I have no problem with that, but would urge you to see a therapist in addition to whomever else you see, at least for a while.

The Pulitzer Prize–winning writer Richard Rhodes draws a direct line between his therapy (for post-traumatic stress syndrome resulting from an abusive childhood) and his professional success:

> I started therapy for myself, not for writing, but it was through that
> process that the breakthrough came. . . . Seven years of therapy was
> no more expensive than graduate school would have been, and I've
> come to think of therapy as graduate school for the emotions (or
> was it remedial?). When I groaned at the expense, my therapist, a
> good man trained at the Menninger Clinic, expressed the hope that
> therapy would pay for itself. Since I've made a good living writing
> now for more than twenty years, it did. (*How to Write: Advice and
> Reflections;* Quill, 1995)

I don't know about Rhodes, but one reason therapy worked for me was
that I made it one of my top priorities. Nothing but a real emergency would
cause me to miss a therapy session, and I always took my therapist's recom-
mendations very seriously. That's because I saw that the insights and lessons I
was learning in therapy could help me in all of the important areas of my life.

So I urge you to try therapy. This is particularly true if you have been
thinking about therapy, but dithering. Stop dithering, and go out and find
a therapist. Here are two tips to help:

1. **Shop carefully.**
Therapists vary tremendously in training, background, approach, competence and cost. A therapist is one of the most important professionals you
will ever hire, so try to find a great one. Don't settle for someone who is
merely OK—and certainly not someone who is mediocre.

   The best way to find a therapist is to ask friends and family, or perhaps
your doctor, if they can recommend someone.

   When you contact a therapist, ask what kind of clients she or he likes
to work with. The answer should be people like you, facing problems or
challenges similar to the ones you yourself are facing. Some therapists specialize in helping creative people, while others specialize in helping people
who themselves work in helping professions. Still others specialize in working with trauma victims, including people suffering from Compassion
Fatigue. And still others position themselves as "career coaches" or "success
coaches." Any of these could be a perfect fit for you.

2. **Give the relationship time to develop.**
In many therapeutic relationships, you spend the first two or three sessions
detailing your history and current situation for the therapist. These sessions

can be kind of boring because the therapist doesn't have much to work with until she or he has all this information. So be patient while the relationship is developing.

If, however, you've seen a therapist for a few sessions and you two do not seem to be "clicking," or if the sessions themselves do not seem productive, then tell the therapist your concerns and hear what she or he has to say. You can decide to stay for a few more sessions, or look for someone else. Don't hesitate to do the latter, if the little voice in your gut is saying "this isn't working." Many people try two, three or even four therapists before striking gold.

Self-Care

Therapy, along with good nutritional, sleeping and exercise habits, is an important aspect of *self-care*, a topic I discussed in Part I, Chapter 10.

As my excellent therapists have taught me, self-care should come before everything except emergencies. If your physical or emotional being is not healthy, then you can't hope to be productive at activism or anything else. It is also hard to take care of others, or advocate for them, when your own needs are going unmet.

Activists need to keep hearing this message, as it is very easy for us to buy into the myth that we are supposed to sacrifice our all for our movement. While there may be isolated examples of activists who did just that, achieving great things thereby, most of us are incapable of making such a monumental sacrifice and still remaining productive.

So, take care of yourself, and don't deny your physical, emotional or material needs. The act of discovering and meeting those needs forms the foundation for a happy and productive life. Schedule regular appointments with your doctor, dentist and ophthalmologist. Eat nutritious meals, get plenty of exercise and get a full night's sleep. Don't waste your time on perfectionist housekeeping, but also don't let your living space deteriorate into a disorganized pit. (A wise student of mine once put it this way: "Depression is disorganizing, and disorganization is depressing.") If a polished personal appearance is important to you, make sure to build haircuts, clothes shopping, etc. into your Mission and Schedule.

On a related topic: deal with your issues. **Studies[7] have shown that creative people (a group that surely includes many activists) suffer from above-average rates of attention-deficit disorder (ADD), attention-deficit hyperactivity disorder (ADHD), obsessive-compulsive disorder**

(OCD), depression, addiction, bipolar disorder (formerly called manic depression) and other cognitive and emotional problems. **Failure to deal decisively with these issues is one of the most fundamental forms of self-sabotage.** So, if you even suspect that you suffer from one or more of the conditions mentioned, or another similar one, see a doctor. If the doctor suggests therapy, get some. If a doctor you trust prescribes drugs, and you agree with that approach for solving the problem, take them.

Self-care doesn't have to be a major effort: it can be as simple as taking time out for a movie, a meal with friends, a walk in the park or a stroll through a department store. It can also mean buying a colorful new sweater that pleases you, or taking a taxi instead of a bus once in a while. The key is to generally treat yourself well, and also to give yourself little "treats" as often as possible—once a day or more is great—without experiencing even the slightest twinge of guilt. Treat yourself well whenever you've had a "success," no matter how minor, and treat yourself especially well whenever you've had a "failure" or disappointment. And treat yourself well whenever you feel like it, just for the heck of it.

Just treat yourself well, OK?

CHAPTER 25

Tools for Change #III: A Created Community

As you have by now heard me say numerous times, a key factor separating successful from unsuccessful people is that the former surround themselves with supportive, encouraging people, while the latter surround themselves with skeptics and nay-sayers. Whom we choose to associate with is one of our most crucial life decisions, for two reasons:

- We tend to live up, or down, to the expectations of those around us.
- It takes tremendous energy and toughness to maintain a positive view of yourself and your values when you are surrounded by people who constantly criticize you or put you down. Defending yourself from these kinds of attacks is not only draining, but a misuse of your time and energy, which would be better spent doing activism or some other part of your Mission.

That's why you have heard me say repeatedly throughout *The Lifelong Activist* that it is vital to "dump" unsupportive people from your life, and as quickly as possible. If they are friends, acquaintances or coworkers, ease out of the relationship. If they are family members, try to scale back the relationship—although, if they are really toxic and unsupportive, you may need to cease all contact, at least temporarily. One friend of mine, who was raised in a family that is highly conservative, moved three thousand miles away so that he could have the mental freedom and space to develop into his own person. That takes courage and determination, and I am filled with admiration for him.

Please note that, although I use the harsh-sounding word "dump" in the above paragraph to indicate urgency, I always advocate acting with compassion. If you have to leave a relationship behind, ease out of it gently, and always open the possibility of reconciliation. The person you are leaving behind is traveling his own path, and—who knows?—maybe your paths will one day lead you back in each other's direction, especially if he sees you leading a happy, fulfilled, balanced life. If that happens, you want to be there to welcome and encourage him.

Getting rid of naysayers is only half the battle, however. You need to replace them with a supportive community. Don't make the mistake of thinking that this community will magically accrue around you if you just do your own thing. You need to create your community, and manage it.

The major categories of people you want in your Created Community include mentors, family, friends, colleagues and helping professionals. Mentors are a very important topic that I discuss separately in the following chapter, but I discuss the other categories briefly below.

Family

Family is such a delicate topic for activists, since many of us have families who are hostile to our values and life choices. I hear more anguish from activists on the subject of families than anything else.

Most people have two families: the one they grew up in, and the one they create as adults. Psychologists and sociologists theorize about what constitutes a "family," but for the purposes of this discussion, let's just say that "family comes first." If a family member is in need, that trumps all other requests for your time and attention.

We are all familiar with the traditional type of "created family": a spouse or partner; perhaps some kids or companion animals. If this is the kind of family you aspire to, please make sure that the person you choose for your spouse or partner is 100 percent supportive of your Mission. An unsupportive spouse is one of the worst, most painful and hardest-to-solve Situational Obstacles.

Many activists create a different kind of family. They cultivate a group of very special friends whom they know will support them in good times and bad; and whom they, in turn, commit to supporting. This can be an informal, or formalized, family relationship.

Especially if you are distanced from your birth family, it is very important for you to create some kind of family for yourself. Although rare individuals are able to thrive and be productive in isolation, most of us cannot, and we suffer if we remain too long in isolation.

Friends

People are social to varying degrees, and so you may seek out only a few very close friends, or a wider circle. Either is OK, provided your relationships are healthy and don't interfere with your personal growth and success. Just three reminders:

1. As discussed in Part II, a "party animal" lifestyle is generally inimical to success at an ambitious endeavor.
2. So is a "doormat" or "go-to person" lifestyle in which you cannot or will not say "No" to requests that interfere with your ability to Manage your Mission or Time.
3. Someone who undermines or harshly criticizes you is *not* a friend, regardless of what they say their motives are. Friends have a responsibility not just to objectively state the truth—including, perhaps, unpleasant truths—about your behavior, but to do so in a compassionate, supportive way. They also have a responsibility to praise you and acknowledge your achievements.

Wonderful friendships not only bring light and color to our lives, they sustain us through the inevitable dark moments. Don't settle for less!

Colleagues

It's a sad fact that some of the people who treat activists worst are other activists.

Don't let *anyone* abuse you. That includes other activists, and I don't care how illustrious their achievements or credentials are, or how awe-inspiring their intellectual framework. Recognize that it is possible, and all too common, for someone to be highly effective and evolved in some areas of life, and highly ineffective and unevolved in others.

Many activist organizations are badly run, and treat their employees and volunteers badly as a result. If you are involved with an organization and are being treated badly, leave it. Get a non-activist job if you have to, and do activism part-time. Don't worry: another opportunity to do full-time activism will eventually present itself.

If another activist criticizes you harshly for being insufficiently committed or dedicated, or for any other reason, ignore her. If you want, you can try to help her examine her own problem of intolerance, but if she's resistant, don't waste too much time on this—just walk away. It's probably more of a job for a therapist, anyw,

And, needless to say, **don't abuse or attack others**—especially other activists. There is simply no excuse for doing so. Recognize that your anger and intolerance probably stem from childhood, and that you may be using your activism as a rationalization to support this ingrained defensive behavior. As someone who has spent years dealing with her own anger issues, I urge you to deal with yours—not just for your own sake, but for the sake of those around you, and your movement.

Helping Professionals

By helping professionals, I mean, first of all, a doctor and therapist. Add to that, perhaps, a dentist, ophthalmologist, nutritionist, massage therapist, spiritual advisor or anyone else you consult about your physical and mental health.

I also mean good personal-finance and insurance help. You may not like to focus on these issues, but, as discussed in Part I, they exist whether you focus on them or not, and ignoring them inevitably leads to trouble. You may have to hire someone with these forms of expertise, or you may be able to consult a family member, coworker or friend for free. Just make sure you're getting quality advice—and getting it as part of your life planning, not only after you find yourself in a jam—recalling, once more, that poverty has probably ended more activist careers than anything else.

CHAPTER 26

Finding and Cultivating Mentors

Mentors are people who have already achieved some of the things you want to achieve. They are where you hope to be next year, five years from now or twenty years from now. And they are available, and willing, to tell you how to do get there, and to guide you along the way.

Mentors typically offer one or more of the following benefits:

- **Information.** Because they've done what you are trying to do, they have a lot of knowledge about how to do it.
- **Wisdom.** They don't just have the information, they know how to apply it. They have a good grasp of the "big picture," of strategy, and of what could go right and wrong.
- **Opportunities.** Mentors often know about jobs, grants and other opportunities that can help you.
- **Contacts.** This is a very important and underrated contribution of mentors. They often know lots of people, and they often know important, influential people. Your mentors' contacts can be of enormous help to you as you build your career.

Mentors are probably the most powerful "success catalysts" around, meaning that they can help you reach your goals more quickly than anything else. The right mentor can literally take years or even decades off the time it takes you to succeed; and without mentors, you are almost certainly doomed to failure, or at least to time-wasting and frustration.

Finding and cultivating mentors should be a primary goal of all activists. You're never too successful or accomplished to need mentors.

Here's how to find and work with them.

Who Are Mentors?

Some people may be mentors for you in one area (e.g., public relations), while others may be mentors in another (e.g., strategy). Some might be experts in your particular movement or in activism and/or activist career paths in general. You could, and should, have as many mentors as possible in as many different specialties or fields relevant to your career as possible. You should also have mentors for your personal life: for dating, marriage, parenting, home ownership, personal finance, health and fitness, etc.

All of your mentors should not just have specific information and other resources that you need, but should also be kind people who like to help. In other words, they should understand, and enjoy, the process of mentoring.

Anyone and everyone who meets these criteria could be a mentor. Although many teachers, bosses and other authority figures are natural choices, you should cast as wide a net as possible. Some of my most important mentors are activists who are much younger than I am, but who have knowledge, experience and skills I lack. Others are people I disagree with politically, but whose attitudes and life choices I admire. I am grateful for mentoring from whatever source it comes.

How to Establish a Mentor Relationship

Below are examples of the wrong and right way to establish a mentor relationship:

> **Wrong Way:** Ian is attending a reception at an activist conference when he spots the celebrated activist Jane Smith across the room. He's always revered her and now, he thinks, is his chance to meet her. So, without thinking, he barrels across the room and introduces himself to her and says he's always admired her and her work. She thanks him, but then he can't think of anything else to say. The conversation languishes, and after a few moments, she excuses herself to talk with someone else.

Not very encouraging, but it could have been worse. Had Ian naïvely said, "Would you be my mentor?" Jane would have probably been surprised and then given him a polite refusal. You can't go around asking strangers whom you've just met to mentor you, just as you can't go around asking them to marry you. Both relationships imply a serious long-term commitment and should thus be approached gradually and with caution. Even if the potential mentor is someone who already knows and likes you and wants to help you, the word "mentor" can imply more of a serious, long-term commitment than she may be ready for.

Here's a better way to get someone on board as a mentor:

Right Way: Another activist, Pete, studied the speaker list at the conference before coming. Noting that Jane Smith would be there, he decided to introduce himself to her during the reception. Before showing up, he reviewed her most recent writings and found an article of hers that he particularly liked. He gave it some thought and came up with some follow-up questions about it.

Doing a bit of research, he discovered that an activist he knows is actually acquainted with Jane, so he got that activist to agree to come to the reception with him and introduce him. When it came time to attend the reception, Pete wore a suit, even though he typically prefers to dress more casually. He knew, however, that the suit would convey an impression of seriousness and professionalism.

At the reception, his friend made the introduction, and Pete told Jane how much he liked her work and her last article in particular. He spoke in a relaxed voice and didn't ramble on and on. (He had rehearsed what he was going to say ahead of time.) Then he asked his questions. Jane appreciated his interest, and also found the questions insightful, and so was happy to answer.

The conversation continued for a few more minutes. Then Pete said: "This has been a great conversation, but I know you're busy and that there are lots of people here who want to talk with you. I don't want to monopolize your time. But I'm working on a fair housing campaign that's very similar to the one you ran in Cincinnati, and we're having trouble getting the attention of the local legislators. Would it be okay if I contacted you after the conference to get some advice on how to do this?"

Jane gave him her business card and invited him to get in touch.

Jane is not yet a mentor for Pete, but she has agreed to give him at least some help, which is the first step toward establishing a mentor relationship. If Pete develops the evolving relationship well (see below), Jane could easily develop into a mentor for him.

Pete did many things right, including:

- Planned ahead (studied the conference agenda).
- Didn't approach Jane "cold" (i.e., arranged an introduction).

- Presented himself in a professional manner.
- Was prepared—he had studied up on Jane's work, and also rehearsed what he was going to say. Pete knew that **every first meeting, and some second and third ones, is an audition**.
- Demonstrated specific knowledge of Jane and her work. Many famous or important people are constantly approached by people who want their help, but know little about them or what they do. It's a drag and it turns many of them off from meeting new people. However, by demonstrating that he really, truly knows Jane and her work, Pete set himself apart from the crowd.
- Was conscious of her situation and respectful of her time.
- Made his request only after a friendly dialogue was established.
- Made an appropriate request—i.e., one that was both within her field of expertise, and not too time-consuming.

Oh, and by the way, Pete took a similar strategic approach with several other VIPs who were attending the conference and as a result wound up with several potential mentors.

Working with Your Mentors

You want to **stay in regular touch with your mentors**. That could mean once a month, once every six months, once every year or even less often, depending on who the mentor is and the specific nature of your relationship with him. Or, you might consult your mentor intensively during a specific project that lasts a week or a month, and not for a while after that.

But regularly. What you don't want to do is drop out of sight and then, when a crisis emerges, contact your mentor frantically for advice. If your mentor is nice, he will help you out, but he might also feel used, so send regular updates, preferably containing good or at least useful news. E-mail works well for this.

You want your interactions to be meaningful—**above all, you don't want the mentor to feel you've wasted his time**. That means you have a defined goal for each interaction—be it over the phone, or in person at his office, or over coffee. It also means you have done all the thinking and preparation you need to do ahead of time, so that the interaction is efficient.

And you need to **be appreciative**. Thank-you notes are required after every meaningful exchange or bit of assistance your mentor gives you— and not a dashed-off thank-you note, but a carefully written one. Note that a handwritten note or card is often more meaningful and valued than an e-mail, but an e-mail is *way* better than nothing.

And, of course, you should always seek to **reciprocate**. Even though you may feel that you have little to offer your mentor, that is probably not the case. Sooner or later, you'll see a newspaper article, or get some information at a meeting, or make a contact, that your mentor will find useful. Be sure to get that information or contact to him. Or, you may be able to assist the mentor in some difficult project he's involved with. Even if your contribution is just doing some typing or picking up the bagels and coffee for a meeting, he will appreciate your willingness to reciprocate.

Mentoring Others

Mentoring is, as I'll discuss in Chapter 28, one of the most fantastic growth experiences you can have, which is why a lot of even very busy people welcome the opportunity to mentor a few select protégés. It's also why you should also be a mentor to others.

Yes, *you* should mentor! Regardless of how inexperienced or unaccomplished as you may feel, there are still plenty of people who would benefit from your wisdom and guidance. If someone comes to you seeking advice—and it will happen sooner or later, especially if you work on your mission, time, and fear and relationship management—and you feel comfortable with them and their request, by all means mentor them.

If you don't want to wait until someone approaches you, you can always join a mentor program at a nonprofit organization or charity. Many youth-oriented programs and schools have mentor programs, for example. Or you could start a mentor program within your movement or activist organization. There is probably *no* activist organization that wouldn't benefit from having a mentor program in place.

Don't dither on this: the one thing almost every mentor eventually winds up saying is that they feel they got more out of the relationship than the person they were "helping."

For more information on mentoring, visit www.lifelongactivist.com/mentoring.

CHAPTER 27

The Ultimate Solution to Managing Your Fears: Develop an Empowered Personality

When you start making progress on your procrastination problem, your personality will change. That sounds scary, but it is actually a good thing, because it means that you will be becoming more effective and successful. In fact, you'll be developing what I call an "empowered personality."

An empowered person is someone who has made great strides in conquering her obstacles and, as a result, is actually achieving what she wants to achieve. There are empowered people in every field, and you should seek them out and enlist them as role models and mentors.

Below, I describe the empowered mindset and compare it with its opposite, the unempowered mindset.

Empowered People versus Unempowered People

Empowered people tend to be . . .
- Positive
- Action-oriented
- Planning-oriented
- Solution-oriented
- Optimistic

They tend to . . .
- Feel empowered and in control
- Take responsibility
- Not take difficult situations personally
- Help others

Unempowered people, in contrast, tend to be . . .

- Negative
- Passive (not action-oriented)
- Planning-averse
- Blame-oriented (not solution-oriented)
- Pessimistic

They tend to . . .

- Feel powerless and out of control
- Evade responsibility
- Take difficulties personally
- Not help others

Empowered people tend to be self-actualized and, like all self-actualized people, tend to have an expansive world view. They are at home in the universe and in their own skins, and their power, passion, wisdom and tenderness makes them highly attractive to others.

Some empowered people may even strike you as *too* happy and high-energy, if you yourself are low-energy or haven't met that many empowered people. (A sure sign, by the way, that you're hanging around with the wrong crowd. . . .) But hang in there and get used to the energetic new vibe.

You shouldn't hesitate to approach empowered people because most of them understand the importance of networking and mentoring. Of course, you always want to time your introduction carefully and be well prepared for the encounter. Remember: *every introduction is an audition*, and empowered people, because they value their time highly, tend to be highly selective about whom they choose to work with or mentor.

Note that while many empowered people are successful in the conventional sense, not all successful people are empowered. There are plenty of successful people who run large organizations, command great salaries or have developed awesome intellectual frameworks, and yet have not conquered their internal demons. They remain subject to a fear-based, zero-sum, deprivational mentality that causes them to shut out—or, worse, exploit—younger, less-experienced or less-powerful activists. People like this are *not* empowered and should be avoided in your search for mentors.

CHAPTER 28

What Empowered People Do

Working to empower yourself is one of the best things you can do for your-self, your movement, and the world at large. Doing so is largely a matter of forming certain intellectual, emotional and behavioral habits. Below is a list to get you started; as always, take it slow, applaud every bit of progress you make, and never bash yourself for perceived "failures."

Empowered people build infrastructures to support their success.

When you take a job in a corporation, you automatically acquire, on your first day of work, and with little or no effort on your part, most or all of the follow-ing: a desk, office, computer, computer assistance, electricity, lights, a bath-room, phone, schedule, rule book, records of your predecessor's work, a salary, benefits, reference books and other materials, colleagues, a boss, a boss's boss, a human resources department, and a budget for additional purchases.

I call all of the money, things and people that make it possible for you to do your job your "success infrastructure." As you can see, success infra-structures tend to be big, complex and expensive.

Activist work is as hard, or harder, than corporate work, which means you probably need an equivalent, or better, infrastructure for it. In activism, however, it's often the case that no one gives you your infrastructure; rather, you need to create it yourself. That is not so much a task as an ongo-ing process, and it should be one of your top priorities at all times. An unempowered person will sit around bemoaning all the resources he needs but doesn't have. An empowered person, in contrast, will identify a need and quickly start working the phones to get it met. In doing so, he creates his success infrastructure.

Empowered people educate themselves.

They are lifelong learners, and constantly reading, attending classes, and consulting experts and others. They are naturally curious about a wide range of topics, and not biased against non-political or "soft" subjects such as personal finance and self-help.

Empowered people welcome challenges.

Many people avoid challenges and the unknown, but empowered people welcome them as growth opportunities. They also know that success often comes from pushing oneself just a little bit beyond one's "comfort zone."

Here's what Christopher Reeve, in *Nothing Is Impossible: Reflections on a New Life* (New York: Random House, 2002), had to say about comfort zones:

> The vast majority of people live within a comfort zone that is relatively small. The comfort zone is defined by fear and our perception of our limitations. We are occasionally willing to take small steps outside it, but few of us dare to expand it. Those who dare sometimes fail and retreat, but many experience the satisfaction of moving into a larger comfort zone and the joyful anticipation of more success. A person living with a disability may find the courage to leave the comfort zone of his own house for the first time. An able-bodied individual might decide to face claustrophobia by taking up scuba diving. Even as our country tries to cope with terrorism, most of us know intuitively that living in fear is not living at all.

Fortunately, activism provides no shortage of opportunities to be challenged! Even worthwhile challenges can be scary, however, which brings us to . . .

Empowered people anticipate, and learn to deal with, fear and anxiety.

Recall Steven Pressfield's story about how Henry Fonda threw up before every performance. For forty years, he threw up; and then, each time, he went out and gave his performance.

Unsuccessful people often assume that successful people find success easy, or are unusually good at coping with stress. That's often not the case, however. Successful people may get just as scared or anxious as anyone else, but they figure out ways to cope. In fact, they are determined to cope. They understand that the negative feelings are transient and relatively unimportant in the larger scheme of things.

Empowered people seek out not just mentors, but protégés.

Empowered people seek out protégés—people to mentor—not just because they know that the world runs better when everyone gives back, but also because they know that mentoring is one of the best uses of their time. Mentoring helps you identify and reinforce your strengths, and also increases your base of knowledge. And because the goal of mentoring is to help your protégé evolve into an empowered person, mentoring is also one of the best ways to expand what Stephen Covey, author of *The Seven Habits of Highly Effective People* (see Bibliography), calls your "circle of influence."

Empowered people reprogram their thoughts for success.
They make a conscious effort to replace dysfunctional thought patterns with functional ones. For instance, they try to replace

Negative thinking	*with* . . . Objective, or positive, thinking
Self-criticism	*with* . . . Self-acceptance or self-praise
Judgmental thinking	*with* . . . Compassionate observation and objective analysis
Perfectionist thinking	*with* . . . Reasonable goal setting and tolerance of error
Hypersensitivity	*with* . . . Resilience
Panic	*with* . . . Calm and perspective

So, if an empowered person who happens to be an activist screws up at a press conference and then catches himself thinking, "What a jerk I am . . . " he immediately and consciously stops that line of thought and replaces it with another, more functional one. For example: "That press conference didn't go well because I didn't have time to rehearse my points. In the future, I will make sure to spend a few hours rehearsing the day before. But, it wasn't all bad: several of the writers who attended said they would use our story. I will call them this afternoon to confirm that and to clear up any misunderstandings I may have caused."

Empowered people deal quickly and decisively with their obstacles.
That's because they know that, not only are obstacles a serious impediment to success, but that they tend to worsen over time. Empowered people also know that success, which brings its own busy-ness and stresses, can worsen many Situational Obstacles in particular. Many people, for example, let their health or relationships deteriorate as they become more professionally successful.

Don't let something like that happen to you—start dealing with your obstacles *now*.

Empowered people understand that success is often a performance.

Most people feel empowered at least part of the time. We all have moments when we operate at peak performance (or have a peak experience, see Part IV, Chapter 2) and feel on top of the world.

The crucial question is: What do you do in between those moments?

My suggestion is that, even in moments of non-motivation, you should act as if you are highly motivated. This is because of a wonderful thing that behavioral scientists have discovered: that not only do our emotions dictate our actions, but our actions often dictate our emotions. Research has shown, for instance, that we don't just smile because we're happy, we actually become happier when we smile. That's because the smile initiates a sequence of hormonal and other events that relaxes us and makes us feel good.

Professional salespeople, who must be "on" close to 100 percent of the time in order to make their quotas, are very familiar with this phenomenon. They are taught that their posture, facial expression and other physical attributes affect not only their mood but their customers'. Salespeople are taught to smile even when talking over the telephone, because although the customer on the other end of the line can't see them do it, the salesperson's voice sounds much more forceful and dynamic when she smiles. Try it.

Many salespeople, performers, athletes and other peak performers develop a personal collection of tricks, rituals and physical and mental exercises to help themselves get and stay pumped for their workday.[8] You should do the same thing.

And here's the icing on the cake, the amazing secret that empowered people in every field eventually learn: that **with enough practice mimicking peak performance, you will actually start experiencing the real thing more often.** Experts say that while we probably can't operate at peak all the time, we can probably do so much more frequently than we realize.[9] Simply by becoming more familiar with the state of performing at peak, you train yourself to enter into that state more easily and frequently.

And that will be the most amazing reward of all, for all of your hard work.

By now, you've learned to Manage Your Mission, Manage Your Time and Manage Your Fears. One more challenge remains, arguably the toughest, but also the most rewarding: Managing Your Relationships. In *The Lifelong Activist* I've divided this challenge into two parts: Managing Your Relationship with Self; and Managing Your Relationship with Others. First is . . .

PART IV. MANAGING YOUR RELATIONSHIP WITH SELF

PART IV

Managing Your Relationship with Self

PART IV. MANAGING YOUR RELATIONSHIP WITH SELF

CHAPTER 1

Your Most Important Relationship

I call the process by which one goes about acquiring an empowered personality **self-actualization**. The term was coined by the influential psychologist Abraham Maslow, who, in his 1962 book *Toward a Psychology of Being* (New York: Wiley, 1998), and other works, wrote that a self-actualized person exhibits many or most of the following characteristics:

- **Realistic.** Has a more accurate, objective and "efficient" perception of reality; more comfortable with complexities and contradictions than non-self-actualized people are.
- **Accepting of self, others and nature.** Not crippled by guilt or shame; able to enjoy himself without regret or apology.
- **Unhampered by convention.** Has a strongly autonomous and individualistic, but not isolationist, nature. Relies on inner self for satisfaction and has a strong inner sense of what's right and wrong.
- **Problem-centered.** Likes to solve problems, and likes to have an ambitious mission. Stable in the face of adversity. Resilient.
- **Spontaneous/Maintains a fresh view.** Has a fresh rather than a stereotyped view of the world, and an authentic appreciation for it.
- **Spiritual.** Tuned in to a "deeper wisdom."
- **"Gemeinschaftsgeuhl."** "Identification, sympathy, and affection for mankind, kinship with the good, the bad and the ugly."
- **Democratically oriented.** "The self-actualizing person does not discriminate on the basis of class, education, race or color. He is humble in his recognition of what he knows in comparison with what could be known, and he is ready and willing to learn from anyone."
- **Possessing a philosophical, unhostile sense of humor.** Can laugh at himself, but never makes fun of others.
- **Creative.** Can express his "inborn uniqueness."

Maslow characterized self-actualization as "the intrinsic growth of what is already in the organism, or more accurately, of what the organism is." He believed that people are fundamentally good, and that "psychopathology generally results from the denial, frustration or twisting of our essential natures." As you will learn in Chapter 5, this description is in line with what many progressives believe and how they strive to live their lives and treat others. Although some feminists and others criticize Maslow's model for, among other things, overvaluing autonomy and undervaluing interconnectedness and relationships, both among individuals and between individuals and the natural world,[1] I believe it remains a valuable guide, and I particularly like the way the term "self-actualization" doesn't just define an end point (the self-actualized personality), but a process (self-actualization) that one can use to get there. When I use the term in this book, I am using it to refer not to Maslow's exact model, but to a broader concept that largely, but not entirely, overlaps it.

As a human being and an activist, your most important goal should be to work on your own self-actualization, because in the process of becoming self-actualized you will gain the qualities you need to work on all of your other goals. Self-actualization creates strength and character and commitment: it is a political act, really, and the foundation for all of your future political acts. Let's remind ourselves of what Confucius said: "To put the world in order, we must first put the nation in order; to put the nation in order, we must first put the family in order; to put the family in order, we must first cultivate our personal life; and to cultivate our personal life, we must first set our hearts right." Let's also not forget that Gloria Steinem titled her autobiography *Revolution From Within*.

I would go so far as to say that one of the key differences between effective and ineffective activists is that the effective ones are more self-actualized, i.e., more empowered and able to express more of their unique selves. As Saul Alinsky puts it in *Rules for Radicals*:

How can an organizer respect the dignity of an individual if he does not respect his own dignity? How can he believe in people if he does not really believe in himself? How can he convince people that they have it within themselves, that they have the power to stand up to win, if he does not believe it of himself? Ego must be so all-pervading that the personality of the organizer is contagious, that it converts the people from despair to defiance, creating a mass ego.

Despite Alinsky's and my exhortations, however, you may still be wondering, "How can I justify spending time working on my own tiny problems when so many others are suffering so horribly?" That's a legitimate concern, and I'll address it in the next few chapters. First, however, let's explore the concept of self-actualization in more depth.

CHAPTER 2

A Vision of the Actualized Self

Maslow maintained that a person's degree of self-actualization correlates with the number of "peak experiences" he or she has. The phrase "peak experience" has been defined in many ways by Maslow and others—and sometimes used in a recreational drug context—but most descriptions come down to something like this: during a peak experience, you are using your skills and talents in the service of something you truly enjoy and feel is worthwhile. You're "in the zone": not blocked at all, and able to work and create almost effortlessly. You lose track of time. You forget to eat or e-mail or watch television, or whatever else it is that you do when you procrastinate. You feel great, and maybe joyful.

You want as many peak experiences in your life as possible—and if you follow through with your Mission Management, Time Management, Fear Management and Relationship Management, you will have lots of them. In fact, you want your life, as much as possible, to be filled with peak experiences and joyfulness. While this may sound like an unrealistic goal, it isn't, even (especially) for activists. **Please don't fall into the common trap of believing that the most we humans can aspire to is the rare peak or joyful experience in a life otherwise characterized by long stretches of suffering or, at best, boredom.** That tragic and defeatist view holds many people back from living a happy life. It is also, as we shall see in Chapter 7, a hallmark of *conservative* thinking.

Make the Shift From "Survival" to "Self-Expression" Values

Gay Hendricks and Kathlyn Hendricks, authors of *Conscious Loving: The Journey to Co-Commitment* (see Bibliography) identify the above-described tragic mindset as a major barrier to personal happiness:

We are programmed that we cannot feel good for very long without invoking some negative experience to bring us down. Our programming tells us that we must have fun/have a crash, get close/get sick, be close/start a fight. We have an old association between feeling good and pain, so that when we feel good for a little while we find some way to create pain. . . .

The Upper Limits Problem is the phrase we use to describe this unique human tendency. It is the only problem you have to solve . . . how to let yourself expand continuously into more positive energy. . . .

Human beings have been suffering and struggling for millions of years; we are highly skilled at handling negative energy. We believe that at this time in evolution our species is actually creating new channels in ourselves for experiencing positive energy. How to feel good naturally, without chemical assistance, is a new task in evolution.

The Hendricks are mostly writing about shifts within the individual human psyche, but the World Values Survey project (www.worldvaluessurvey.org) documents a similar shift toward positive energy that takes place across entire societies. The WVS is a highly respected, decades-long series of surveys documenting shifts in sociocultural and political thinking and mores in nearly eighty societies around the globe. The sociologists conducting the surveys have identified a key shift in values that occurs as societies become more affluent: a shift from "survival values," such as political caution, stoic acceptance of the status quo and wariness toward outsiders, to "self-expression values," such as an openness to new people and ideas, political activism and creative exploration. In other words: toward self-actualization and, as you will learn in Chapter 5, progressivism.

A shift from "survival" to "self-expression"—what a wonderful project to be working on, both in one's own life and as a society. And the truth is that, absent severe disability, illness, oppression or some other very negative factor, we can feel happy and free and even joyful for much of our lives. And even in the presence of those kinds of negative factors, we can still work to feel as happy and free and joyful as possible. Recall Part III, Chapter 14, and our discussion of Christopher Reeve and Dr. Viktor Frankl.

We can even feel happy and free and joyful while knowing that there are billions of people and animals around the globe who are suffering horribly. The reason we should strive for happiness in the face of this ongoing calamity is this: **our being miserable isn't helping those suffering beings at all—not one bit. But our being happy, free and joyful will help us to become better activists, so that we can help them more.** All this is not to say that we should repress or ignore our sadness and other "dark" emotions; they are often appropriate responses to what we see and experience, and we shouldn't be repressing anyway. But it is important to not let those feelings overwhelm us, and one way to do that, besides dealing with them directly via therapy or other tools, is to work consciously and conscientiously to locate, and grow, our more positive feelings.

I discuss how self-actualization will help you be a better, more effective activist in Chapter 4. First, however, let's discuss the work you need to do to self-actualize.

CHAPTER 3

How to Self-Actualize

As you start to Manage Your Mission, Time, Fears and Relationships, you will be doing the work of self-actualization. This work will take time—a lifetime, really—and there will inevitably be plateaus and backsliding. The important things, as discussed in Part III, are not to rush it; to always aim to improve in "baby steps"; to celebrate every victory or achievement, no matter how trivial-seeming; and to never, ever put yourself down for any perceived failures. Remember that growth is achieved not from blame or shame or self-criticism, but from recognizing and reinforcing your strengths and accomplishments.

Maslow himself claimed to know of only a handful of people who had achieved self-actualization, but I see no reason to set such a high standard. In my view, self-actualization is not about perfection, but about (1) finding your unique path; (2) following it to the extent you're able; and (3) having the most fun possible while you're doing it. I know plenty of people who qualify. Still, most of the time I prefer to use the adjective "self-actualizing" instead of "self-actualized," to reflect the reality that there is no official "finish line" and that we're all works-in-progress.

As you start to work on your self-actualization, you should see yourself not just achieving more of your goals, but starting to develop the empowered personality described in Part III. This, in turn, should lead you to achieve still more goals, including the bigger and scarier ones. Whether your "scary" goal involves a new job, new relationship, new living place, new form of activism or something else, self-actualization will give you the strength and other qualities you need to make progress on it.

Please remember that self-actualization is not something extra you do on top of all your "normal" obligations and responsibilities. It is the act of meeting those obligations and responsibilities in an empowered and joyful way. It is a life strategy, and an amazingly effective one. And Mission, Time, Fear and Relationship Management are the keys.

Surround Yourself with Self-Actualizing People

As discussed numerous times throughout *The Lifelong Activist*, you want to surround yourself with supportive people. More specifically, you want to surround yourself with self-actualized and self-actualizing people, since they are the ones who will most understand and support your own self-actualization process. Also, make sure that any organizations you work with or for support your self-actualization efforts. (See next chapter.)

All of this is particularly important in the context of your activism. So much activist time and energy gets wasted in pointless work, as well as in infighting, personality clashes and other drama. Working with self-actualizing people is the best way to minimize the odds of your falling into one of these traps, and of ensuring that you will one day look back at your activist career with satisfaction.

That doesn't mean you seek out, or only work with, people who are "perfect." Perfection is never the goal, and it's a particularly unrealistic standard when applied to human beings. Self-actualization, as I mentioned above, is a lifelong process, and even highly self-actualized people have issues they need to continue to work on. The difference between them and non-self-actualizing people is that they are actually committed to working on those issues, and to helping others work on theirs. Non-self-actualizing people, in contrast, often put much of their energy into denial, repression, blaming (of themselves or others), and other ineffective coping strategies. As a result, their problems remain unsolved, and they tend to lead unhappy lives, and to make others unhappy as well.

You should always encourage other activists to self-actualize, and support them as they do. Right now, you could team up with one or two of your friends, classmates or colleagues to help each other with Mission, Time, Fear and Relationship Management. (For guidance on how to do this, check out www.lifelongactivist.com/workgroups.) And you can start mentoring one or two others—mentoring, as we discussed in Part III, not just being a great way to support someone else, but to reinforce your own knowledge and growth. Just be sure to pick protégés who are committed to the process, and to include the time you spend mentoring them in your Personal Mission Statement, Mission Plan, Time Budget and Weekly Schedule.

EXERCISE

Come up with a list of those people you know whom you consider to be self-actualizing. They could be activists or non-activists, and most will be more successful in some areas of their lives or careers than others. They may not even identify what they're doing as self-actualization, but will nevertheless be working hard to live their lives according to their values.

Think about the qualities these people possess that make you see them as self-actualizing and, in particular, how they manage their Mission, Time, Fears and Relationships. Start thinking of them as mentors and make plans to build that relationship (see Part III, Chapter 26).

CHAPTER 4

Self-Actualize to Become a Better Activist

Self-actualizing will help you to become a better activist, for these reasons:

- Self-actualizing people don't just have a clearer sense of their Mission, but are also able to use their time better. They also tend to suffer less from fear, including the fear-based habits of perfectionism, negativity, hypersensitivity and panic, and to form more effective personal and professional relationships. These relationships not only provide them with needed support and resources, but also allow them to expand their "circle of influence," as Stephen Covey puts it. In other words, self-actualization lets you leverage your strengths and talents to the greatest extent possible.

- A self-actualizing activist is a happier activist, and a happier activist is usually a much more effective advocate for his values. See Part V, Chapter 30, for more on this topic, but the simple explanation is that people who are happy, upbeat and enthusiastic tend to attract others to themselves and their way of thinking, while those who are unhappy, bitter or unmotivated tend to repel others.

- Self-actualizing people also tend to be emotionally stronger and more resilient than non-self-actualizing ones. Strength and resilience are great qualities for anyone to have, but are especially useful for activists who work on stressful projects or lead stressful lives.

- Because of their emotional strength, self-actualizing people also tend to be less egocentric than non-self-actualizing people, meaning that they are better able to accept others on their own terms. This is also an extremely valuable quality for any activist to possess, as it aids you in relating to, and influencing, diverse audiences. An activist who isn't self-actualizing is more likely to react with confusion, contempt or even hatred to someone who thinks differently than she does, while a self-actualizing activist is more likely to stay in control of her emotions and also retain the compassionate view that is the foundation of effective activism. See Part V, Chapter 10, for more on this point.

As discussed in Part I, your self-actualization work may result in your temporarily or permanently doing less, or even no, activism. If this turns out to be the case, be true to your Mission and do not feel bad about your choice. There is an excellent chance that you'll one day return to activism, and that when you do you'll make a far more valuable contribution than if you had spent years doing half-hearted activism that conflicted with your true values and needs.

Mission for Activist Organizations

One of the top goals of any activist organization should be to help its employees, volunteers and other participants self-actualize. If you belong to such an organization, encourage it to do so by:

- Providing tools, training and other support for participants who wish to do Mission, Time, Fear and Relationship Management.
- Actively encouraging mentor relationships. These can be between people working within your organization, or between your organization's members and outsiders. See Part III, Chapter 26, and www.lifelongactivist.com/mentoring.
- Establishing a lending library of books listed in the Bibliography, and sponsoring a book group or discussion group on issues related to self-actualization.
- Setting up a Lifelong Activist Workgroup. See page 385 and www.lifelongactivist.com/workgroups for more information.

An organization consisting of happy and effective self-actualizing activists will probably attract much more attention and support—including financial support—than one consisting of miserable, depressed and ineffectual non-self-actualizing ones. It is also likely to be much more successful at its goals of influencing people to effect positive social change.

The more activists who self-actualize, the better off we will all be.

CHAPTER 5

Self-Actualization: A Progressive Value

In his books *Moral Politics* and *Don't Think of an Elephant!* (see Bibliography), and other works, cognitive linguist George Lakoff explains how humans use metaphors, or models, to organize information and better comprehend the complex world around them. One of the primary metaphors we use for comprehending society and the political arena, he says, is that of the *family*—our own birth family, of course, being the first social and political system we experience. Progressives, Lakoff says, tend to use what he calls a "nurturant parent" model for interpreting politics and society, while conservatives tend to use a "strict father" model. The gender asymmetry between "nurturant parent" and "strict father" is deliberate because, "In the strict father model, the masculine and feminine roles are very different, and the father is the central figure. . . . In the nurturant parent model, there just isn't a gender distinction of this sort."

I'll discuss the strict father model in Chapter 7, but first, from *Don't Think of an Elephant!*, here's Lakoff's description of the nurturant parent model:

> The nurturant parent family assumes that the world, despite its dangers and difficulties, is basically good, can be made better, and that it is one's responsibility to work toward that. Accordingly, children are born good and parents can make them better. Both parents share responsibility for raising the children. Their job is to nurture their children and raise their children to be nurturers. Nurturing has two aspects: empathy (feeling and caring how others feel) and responsibility (for taking care of oneself and others for whom we are responsible). These two aspects of nurturance imply family values that we can recognize as progressive political values: from empathy, we want for others protection from harm, fulfillment in

life, fairness, freedom (consistent with responsibility), and open two-way communication. From responsibility follow competence, trust, commitment, community building, and so on.

Is self-actualization a progressive value? I believe so, because Maslow's characterization of self-actualization closely resembles Lakoff's nurturant parent model. Reread the description of the self-actualized individual in Chapter 1, and you will see that both self-actualization and the nurturant parent model emphasize:

- The intrinsic goodness of the individual.
- The intrinsic goodness of other people.
- Independence of thought and action.
- Equality and freedom.
- Creativity and other expressions of "self."
- The importance of treating others with respect, tolerance and kindness.

Moreover, as you will see in Chapter 7, these qualities are in direct opposition to those associated with the conservative strict father model.

Although Lakoff doesn't use the exact phrase "self-actualization" in *Don't Think of an Elephant!*, he does urge progressives to work toward a mindset that sounds very much like it:

> If you empathize with your child, you want your child to be fulfilled in life, to be a happy person. And if you are an unhappy, unfulfilled person yourself, you are not going to want other people to be happier than you are. The Dalai Lama teaches us that. **Therefore, it is your moral responsibility to be a happy, fulfilled person. Your moral responsibility.** Further, it is your moral responsibility to teach your child [and others] to be a happy, fulfilled person who wants others to be happy and fulfilled. (Emphasis added.)

There is perhaps no better example of the nurturant, progressive mindset than a wonderful quote from Spanish prime minister José Luis Rodríguez Zapatero. In June 2005, after Spain's parliament legalized same-sex unions, he said: "We are expanding opportunities for the happiness of our neighbors, our work colleagues, our friends, our relatives."

This really is the mission of all progressives, especially if you expand the circle to include not just our neighbors, etc., but every person and all beings who share the planet with us. Our goal is to help them all self-actualize.

It's a glorious mission, but as Confucius says, you have to begin with yourself. So start working to self-actualize, and never feel guilty about your efforts to do so. Rather, let your joyous example inspire others to do the same.

EXERCISE

Do you still feel guilt or other negative emotions around the topic of self-actualization, or around your own need to, or desire to, self-actualize? If so, try journaling to see if you can define and defuse those feelings—or consult a mentor, therapist or other advisor.

CHAPTER 6

The Right's Big Lie

There is one barrier that, perhaps more than any other, stands in the way of many progressives living a happy, self-actualized life: the view that being a progressive automatically dooms you to a life of unhappiness, or sets you tragically apart from the mainstream of humanity. This view is promoted by people on both the Right and the Left, for different reasons.

It's obvious why the Right wants to convince people that being a progressive makes you miserable: it supports their agenda. The more people who believe that progressives are losers, loonies, flakes, tree-huggers, bleeding-hearts, impractical dreamers, "out-of-touch with the common man," "Hollywood elites," "Eastern elites," etc., the easier the Right's job is. These and other misconceptions have been deliberately and aggressively promoted by rightwing strategists all the way back to at least the 1950s (cf. McCarthyism and the demonizing of Democratic presidential candidate Adlai Stevenson as an "egghead" intellectual). "Liberals as losers" can, in fact, be considered one of the Right's most successful pieces of propaganda: successful because vast numbers of people, including many progressives, believe it.

It's trickier to figure out why some on the Left would promote this misconception. Some activists have probably unthinkingly bought into the Right's propaganda, while others may use the misconception to justify their own failure to self-actualize and build happy lives. Still others may mistakenly feel that they don't deserve to be happy, or shouldn't be happy, in a world in which so many others are suffering. Misguided viewpoints such as these are also often used as a cover-up for a deeper problem that keeps activists unhappy: low self-esteem. People suffering from low self-esteem often feel they don't deserve to be happy or have their needs met, and so they often build lives for themselves that are characterized by deprivation. (Recall Gloria Steinem's story, and also the discussion on voluntary poverty, in Part I, Chapter 13). There is simply no reason to live this way, however—and doing so will probably make you a worse, not a better activist. So:

- If you suffer from low self-esteem, work to create a healthier self-image for yourself. This may require therapy and the other tools discussed in Part III.
- If you've bought into the misconception that progressives should be unhappy, work to embrace a more positive vision.

Remember that many of the most joyful and empowered people around are progressive activists—people like Granny D, Julia Butterfly Hill, Jim Hightower, Frances Moore Lappé and Dr. Patch Adams. (You can probably think of other examples in your own community or movement.) These people, and not any unhappy activists you happen to know or hear about, are the ones whom you should be modeling your life and career after. Remember that working to be happy is not only not selfish, it is, according to Lakoff, your moral imperative.

What about the undeniable fact that many progressives are unhappy? Well, examine any population and you'll find many unhappy people. If progressives have their characteristic woes—many of which derive from the strain of living in, and being in constant struggle against, a society at odds with their values—so do corporate executives or any other group you can name. For every progressive struggling with poverty or alienation, there's a middle manager trying to figure out how she can escape the fate of being "just one more meaningless cog in the wheel."

The reality may be that most progressives—and, especially, the older, "settled" ones—are actually happier than most conservatives. This is certainly one conclusion that can be drawn from the "strict father" model Lakoff says is common to conservative thought, and which I discuss in the remaining chapters of this section. It's important to understand the roots and framework of conservative thought, not just as an antidote to conservative propaganda, but so that you can more persuasively present your progressive ideas, both to the conservatives themselves and those in the political middle.

CHAPTER 7

The Strict Father Model

In Chapter 5, I discussed the "nurturant parent" model that George Lakoff says underpins much progressive thought. Here, again from *Don't Think of an Elephant!*, is its conservative equivalent, the "strict father" model:

> The strict father model begins with a set of assumptions:
>
> The world is a dangerous place, and it always will be, because there is evil out there in the world. The world is also difficult because it is competitive. There will always be winners and losers. There is an absolute right and an absolute wrong. Children are born bad, in the sense that they just want to do what feels good, not what is right. Therefore, they have to be made good.
>
> What is needed in this kind of a world is a strong, strict father who can protect the family in the dangerous world; support the family in the difficult world; and teach his children right from wrong.
>
> What is required of the child is obedience, because the strict father is a moral authority who knows right from wrong. . . .
>
> A good person—a moral person—is someone who is disciplined enough to be obedient, to learn what is right, do what is right and not do what is wrong, and to pursue her self-interest to prosper and become self-reliant. A good child grows up to be like that. A bad child is one who does not learn discipline, does not function morally, does not do what is right, and therefore is not disciplined enough to become prosperous. She cannot take care of herself and thus becomes dependent.

The strict father model, Lakoff says, "assumes that the world is and always will be dangerous and difficult, and that children are born bad and must be made good. The strict father is the moral authority who has to support and defend the family, tell his wife what to do, and teach his kids right from wrong. The only way to do that is through painful punishment—physical discipline that by adulthood will develop into internal discipline."

This is pure "survivalist" mentality, and couldn't contrast more with the self-actualized individual described in Chapter 1:

- The self-actualized person is independent, while the "good child" in the strict father model is obedient.
- The self-actualized person is born good, while the child in the strict father model is born bad.
- The self-actualized person feels at home in the world, while the strict father model views the world, and other people, as difficult and dangerous.

The strict father model is based on **fear**, but a different kind of fear from those discussed in Part III. Those fears—fear of change, fear of failure and fear of success—are mostly a fear of *self*: a fear that you don't have what it takes to succeed, or can't handle what life throws at you. The strict father model mostly fears *others*. The strict father model explains why so many conservative policies tend to ignore, or even punish, those who struggle economically, while rewarding those who succeed, even if their success is achieved dishonestly. The model presumes that people struggle not because they have been the victims of bad luck or societal inequity, but because they disobeyed the rules. It is therefore not only right, but obligatory, that they be punished, both for their own, and society's, good.

The Wages of Conservative Fear . . . and Progressive Courage

The fear-based strict father model also explains a wide range of dysfunctional behaviors we associate mainly with the Right[2], including bigotry, self-segregation into sterile and isolationist suburbs, and a propensity for joining authoritarian churches and other organizations. Oh, and let's not forget the Right's fabled antipathy to sex, and especially gay sex, unmarried sex and young sex. (Lakoff points out that these happen to be the kinds of sexual relationships that most directly subvert the strict father model.[3]) The Right has also traditionally hated interracial sex, but progressives have succeeded in defeating racism to the extent that, these days, few even on the Far Right will own up to that hatred, at least in public. The Right also routinely employs fear-mongering and hate-mongering as explicit strategies for gaining and keeping power. For decades, the main "enemy" the Right "protected us" against was Communism.

In *Don't Think of an Elephant!*, Lakoff points out, "Fear and uncertainty . . . naturally activate the strict father frame in a majority of people, leading the electorate to see politics in conservative terms." He also writes:

> The vehemence of the culture war provoked and maintained by conservatives is no accident. For strict father morality to gain and maintain political power . . . the conservatives need the support of many of the poor. That is, they need a significant percentage of the poor and middle class to vote against their economic interests. . . . Their method for achieving this has been cultural civil war . . . pitting Americans with strict father morality (called conservatives) against Americans with nurturant parent morality (the hated liberals), who are portrayed as threatening the way of life and the cultural, religious, and personal identities of conservatives.

We currently see this strategy being used not just by America's homophobic and xenophobic Right, but by the Muslim world's fascists.

I am certainly not saying that everyone on the Right, or every Right-wing ideology, is motivated strongly by fear; or that everyone on the Left, or every Left-wing ideology, isn't. Nor am I saying that the Left is immune to authoritarian, hierarchical, isolationist, hateful or puritanical thinking. That would be a ludicrous statement to make in the wake of Stalin and Mao, not to mention the histories of the Communist Party USA and the New Left. The Left, like the Right, is comprised of people in varying stages of self-actualization; and it is perhaps inevitable that some people on the Right are going to be more self-actualized—and, hence, more nurturant—than some on the Left. Like all models, Lakoff's are simplified representations of a more complex reality, and hence should be used as generalized guides, not infallible doctrines. Lakoff himself points out that most people will use both models at different times, although the more you "tilt" toward the Left or Right, the more one model or the other will tend to predominate in your thinking.

Nor do I ignore the obvious point that many of the choices we progressives make have the potential to make our lives harder, and therefore presumably less happy, at least in the short term. There's nothing like standing out in the wind and rain, getting yelled at by passers-by during a demonstration, to brighten your day, after all. . . . And certainly there are plenty of conservatives who remain innocently or deliberately unaware of—or aware of but uncaring of—the inequities and injustices of the system that props them up. As such, they live in a kind of blissful ignorance and affluence unavailable to most progressives.

And yet, despite the innate difficulties of the progressive/activist life, and despite the pervasive anti-progressive propaganda out there, we—meaning you and I—have chosen to live our lives as progressives and as activists. Ask yourself why, and I think you will see that it's not simply because we believe our vision of the world is truer or more moral, but because we see our lifestyle as offering greater opportunities for happiness and self-actualization. Keep that in mind when the going gets rough, and always remember that, if a time comes when the lifepath you've chosen for yourself is making you unhappy, you have the ability to choose another. That is the ultimate luxury of all, and it only available to those of us who live lives not grounded in fear.

CHAPTER 8

The Key Insight

Think back on a time when you felt afraid, truly afraid, and you'll realize what an awful burden it is to live in fear. Then use that knowledge to feel compassion for conservatives whose worldview is founded on fear.

Yes, you must be compassionate to conservatives: even those who appear to be utterly lacking in compassion themselves. This is both your obligation as a nurturant progressive, and an eminently practical strategy, since hatred, even "legitimate" hatred toward a venal opponent, accomplishes nothing and is self-destructive. It will ruin your day and, if left unchecked, your life. "Whenever you feel hatred toward the enemy, think of him as a human being," advises the Dalai Lama. "[Hatred] . . . is not necessarily helping the enemy as harming yourself."

One way to avoid succumbing to hatred is to not concern yourself very much with the conservative "leaders" at the top reaches of government or in the media, the worst of whom are often not principled conservatives so much as craven opportunists. Focus, instead, on the conservatives in your neighborhood, classes, workplace and family. Strive to understand them and their belief systems—which often make sense in the context of their experiences—and to locate your points of commonality with them. Remember that . . .

- As a human being, you have a vast amount in common with all other human beings.
- As a citizen of the United States (or Canada, or another country), you have even more in common with everyone else in that country.
- As a member of whichever political, professional, religious, ethnic, gender, cultural or other groups you belong to, you have still more in common with the other members of those groups.
- Also, as an inhabitant of whatever local community you live in, you

have even more in common with the other inhabitants of that community.

• And, finally, as a member of a family, you have an enormous amount more in common with the other members.

All of this means that you have a vast amount in common even with people you might disagree with, and even with those whose values and actions you consider deplorable. This explains why even a highly committed progressive can admire, like, or even love someone whose values are different from hers, or even diametrically opposed to hers. This is nothing to be ashamed of: it just means you are a human being with a complex, human heart, and that your heart recognizes, even if your intellect does not yet do so, the commonality of all humankind.

The insight that we have vast amounts in common even with those with whom we disagree is so important that I call it The Key Insight. It mandates an attitude of not just compassion but, yes, love toward not just the progressives in your life but the conservatives as well. Accepting The Key Insight as a guiding principle is a truly revolutionary act that will forever change the way you view yourself and the world around you. It will also empower you to do much more powerful activism, since, as you will learn in Part V, people are far more likely to be persuaded by someone who they believe likes and respects them than by someone who they believe is harshly judging them and their ideas.

The Key Insight suggests that there should be many conservatives out there who share significant common ground with us progressives, and this is indeed the case. Many of these conservatives are older people who recall a time when (for all its drawbacks), our culture was less consumerist, our media less corporatist, and our civic institutions were stronger. But there are younger conservatives out there as well, a community and a trend that Rod Dreher documents in his fun book *Crunchy Cons* (see Bibliography). "Crunchy" alludes to granola, and "cons" is short for conservatives, and Dreher's subtitle says it all: "How Birkenstocked Burkeans, gun-loving organic gardeners, evangelical free-range farmers, hip homeschooling mamas, right-wing nature lovers, and their diverse tribe of countercultural conservatives plan to save America (or at least the Republican Party)."

Dreher is a journalist with impeccable conservative credentials—he has written for the *National Review*, the *Washington Times* and other conservative bastions—and yet he writes scathingly of the greed and the consumerist ethic permeating our society, the corrupting influence of corporations on our society and political process, and our devastating failure to nurture the environment and each other. True, he is also pro-gun, anti-sexual freedom and (in my view) fetishizes the traditional nuclear family to an inappropriate degree. Still, there is more than enough here to make common cause with—and the same is true for even many "non-crunchy" conservatives.

The Key Insight does not imply that you accept what the conservatives do, or fight it any less vociferously. It means, rather, that when dealing with people, you always strive to see the person and not the label.

Always remember that stereotyping and vilification are fear-based tactics of the Right, and should not be ours. **Remember, also, that every person has a complex story to tell, and that it is often in the details of that story that you will find your opening to "sell" him or her on your progressive views.**

Remember, also, that even many people who seem to be happily conservative, and happily enjoying the Average American Consumerist Lifestyle (AACL—see Part II, Chapter 3), are living lives of quiet desperation. Few people, when young, dream of being a cog in a corporate machine or living a conformist suburban lifestyle. Most of us start out dreaming of greatness, uniqueness and self-expression, and many people actually try to live out those dreams, until some combination of the AACL and their own fears subvert their plan and trap them into a more constricted existence. This kind of tragedy happens all the time, and while it is entirely appropriate to congratulate yourself (silently) for having the courage and fortitude not to get sucked in, it is also appropriate to feel compassion for those who, for whatever reason, were unable to avoid that fate.

Or unable to avoid it until now. For it is also appropriate for you to do what you can to lessen the sense of fear and increase the sense of hope and freedom and possibility in those around you, and in your society and the world as a whole. That is the essence of progressive activism, and I discuss how to do it in the final section of *The Lifelong Activist*. . . .

Activism and Joy:
A Meditation

It's sometimes hard to remember it, but the activist life provides many opportunities for joy.

There's the joy of living a self-actualized, authentic life, where your unique personality is being expressed, your unique needs are being met, and your unique talents and skills are being used to their fullest.

There's the joy of living a life that's devoted to important, even historic, things.

There's the joy of participating in a lively and intelligent and engaged community. Of helping others and then watching them, in turn, help others. Of watching your ideas and influence spread throughout your community, your society and the world.

There's also the joy of believing and acting passionately, and the joyful excitement of planning and executing a campaign. In *Letters to a Young Activist,* Todd Gitlin writes of, ". . . the almost sinful pleasure of being right, to see people surge into your ranks, to feel that your analysis penetrates to the heart of things."

Locate your joy, and nurture it. Practice feeling joyful even in situations where you might not ordinarily experience that emotion, so that you can increase your capacity for experiencing it. This will not only help you cope with the inevitable disappointments and discomforts of the activist life, but provide you with one of your most persuasive tools. People are naturally attracted to, inspired by, and driven to emulate joyful people—and are naturally repelled by those who are morose, bitter, sad or otherwise afflicted.

Which is what Part V, coming up next, is all about.

If every activist could access more of his or her joy, it would probably help the cause of progressivism more than anything else.

And you know what? Every activist can.

PART V

Managing Your Relationships with Others

PART V. MANAGING YOUR RELATIONSHIP WITH OTHERS

CHAPTER 1

What Activism Is—or Should Be

Activism is the act of influencing a person or group of people with the goal of eliciting a desired behavioral change. That change might be that the person votes for your candidate or ballot initiative; joins, donates to or participates more fully in your organization; or adopts a new habit such as energy conservation or vegetarianism.

The word *behavioral* is crucial because it is behavioral change, not simply a change of heart or mind, that leads to a more progressive society. Some activists don't get this; they think they've done their job if they can get their audience to agree with them. As meaningful as agreement is, however, and as good as it feels to both you and your audience, it does not in itself change the status quo: only behavioral change does. Getting your audience to change their behavior is harder than simply getting them to agree with you, but a dedicated activist will work diligently toward that goal, knowing that it will benefit not just the planet and society but, as I discuss below, the individual himself or herself.

Two other activities that aim to influence people with the goal of changing their behavior are **marketing** and **sales**. These are anathema to many activists, who consider them inherently exploitative, and the essence, really, of all that's wrong with capitalism. There's some truth to this viewpoint, but it is also somewhat of an oversimplification, since marketing and sales can, in fact, be used non-exploitatively and to positive ends. In business classes, and in this section of *The Lifelong Activist*, I teach what is called "consultative sales," where you're not manipulating the customer, but working alongside of him to arrive at a solution to a serious need he has. That need might be "I need a computer," "I need a birthday gift for my girlfriend," or "I need a government that represents the interests of everyone, and not just the top one percent." The salesperson's/activist's job, in consultative sales, is not to manipulate the customer but to guide him toward an informed choice, and the outcome is not zero-sum, but win-win: the customer gets what he needs, and the salesperson/activist gets what she needs, be it cash, a vote or a petition signature.

The bottom line is that activism is, or should be, marketing and sales. Meaning, that you should use the same marketing and sales techniques that corporations use to sell products to sell your activist cause, and progressivism in general. You should, moreover, use these techniques wholeheartedly and without shame or embarrassment, for two main reasons:

1. **Modern marketing and sales are, literally, the most powerful persuasive techniques ever devised.**

They are responsible for the fact that hundreds of millions of people around the globe willingly eat at McDonald's, listen to Madonna or U2, wear Nikes and use Microsoft Windows.

These techniques are too powerful to ignore and, in fact, it is folly to do so—folly, and a disservice to those on whose behalf we say we're working. This is especially true given that our opposition generally embraces marketing and sales wholeheartedly, and uses them to powerful effect.[1]

In her book *Bridging the Class Divide and Other Lessons for Grassroots Organizing* (see Bibliography), activist Linda Stout says:

> It is important for [activist] organizations to have a marketing plan. Marketing is usually thought of in terms of selling products. But I think of marketing as figuring out how to talk about your work and get the message of what you are doing across to particular groups of people. When you are organizing, you are literally marketing a message.

All successful activists do, in fact, use marketing and sales, even if they don't recognize or identify their activities as such. Fundraising and volunteer-recruitment are quite obviously marketing and sales endeavors, but so is any activity where you seek to persuade others. That's why, throughout this section of *The Lifelong Activist*, I am able to quote business experts and activist experts side-by-side, giving essentially the same advice.

2. **What corporate marketing and sales harms, progressive marketing and sales heals.**

Many progressives believe that ubiquitous corporate marketing has largely replaced authentic expressions of identity, culture and community, resulting in a citizenry that is alienated from self and others. Corporations create that alienation, then profit when they sell people on the (false) idea that buying things will heal the alienated, hurting soul.

That's not what you are doing when you market and sell progressivism, however. What you're doing is offering a cure for that alienation.

Convince someone to support a progressive cause and you help heal society.

Convince someone to become an activist, with all the self-determination and self-expression and community that that role encompasses, and you help heal *him*.

How to Save the World

Sometimes, the healing referred to in point #2 extends beyond "emotional" and "community" healing to actual physical healing. That was certainly the case with one of the most successful activist movements of recent decades, the AIDS treatment movement. In the early and mid 1980s, AIDS remained a terrifying mystery. Because it preyed mainly on gays and drug users, it was considered by many a "disreputable" disease; and it wasn't until mid-1987—nearly the end of his second presidential term—that Ronald Reagan finally gave a public address on the epidemic. Jerry Falwell and others even claimed that AIDS was God's retribution for the supposedly sinful homosexual lifestyle.

Needless to say, there was little societal impetus to fund a cure—until a vocal and determined activist community started demanding one. Many of these activists worked in fields related to marketing: for instance, the group of six activists that created the famous "Silence=Death" pink triangle included a book designer and two art directors.[2]

The achievements of these activists were stunning. First, they succeeded in largely removing the stigma from AIDS and making it a topic of general conversation. That in itself made life much more bearable for many AIDS sufferers. The activists also managed to educate Americans—and, later, much of the rest of the world—on the need for, and mechanics of, AIDS prevention and safe sex. Finally, these activists managed to focus the attention of the medical establishment on AIDS, and to garner substantial funding for research into the disease and its treatment, resulting in the development of azidothymidine (AZT) and other palliative drugs.

While it's true that AIDS remains a vast problem, especially in Africa, there is no denying the spectacular achievement of these "first-generation" AIDS activists whose work saved millions of lives. They serve as an inspiration to all progressive activists.

So, for your sake, the sake of those around you, and the sake of the planet, please market and sell your progressive ideals boldly and effectively.

The rest of this section of *The Lifelong Activist* tells you how. First, in Chapters 2 through 23, I discuss some fundamental principles you need to know to market effectively. Then, in Chapters 24 through 36, I discuss sales.

Of course, marketing and sales are highly complex endeavors, about which entire libraries have been written, so what follows is necessarily just an overview. See the Bibliography for suggestions for follow-up reading.

A CUSTOMER BY ANY OTHER NAME . . .

Yes, I sometimes use the word "customer" in this part of *The Lifelong Activist* to refer to your audience, or the person or persons whom you are trying to influence. This may sound odd, in an activist context, but it's hard to talk about marketing and sales without at least occasionally using that word. I also find that using it reminds us that, when we are doing activism, what we really are, or should be, doing is marketing and sales.

For the same reasons, I sometimes use the word "product" to describe your activist cause, and "sales" or "selling" to describe your activism.

Many progressives are familiar with the term social marketing. As far as I can tell, it is basically a synonym for plain old marketing and sales done non-exploitatively in the service of a progressive or otherwise socially beneficial cause. I think it betrays a certain ambivalence about marketing and sales, however, and so I refrain from using it in this book.

Whether you use the term "social marketing" or not, please be *un*ambivalent and bold when doing your marketing and sales.

CHAPTER 2

Marketing and Sales Defined

Even many businesspeople aren't clear on the difference between marketing and sales, so let's start there. **Marketing** is the work you do that attracts the right customers to you and predisposes them to buy. After that is accomplished, you still need to persuade them to buy, and that process is **Sales**.

Marketing, in other words, is what brings a suburban couple to a Volvo dealership knowing that they want to buy a safe station wagon, that Volvo manufactures such a car, and that people like them buy Volvos. (They don't actually *know* those last two facts, but Volvo's marketing has successfully implanted those messages in their minds.) When the couple enters the dealership, the salesperson doesn't have to sell them on those points, but only to convince them to complete the transaction and buy one of her cars *today*. That's sales: completing the transaction. It's hard work, but far easier than if the saleswoman had to convince the customers to favor station wagons or Volvos in the first place.

Marketing works by giving your audience a positive impression of your cause, your organization, and even of you yourself. And, as you will learn, it also conveys the impression that whatever it is you are selling—whether it's a car or progressive cause—will help the customer meet one or more important needs that he has.

In any business or activist endeavor, if the marketing is done right, it becomes *much* easier to make the sale—i.e., to get the customer to take the specific action you want. In a car dealership, that action is for the customer to pull out her checkbook and write a check for the car. In activism, that action could be for the customer to sign a petition, vote for a candidate, make a donation or attend a meeting.

The **marketing** process, which I discuss in detail starting in Chapter 4, involves three basic steps:

1. **Identify** the group of customers ("target market" or "market segment") most likely to buy your product.
2. **Rework** ("repackage") your product so that it will appeal even more to those customers.
3. **Connect** the customers with your product via a marketing campaign consisting of advertising, public relations, Internet marketing, word of mouth, and/or other tactics. A good distribution strategy—so that the customer can actually get his hands on your product—is also an important part of this step.

It's not rocket science.

Sales is the process of interacting with a customer with the goal of persuading her to complete a transaction. Many people think of it as an intuitive, seat-of-the-pants activity, but nothing could be farther from the truth. Sales is actually a complex process consisting of multiple well-defined steps, each of which is grounded on a solid foundation of human psychology. The sales process I discuss starting in Chapter 24 consists of six steps: Prospect; Qualify; Needs Assessment; Restate; Ponder & Present Solution; and Ask for the Sale & Supervise the Result.

It's not rocket science, either.

Expert salespeople, who are often paid based on how much money they earn for their company, take their skills and education very seriously. They often spend weeks or months in classes at the beginning of their careers, and many take classes throughout their careers. Many are also inveterate readers of business literature, self-help books and current events. And, as you will learn in Chapter 25, many practice intensively and prepare exhaustively for all important customer interactions.

Marketing = Nine-Tenths of the Sale

Although sales seems more glamorous than marketing, and thus appears to attract all the attention—no one's written a play called *Death of a Marketer*, after all—marketing is actually the most crucial part of any sale. It is, remember, what actually gets the customer interested in the product to start with. In classes I teach that a sale resembles an iceberg, nine-tenths of which is hidden under water. Marketing is that nine-tenths: you may not see it, but it is the foundation of the successful sale. Think of that Volvo saleswoman again, and how grateful she is that she doesn't have to explain to each customer (a) what a station wagon is, (b) who Volvo is, and (c) the fact that Volvo makes safe station wagons. Volvo's marketing takes care of all that.

Perhaps because sales is more glamorous than marketing, many people use the term "sales" as shorthand for the entire marketing and sales process. For convenience, I sometimes do the same thing. If you see a reference to sales in *The Lifelong Activist*, always assume that I'm talking about "sales preceded by marketing."

CHAPTER 3

The Most Important Point about Marketing and Sales

The most important thing you need to know about marketing and sales is that both activities are **easy** and **fun**.

Marketing is a fun, creative activity. A lot of it, as you will see, is brainstorming around your cause and the people whom you hope to influence. Then, you get to convey your ideas in creative and compelling ways, by creating posters, speeches, public service announcements (PSAs), films, fliers and theatrical events.

Sales is also a fun activity, believe it or not. Okay—perhaps not if you're really shy, in which case you might want to stick with behind-the-scenes marketing or other activities. But many people, once they know what they're doing and get in some practice, find that they like sales. That's because, done right, it pretty much comes down to socializing with a defined purpose.

Marketing and sales are also, as you will see, relatively easy and straightforward activities. In other words, they are well within the intellectual and other abilities of almost any activist. The key to success in both activities is not brilliance but discipline, consistency and attention to detail.

Finally, marketing and sales are high return-on-investment (ROI) activities. That means that if you add just a little marketing and sales to your activism, it will be *way* more powerful and effective.

And if you add a lot—as the AIDS example illustrates—you can change the world.

And there's nothing more fun than that.

CHAPTER 4

How Marketing Works: An Activist Case Study

The September 20, 2005 issue of *The New Yorker* offered a report on an evening vigil in New York City memorializing the (at that time) more than 1,000 American soldiers and tens of thousands of Iraqis who had died in the second Gulf War. Here's an excerpt:

> While the crowd shrank to a few dozen, watched over by a handful of policemen, some protesters attempted to engage passersby. "Come join us, no matter what you think of the war," [Jane Doe] pleaded. "These are the dead." [Doe], a performance artist with R. Crumb hair who lives in the East Village, was having no luck recruiting people. "They just think we're obnoxious, like we're saying, 'Come love Jesus,' " she said.
>
> Patricia McHugh took a different approach. A gray-haired librarian who lives in the neighborhood, she was pronouncing the names of the dead, and their ages, with unusual precision. She spoke not into the center of the dwindling crowd of protesters but outside the circle, into the faces of those pedestrians who would consent to meet her gaze. She got strong responses, she reported, especially from young men. "When I say the name of a young American man, and his age, to young males, they get it immediately."

(I changed the name of the first activist to spare her further embarrassment. She was doing her best, after all, and also deserves credit for being candid about her lack of success.)

This anecdote shows both good and bad marketing in action. I don't know if Patricia McHugh ever studied marketing, or whether she did some conscious market strategizing before she participated in the vigil, but she is clearly an ace marketer. Here are the three basic marketing steps again, with an explanation of how she succeeded at them:

1. **Identify** the group of customers ("target market" or "market segment") most likely to buy your product. *What McHugh did:* She surmised that, out of all of the diverse people passing by on the streets of New York, young men of approximately the same ages as most of the dead soldiers responded most strongly to her message about the human cost of the war. Although this seems obvious in hindsight, it probably wasn't at the time. McHugh could have aimed her message at, for instance, baby boomers who lived through the Vietnam War years, and are old enough to be the parents of the dead soldiers.

    Or, like many of the other activists in her group, she could have targeted no one, keeping her gaze directed inward into "the center of the dwindling crowd of protestors." As someone who has participated in demonstrations and vigils, I know how scary it can be to reach out to strangers, but doing so is the very essence of effective activism. In contrast, maintaining your focus safely on your "already converted" colleagues is a perfect example of ineffective activism and "preaching to the choir."

2. **Rework** ("repackage") your product so that it will appeal even more to those customers. *What McHugh did:* She shrewdly mentioned not just the name but the age of each dead soldier—crucial information that provided the "bridge" her audience needed to identify strongly with her message.[3]

    Also, unlike Jane Doe and perhaps the other activists, McHugh didn't beg, plead or cajole her audience into caring about her viewpoint. Nor did she frighten them with the demand that they "come join us." Rather, McHugh spoke directly to the experience and perspective of her "customers," and made no excessive demands on them. As a result, they let down their fear, skepticism and other barriers to communication, and were receptive to her message.

3. **Connect** the customers with your product via a marketing campaign consisting of advertising, public relations, Internet marketing, word of mouth and/or other tactics. *What McHugh did:* Much

of this work was done prior to the start of the vigil, by the activists who decided the format of the event, when and where it would be held, and how it would be publicized. But McHugh improved on the event's format, not just with her focus on the passersby, but with her clear enunciation, which catches people's attention and heightens the importance of what you are saying. Even McHugh's personal appearance, as we'll see in the next chapter, probably contributed to her ability to connect with her audience.

NOTE

I'll be discussing the three marketing steps in greater detail starting in Chapter 21.

CHAPTER 5

More Lessons from the Case Study

The case study in the previous chapter teaches us the powerful importance of marketing to activist success. Here are some other lessons we can draw from it:

- **If good marketing powerfully attracts people, bad marketing repels them with equal or more strength.** Hence, Doe's no-doubt-correct impression that passersby found her pitch "obnoxious." It is essential, therefore, that even if your marketing isn't expensive—and McHugh's cost nothing, except for her time—it better be good. I regret to say that I believe much progressive activism is built around bad marketing, and that is a major reason for activist failure and frustration. The good news, however, is that if progressive activists can improve their overall rate of marketing success, progressive social change should happen at a much faster rate. (Keep reading and you'll learn how!)

- **There is no such thing as "no marketing" because "no marketing" is equivalent to "bad marketing."** That is because, even in cases where you don't consciously market, a message is nevertheless being conveyed to your customer—and that message is likely to be either repellent, or so weak that your opposition can easily counter it.

- **If your activism is annoying, alienating or angering people, it is (usually) not because they resent you or your message, and not because they resent the fact that you are marketing and selling to them: it is because you are marketing and selling to them *badly*.** Good marketing and sales, by definition, seeks to form a positive bond with the customer, and it *never* seeks to annoy, anger or alienate him or her. So if that's the reaction you're getting, you should assume that your marketing and sales approach is flawed. "What am I doing wrong?" should be the question you ask on such occasions, *not*, "What the heck is wrong with these people?" (I.e., the people you are trying to reach.) More on how-not-to-blame-the-marketing-victim in Chapter 9.

- **In marketing, the details count.** In classes, I teach that marketing that hits the center of the target—that is executed with great precision, with all the details in place—is far more effective than marketing that is even slightly "off." If McHugh hadn't made eye contact, or mentioned the soldiers' ages, or spoken in a clear voice, she probably would have been far less effective at conveying her message.

- **Simply speaking from your heart, or simply narrating your truth, usually isn't enough.** That's because, as I'll discuss in Chapter 16, you need to speak to *your customer's* heart, and tell the truth in a way *your customer* can relate to. That's why Jane Doe's heartfelt pleas did not move passersby nearly so much as McHugh's dispassionate recitation of names.

- *You* **are part of the packaging.** Because customers are easily confused or frightened, professional salespeople go to great lengths to fit in with their customers' cultural norms, or at least to appear as non-threatening as possible.

  Pardon the stereotype, but as a "gray-haired librarian," McHugh probably had the "non-threatening" thing down, and it also helps that she lived in the neighborhood where the vigil took place, so that many passersby probably perceived her as being a familiar neighborhood "type." Her appearance, in fact, probably sent a strong double message that (1) "I am not scary, and therefore you can safely listen to my viewpoint," and (2) "your neighbors support this cause, and therefore it is appropriate for you to do so, too."

  In contrast, Jane Doe, with her "R. Crumb hair" and (I'm guessing) East Village artsy clothes and attitude, was probably perceived by passersby as being at least a little unusual and, therefore, threatening. If so, they would have naturally been inclined to resist her pitch.

If even New Yorkers—who inhabit one of the most diverse and cosmopolitan communities on Earth—are put off by salespeople who look a little different, imagine how much more people from less diverse places are likely to be put off. OK, don't imagine it— here's a real-life example. During the 2004 Democratic presidential primaries, National Public Radio's news show *All Things Considered* ran a segment on the culture clash between the Iowa voters who were soon to be holding their caucuses, and the legions of Howard Dean supporters who descended on the state to try to sell those voters on their candidate. The Iowans (at least as portrayed on the segment) tended to be older, rural, socially conservative and somewhat sedate and measured in their social interactions. The "Deaniacs," in contrast, were mainly young, urban, hip and hyper-enthusiastic and energetic. The culture clash was obvious in the taped encounter between a voter and a Deaniac that was featured on the segment, and another problem was that the clash appeared not to have been noticed by the Deaniac herself, who plowed on with her enthusiastic canvassing, oblivious to the fact that she was putting off the local.

Linda Stout tells a related story in *Bridging the Class Divide*: "We both had a vision of working for peace. I guess I was looking for someone to be the leader, and I assumed Carol would be willing to do it. But she said, 'Linda, look at me. Do you think people would take me seriously as a leader?' And I looked at her wild hair and 'hippie' clothes and said, thinking out loud, 'No, you're not the leader we need for Charleston, South Carolina.' We both knew she would not be trusted by local Charlestonians because of the way she looked and because she was not from the area."

I like my look as much as the next person, but if I were canvassing in Iowa or Charleston, I would swallow my pride and break out the conservative duds. I would also do whatever else I could to be accepted, and seen as non-threatening, by the locals. Otherwise, what's the point?

- **Good marketing is 90 percent of the sale.** McHugh reported that, after she spoke her piece, the young men in her audience "[got] it immediately." Not "somewhat," or "in a while," or "after some consideration," but "immediately." *That's* how easy it becomes to make

the sale, if you do the marketing right. Had the event involved peti-
tioning, voter registration or some other activity, there is also no
doubt that McHugh could have convinced many of the passersby
to take the next step. In any case, she accomplished the most difficult part of any sale: getting the customer's attention.

There are also three fundamental and highly important truths about
marketing and sales that can be gleaned from the case study. People generally don't like to hear them, so I call them Bitter Truths. Accept these truths,
and start incorporating them in your activism, and you will become vastly
more effective.

I discuss them individually, starting in the next chapter.

CHAPTER 6

Bitter Truth #1

Both McHugh and Doe were advocating for the exact same cause, but McHugh's marketing technique made her much more effective at reaching her audience. From this and countless other examples, both in activism and business, we can regretfully conclude the following:

> ### BITTER TRUTH #1
>
> The success of your venture depends much less on the quality of whatever it is you are selling than on the quality of the marketing and sales you use to sell it.

I refer to this as a Bitter Truth—the first of three Bitter Truths discussed in *The Lifelong Activist*—because, in my experience, no one likes to hear this.

- My programming students would prefer to hear that it's the quality of their code that will determine their success.
- My cooking students would prefer to hear that it's the quality of their cuisine that will determine their success.
- My art students would prefer to hear that it's the quality of their painting, writing, sculpture or music that will determine their success.
- And my activism students would prefer to hear that it's the quality of their cause that will determine their success.

But it's true. As Al Ries and Jack Trout point out in *The 22 Immutable Laws of Marketing* (see Bibliography):

Many people think marketing is a battle of products. In the long run, they figure, the best product will win.

Marketing people are preoccupied with doing research and "getting the facts." They analyze the situation to make sure that truth is on their side. Then they sail confidently into the marketing arena, secure in the knowledge that they have the best product and that ultimately the best product will win.

It's an illusion. There is no objective reality. There are no facts. There are no best products. All that exists in the world of marketing are perceptions in the minds of the customer or prospect. The perception is the reality. Everything else is an illusion. . . .

Most marketing mistakes stem from the assumption that you're fighting a product battle rooted in reality. All the laws in this book are derived from exactly the opposite point of view. . . .

Marketing is not a battle of products. It's a battle of perceptions.

Note that word, "perceptions." Along with its verb form, "perceive," you will see it used frequently throughout this section of *The Lifelong Activist*. Ries and Trout are absolutely right: **in marketing, there is no objective reality—it is all about perception.**

The Evidence is Overwhelming

We all wish the world worked differently, and that it were the quality of whatever it is you are selling that determined your success. Unfortunately, however, the evidence in support of Bitter Truth #1 is overwhelming. Just look around you, and you will see that the world is filled with shoddy, useless or even destructive products that are far from being "quality," but that millions of people have been marketed and sold into believing they need.

For some more evidence in support of Bitter Truth #1, answer these questions:

- Is McDonald's the best restaurant in the world?
- Does Microsoft produce the best software?
- Is John Grisham the best writer?

The answer in all three cases is, of course, "No," but that doesn't stop McDonald's, Microsoft and John Grisham from being perennial best sellers, largely on the basis of their marketing and sales efforts.

Let's also be clear, however, that "quality" means different things to different people. McDonald's may not win any *haute cuisine* awards, but the company isn't going after the gourmet market. Rather, it's going after the cheap food/comfort food/consistency of menu/convenience of service-/child-friendly markets, and if one or more of these criteria are important to you, then McDonald's does indeed offer a quality product. You can make a similar argument for Microsoft software, John Grisham's novels, or any other popular consumer product. The very fact that the product *is* popular proves that a lot of people see it as "quality" in at least one crucial attribute.

Needless to say, **Bitter Truth #1 also applies to the political and social arenas.** It explains why some people become president, and some do not. It also explains why you sometimes have trouble selling your "common-sense" or "obvious" viewpoint to audiences. While your cause may indeed be "gourmet," your audience may well be craving "comfort food." Whether they truly want that comfort food (or "comfort politics"), or have simply been convinced they want it by the opposition's zillion-dollar marketing-and-sales campaign, is irrelevant to our discussion. Marketing is about perception, not truth.

In business and in activism, expecting the customer to automatically share your standard of quality is a classic screw-up, and usually fatal to the endeavor at hand. Your job is not to dictate to the customer what he or she ought to think or like, but to adhere to the three-step marketing process described earlier: locate your likeliest customers—meaning, the ones most predisposed to like your viewpoint; repackage your viewpoint to appeal to them further; and connect the customers with your viewpoint.

CHAPTER 7

At the Heart of Bitter Truth #1

Here's an example of Bitter Truth #1 in action from another marketing classic, *Selling the Invisible: a Field Guide to Modern Marketing* by Harry Beckwith (see Bibliography):

> Joel and Judy Wethall are driving from Tampa to Disney World when they are struck with hunger. They begin watching for places to eat, then choose a Burger King restaurant.
>
> Their choice seems odd; they dislike Whopper hamburgers. Why *did* they choose Burger King?
>
> Their alternatives were two unknowns: two local restaurants with nice facades and hints of quality. Had they tried either restaurant, they would have enjoyed juicier hamburgers, fresher salads and friendly personal service, right to their table.
>
> What were the Wethalls thinking? What almost every prospect for every service thinks. **They were not looking for the service they wanted most but the one they feared least. They did not choose a good experience; they chose to minimize the risk of a bad experience.**
>
> This intelligent couple was duplicating what happened all over the country that day, among people choosing accounting firms, remodelers, dry cleaners, cleaning services, human resources consultants and thousands of other services. They were not expressing their preference. They were minimizing their risk." (Emphasis added.)

At the heart of Bitter Truth #1 is **fear:** the customer's fear of wasting her money, making a bad decision, having a bad experience or otherwise getting ripped off. Despite the fact that we live in a hyper-consumerist society—or perhaps because of it—most people have a natural reluctance to, or fear of, spending their hard-earned money. "People do not look to make the superior choice," says Beckwith. "They want to avoid making a bad choice." That's a big reason why companies need to spend billions of dollars marketing and selling in the first place: to overcome that fear. Believe me, they wouldn't spend it if they didn't have to.

In his book, Beckwith points out that the fear can be particularly strong when what you're selling is not a tangible product but an intangible service. A product, after all, can be examined, inspected, tested (for instance, by *Consumer Reports* or the consumer herself) and warranted. A service cannot. You don't know what your new haircut will look like before you actually get it done, for instance; and even if you go to a top stylist, he may be having an off day. Ditto for restaurant meals, home construction, auto repairs, legal services and any other service you can think of.

And for politics.

Fear and the Political "Sale"

The fear factor described above also applies to "sales" of political and social viewpoints. Politics is intangible—although, like most intangibles, its consequences are very tangible. When selling an intangible, one of the salesperson's primary duties is to paint as vivid an "advance picture" of its benefits as possible, so as to relieve as many of the customer's uncertainties and fears as possible. That's why the hairdresser shows his customer a picture of a haircut in a magazine and asks if that's what she wants, and why the activist works to connect the dots, for her audience, between a political viewpoint and its consequences in the "real world."

Regardless of how good a job the activist does, however, the act of "buying" a political viewpoint remains fraught with fear. It can, in fact, be far scarier than buying a normal "product." Along with the fears mentioned earlier—of making a poor decision or getting ripped off—the political "customer" can fear one or more of the following:

- Family or societal disapproval.
- Inconvenience (for instance, feeling compelled to attend a meeting at the end of a busy or stressful day, instead of simply going home and relaxing).
- Economic loss (for instance, having to forego a lucrative career path because it now seems unethical, or feeling compelled to buy a more expensive hybrid car instead of a less expensive gas-guzzler).

- Cognitive dissonance—the uncomfortable feeling we often get when we realize that two or more of our thoughts or ideas conflict with, or contradict, one other. (In an activist context, this often means a new idea conflicting with an older one.) Cognitive dissonance can be a very uncomfortable feeling, and many people seek to avoid it by consciously or unconsciously shutting out new ideas.
- The realization, and consequent remorse and/or shame, that often arises from knowing one has been wrong in the past.
- The realization, and consequent remorse and/or shame, that often arises from knowing that, through one's errors, one may have caused himself or others pain.

In many cases, these fears are well justified. An article entitled "Swingtime: Former Bush Voters Advertise Their Disaffection" in the August 23, 2004 issue of the *New Yorker* describes how family, friends and neighbors reacted when Mississippian Rhonda Nix decided to switch her vote from Republican George W. Bush to Democrat John Kerry in the 2004 presidential election:

> In January, Nix planted a John Kerry sign in her yard, and in July she found it pulled up and "stabbed to death"—torn and battered, with the words "Burn in Hell" scrawled on it. . . . "When my friends and family realized that my priorities, that my values were shifting in a whole new direction, I found myself arguing a lot with them, almost like I was trying to change what they believe in and trying to give them reasons. But then I realized I couldn't change them. I can only change myself."

A lot of unpleasant consequences devolved from Nix's seemingly "simple" and "common-sense" decision.

The English language itself reflects how challenging it can be to take on a new viewpoint: we merely "purchase" or "own" a new item, but we "adopt," "hold," "embrace," or even "espouse" a new viewpoint—and eventually we become "wedded" to our long-held ideas. And although people can bond very closely with their material possessions, and even grow to identify with them, it's generally not as strong an identification as occurs with a political or social viewpoint. Even the most impassioned car owner, for example, doesn't go around saying, "I'm a Mercedes," the way many people say, "I'm a Democrat," "I'm a Unitarian," or "I'm an environmentalist."

The truth is, when you're asking someone to buy into your viewpoint you are actually asking him to make a profound and scary change. (And we know from Part III how scary even small changes can be. . . .) This, in turn, should give you a greater appreciation and respect for:

- Anyone who is willing to even contemplate such a change, even if he doesn't follow through—or does follow through, but not in the way you would like.
- You and other activists who do the difficult work of selling social change.

A major goal of the marketing and sales processes I discuss starting in Chapter 21 is to help allay your customers' fears so that they are more likely to buy whatever it is you are selling. But why are people motivated to buy in the first place? The next chapter answers that crucial question.

CHAPTER 8

Why People Buy (a.k.a. Bitter Truth #2)

Here's Bitter Truth #2:

> ### BITTER TRUTH #2
>
> People buy a product not because of its intrinsic qualities or characteristics, but because they believe it will either solve a problem or meet a need that they have.

In other words, we don't buy something because we think it is wonderful or beautiful or valuable—although the thing we are buying may possess all of those qualities and more. We buy it because we believe it will help us either solve a problem or meet a need that we have—in other words, as a means to an end.4 There is even a business axiom that neatly conveys this concept: "People don't buy drills; they buy holes."

In my experience, novice businesspeople don't like Bitter Truth #2 any more than they like Bitter Truth #1. They would prefer that people buy their programming, cooking, art and other products because of the products' (and, by extension, *their*) intrinsic excellence. This is especially true if the need the customer is filling seems wholly unrelated to the merits of the product in question. Many artists, for instance, hate it when people buy their work for reasons of status, or "to go with the décor," and many computer programmers hate it when their customers show a lack of interest in the subtleties of their code, and only ask, "how fast can you get it done?" This attitude, by the way, is the exact opposite of that held by most experienced businesspeople, who are thrilled if someone buys their product for *any* reason. They are not inclined to dictate to their customers what their motivations should be.

If you think about it, Bitter Truth #2 actually explains Bitter Truth #1. If we buy something because we believe that it will fill a need, and if marketing and sales are the primary vehicles sellers have for fostering that belief, then it makes sense that it is the quality of your marketing and sales, rather than the quality of the thing you are selling, that will determine your success.

Types of Needs

There are hundreds of needs that people can have that can compel them to buy things. We tend to be very familiar with our pragmatic "surface needs" for things such as clothing, food and transportation, but all of us are also motivated to varying degrees by emotional "deep needs" for love, beauty, youth, virtue, etc. (See Chapter 13 for a longer list.) More precisely, what we crave is the *feeling* or *emotional state* of being loved (or in love), beautiful, youthful, virtuous, etc.

Needless to say, we also strongly crave to avoid negative or painful emotions such as guilt or shame.

Deep needs derive from our individual personality and experiences, and tend to reflect our most profound desires and fears. They are thus extremely powerful motivators; so powerful, in fact, that even manufacturers of mundane products often choose to market and sell by appealing not to the obvious surface need that the product addresses, but to one or more deep needs. Many ads for packaged foods, for instance, feature an image of a traditional family enjoying a meal that Mom is serving them. The image is designed to address at least three deep needs that the purchaser (usually a real-life mom) has:

- The need to feel as if she's succeeding at her immediate goal of feeding her family.
- The need to feel as if she's succeeding at her larger goal of creating a happy and healthy family life.
- The need not to feel guilty about serving packaged foods, as opposed to a home-cooked meal.

These can all be lumped into one "mega-deep-need": the need to feel like she's a good mother, or at least not a bad one.

As this example suggests, we usually act from several needs at once, and often our needs are multi-layered. When making a purchase, we may be conscious of some the needs we are fulfilling, and only semi-conscious, or unconscious, of others. We may download an MP3 music file because we enjoy the music, for instance, but we may also download it because, less obviously, we enjoy the "hip," "affluent," "authentic," or "artsy" feeling(s) we get when we do. In other words, the purchase helps us meet our need to feel a certain way about ourselves.

Smart businesspeople learn to market their products by identifying the customer's most urgent needs and presenting (or "packaging") their product as a solution to those needs. And, as we shall see in the next chapter, smart activists do the same thing.

CHAPTER 9

Bitter Truth #2 and the Activist Sale

Hard as many businesspeople find it to accept Bitter Truth #2, many activists find it even harder. That's because the things activists sell—peace, justice, freedom, equality, etc.—tend to be of extremely high value: the most valuable things on the planet, in fact. This blinds them to the fact that Bitter Truth #2 holds no matter how valuable the thing you are selling is.

Here's Saul Alinsky in *Rules for Radicals*:

> The first requirement for communication and education is for people to *have a reason for knowing*. (Italics his.)

In other words: a need. He also writes elsewhere:

> Communication for persuasion . . . is getting a fix on [your audience's] main value or goal and holding your course on that target. You don't communicate with anyone purely on the rational facts or ethics of an issue.

Notice how neatly he incorporates both Bitter Truth #1 and Bitter Truth #2 into that concise statement.

Activists who don't understand or accept Bitter Truth #2 are usually easily spotted. They tend to be ineffective, and they also tend to go around asking questions such as the following, often in tones of high frustration:

- *What's wrong with these people?!* [Meaning: their audience.] *Can't they see that my cause is in their best interests?*

Usually, the activist is asking rhetorically, which is a shame: if he asked for real, he might have a shot at answering the questions, thus arriving at Bitter Truth #2 and the key to improving his effectiveness.

As activists become more and more frustrated, they often ask more pointed questions, including:

- *How can people be so ignorant?*
- *How can people be so selfish?*
- *How can people be so short-sighted?*

And the ever-popular,

- *How can people be so stupid?!*

At this point, the activist is actively blaming the victim—i.e., his audience—for his own inability, or unwillingness, to market and sell effectively. And the sad truth is that anyone who feels so negatively about his customers is unlikely to succeed at selling them anything. So the more frustrated and embittered an activist gets, the more likely he is to fail.

IF YOU'RE FRUSTRATED . . .

Knowing how hard activism can be, I certainly wouldn't blame any activist for experiencing, and venting, occasional frustration. If you feel frustrated a lot, though, you should take a step back and, with the help of friends, colleagues and mentors, assess the situation. Maybe you need to change the way you do your activism. Or, maybe you're burning out, and need to take a break. Try re-assessing your Mission, and see where that process takes you.

CHAPTER 10

The Primary Requisite of Effective Activism

Are people selfish for focusing on their own needs instead of the community as a whole or the larger principle? Maybe or maybe not, but that's not the point. The point is, that is the way most people—including most activists, by the way—behave. They need a reason to buy, and that reason isn't the intrinsic worth of your viewpoint, it's that they have a need that they perceive your viewpoint can fill.

At the same time, if you do your job properly, people will often surprise you by moving their focus quickly from their own immediate need to the more general principle at stake.

Accept the validity of Bitter Truth #2 and start presenting your causes, candidates and viewpoints in such a way that your audiences can *immediately* and *effortlessly* perceive them as meeting their needs. They shouldn't have to do much thinking or guesswork to make the connection. The primary requisite for doing that—and for effective activism in general—is that you hold a sincere liking and respect for your listener that allows you to see things from her viewpoint (see Chapter 16), and to build a positive relationship with her. In the presence of such a relationship, your listener will feel safe and respected and is therefore likely to be tolerant of your attempts to persuade her; in the absence of one, she will likely (rightfully) be suspicious of you, your motives and your ideas. Again, contrast Patricia McHugh's success at reaching out to people during the New York City memorial vigil, with Jane Doe's and the other activists' failures.

The best salespeople and activists are successful largely because they build those kinds of positive relationships almost effortlessly, and with a wide range of people. They are "people people" who love diversity, not just of race, class, religion, age or gender-orientation, but of mind. They enjoy talking to people—or, more to the point, listening to them—hearing their stories and opinions, and figuring out what makes them tick. They find human nature and human behavior endlessly fascinating.

To be sure, there are many salespeople who are insincere flatterers. I believe the percentage of them is much lower than most people think, however, especially among the top ranks. "Faking it" doesn't work all that well, and it's just too hard for most people to pull off, especially over the long term.

One word for the attitude I recommend you cultivate is "tolerance," and yet tolerance doesn't quite go far enough. If your goal is to influence people, you can't just tolerate them, you have to really like and appreciate them. This is true even in cases where you disagree with some of the person's viewpoints or actions. You gain nothing, absolutely nothing, by blaming or shaming such people, or by lecturing them. As Dale Carnegie said way back in 1936, in his classic book *How to Win Friends & Influence People* (see Bibliography):

> You can tell people they are wrong by a look or an intonation or a gesture just as eloquently as you can in words—and if you tell them they are wrong, do you make them want to agree with you? Never! For you have struck a direct blow at their intelligence, judgment, pride and self-respect. That will make them want to strike back. But it will never make them want to change their minds. You may then hurl at them all the logic of a Plato or an Immanuel Kant, but you will not alter their opinions, for you have hurt their feelings.

Carnegie, whose book every activist should read, and then reread repeatedly throughout his or her career, recommends using a "Socratic" method of gently questioning the customer's ideas and assumptions in order to gradually win him or her over to your viewpoint. And—guess what?—Alinsky also recommends using Socratic questioning. From *Rules for Radicals*:

> Actually, Socrates was an organizer. The function of an organizer is to raise questions that agitate, that break through the accepted pattern. Socrates, with his goal of "know thyself," was raising the internal questions within the individual that are so essential for the revolution which is external to the individual.

This, of course, brings us all the way back to the discussion, at the very beginning of *The Lifelong Activist*, of Gloria Steinem's personal evolution from self-abnegation and self-denial to being able to live Socrates' "examined life." *Revolution From Within*, which is what she called her autobiography, and now you understand that **you don't just start a revolution from within yourself, but also from within your audience.** You can't impose a revolution on anyone—or any society—from the outside, and to attempt to do so is not just folly, but morally reprehensible. (See Chapter 15 for more on this point.) But you can ask the questions that will help your listener achieve her own revolution from within.

Later in his book, Alinsky suggests as proper activist technique a gentle form of interview called "guided questioning":

> Much of the time, though, the organizer will have a pretty good idea of what the community should be doing, and he will want to suggest, maneuver, and persuade the community toward that action. He will not ever seem to tell the community what to do; instead he will use loaded questions. . . . And so the guided questioning goes on without anyone losing face or being left out of the decision.
>
> Is this manipulation? Certainly, just as a teacher manipulates, and no less, even a Socrates.

As you will learn in Chapter 29, at the heart of the sales process is a similar form of interview, or "needs assessment," in which you gently question your customer to ascertain his needs and lead him in the direction you wish. The process may be manipulative, as Alinsky unapologetically points out, but it is not inherently exploitative. Done from the standpoint of a sincere interest in, liking for and respect for the customer—not to mention for society and the planet—it is actually kind and caring.

CHAPTER 11

The Best Activists Do This . . . (Part I)

Dale Carnegie says:

> In talking with people, don't begin by discussing the thing on
> which you differ. Begin by emphasizing—and keep on emphasiz-
> ing—the things on which you agree. Keep emphasizing, if possible,
> that you are both striving for the same end and that your only dif-
> ference is one of method and not of purpose.

Most top salespeople and activists would agree: **the key to effective
persuasion is to emphasize your areas of commonality with the customer and downplay your areas of difference.** This is particularly true
when you have just met someone, and are just starting to build the all-
important positive relationship that is the foundation of most sales. We
tend to like, and listen to, those who seem to like us, and who appear to
have lots in common with us. And we tend not to like, and not listen to,
those who seem not to like us, or don't seem to have much in common
with us. That is a basic tenet of human nature—*not* to be confused with nar-
rowness or bigotry—and it's the activist's job to build her strategy and tactics around it.

Unfortunately, the Right has done this much better than the Left in
recent years, with disastrous results for our country.

In his excellent book *What's the Matter with Kansas? How Conservatives
Won the Heart of America* (New York: Henry Holt and Co., 2004), Thomas
Frank documents how conservative demagogues in his home state of
Kansas convinced many middle-class and working-class voters to vote
Republican even though doing so was clearly against their economic inter-
ests. The demagogues did it using a now-familiar bait-and-switch strategy:
during their campaigns, they sold the voters on a "family values" platform
attacking abortion or gays; then, once they were elected, they ignored those

issues but passed regressive economic laws that penalized the masses of people who voted for them.

This strategy is not unique to modern-day Kansas. The Republican Party has, in fact, worked diligently for decades to portray itself as representing the interests of ordinary people, even though its politicians invariably either derive from the economic elite or act on that elite's behalf—Richard Nixon's claim of speaking on behalf of a fictitious "silent majority" of U.S. voters being a classic example. By portraying themselves as representing the interests of ordinary people, conservatives are able to establish the positive relationship they need with the voters in order to sell them extreme and exploitative viewpoints.

At the same time, as Frank and other writers[5] have documented, and as I discussed in Part IV, Chapter 6, conservatives have worked for decades to paint a picture of progressives, and even centrist Democrats and Republicans, as being financially, morally or otherwise divorced from ordinary voters. The Republican Party's demonizing of Democratic presidential candidate Adlai Stevenson as an "egghead" intellectual during the 1952 presidential campaign again serves as a good example—and, incidentally, it was Nixon himself, then the Republican candidate for vice president, who popularized the term "egghead" in reference to Stevenson.

Through their demonizing, the Republicans create a gulf between Democrats and progressives and the people who logically should be voting for them. This sabotages the positive relationship that progressives need to establish with voters to make their "sale," thus making that sales much more difficult, if not impossible.

How the Left Sabotages Itself

But it's not just conservatives who widen the gulf between progressives and those whom they wish to influence, however. Progressives do it themselves. Every time a progressive...

- Sees herself as smarter, more moral, more hip or otherwise better than her audience, or
- Thinks in terms of "us versus them"

. . . she widens the gulf between herself and those whom she is trying to influence.

Here, too, we can learn from professional activists and salespeople, who not only work strenuously to uncover points of commonality with the customer, but also to minimize points of difference. In particular, they work hard not to see themselves—or, worse, to have the customer see them—as being fundamentally different from, or superior to, the customer. True, they may have information that the customer lacks, but that doesn't mean that the customer is inferior in any way. We all have gaps in our knowledge and deficiencies in our perspective.

Another way to say this is that professionals take the Key Insight discussed in Part IV, Chapter 8—that we have vast amounts in common even with people with whom we seriously disagree—seriously, and incorporate it as much as possible into their work.

Professionals also place most people they meet somewhere along a spectrum that starts at "not too likely to buy my product (or viewpoint)" and moves on to "somewhat likely to buy my product," "highly likely to buy my product," and "extremely likely to buy my product," before ending up at, "bought my product!"

In other words, the pros don't see the world in black-and-white (customer/not a customer), but in many shades of gray. Their goal, consequently, is not to convert customers all at once from "non-customer" to "customer"—an often impossible task—but to help customers move, one easy, non-threatening step at a time, along the spectrum. As a result, the number of people they can sell to is much larger than it might otherwise be, and they also make many more sales than they otherwise might.

You would do well to follow the pros' example in your own activism: i.e., to work to minimize the points of difference and increase the points of commonality between you and your audience; and also to consider everyone you meet to be a potential supporter. As Peter Singer advises in *Ethics Into Action*, ". . . don't divide the world into saints and sinners."

CHAPTER 12

The Best Activists Do This . . . (Part II)

A major stumbling-block for many activists is distinguishing between bad ideologies and the people who support them. Here, again, we can learn from expert salespeople and activists, most of whom are disinclined to harshly judge people who disagree with them, and *highly* disinclined to label them negatively (i.e., "ignorant," "selfish," or "stupid"). They may judge the behavior or ideology, but never the person. That's for several reasons:

1. They understand that we all have areas where we need to grow and improve.
2. They also understand that we tend to judge more harshly those whose "growth areas" happen to differ from our own—and that that's unfair.
3. They also understand that even opinions and viewpoints that they may totally disagree with may have been arrived at reasonably. They may not share the viewpoint of a company owner who resists paying her workers more than the minimum wage, for instance, but that doesn't mean that there isn't a certain logic to her position—a logic that is strongly supported by our society and culture.
4. They also know that they aren't likely to know all the relevant facts about a person's life and viewpoints, especially at the beginning of a relationship—and that making assumptions or jumping to conclusions is not just bad activism, but bad manners.
5. As discussed in Part IV, chapters 7 and 8, fear likely underpins much conservative thought, and the only proper response to fear is compassion. This is not just a moral stance but a pragmatic one: fear is very difficult to overcome, and if you judge or label a fearful person harshly, they are likely to dig in their heels, or move actively *away* from your viewpoint. Experts know that compassion and

kindness are really the best tools for helping fearful people embrace new viewpoints.

And, most important of all,

6. Expert salespeople and activists understand that it's not the customer's job to recognize the merits of their position, but their job to work to comprehend the customer's worldview and then sell "to" that view. Experts never blame the customer for their own failure to make a sale, but always look to see what they could have done differently or better.

Below is an example of how a great activist, through his compassion, understanding and, most importantly, his non-judgmental attitude, can convert even the toughest opponent to his cause.

The Activist and the Pig Farmer

In his book *The Food Revolution* (see Bibliography), animal rights activist John Robbins tells how, in the course of doing undercover work, he wound up having dinner one night at the home of an Iowa pig farmer—not a traditional "Ol' MacDonald" kind of farmer—who are a relative rarity these days, anyhow—but a typical modern "factory farmer" who kept thousands of pigs confined indoors twenty-four hours a day in horribly crowded, filthy and inhumane conditions. Robbins didn't tell the farmer he was an activist, but the farmer deduced it somehow, and midway through the meal, as Robbins relates, "pointed at me forcefully with his finger and snarled in a voice that I must say truly frightened me, 'Sometimes I wish you animal rights people would just drop dead.' "

It would be understandable if Robbins had panicked or gotten defensive or belligerent in return, but he didn't. He kept his cool, just asking the farmer what it was about animal rights people that bothered him . . . and asking . . . and asking. What he was doing, actually, was a classic "needs assessment" interview (see Chapter 29) designed to help him uncover his customer's needs so that he could then sell to those needs. With his gentle, non-judgmental "Socratic" questioning, Robbins was also able to defuse the farmer's hostility, call into question his stereotyped view of activists, and form a relationship with him that allowed for the possibility of persuasion.

Through his questioning, Robbins discovered that:

Part of [the farmer's] frustration, it seemed, was that even though he didn't like doing some of the things he did to the animals—cooping them up in such small cages, using so many drugs, taking their babies away from their mothers so quickly after their births—he didn't see that he had any choice. He would be at a disadvantage and unable to compete economically if he didn't do things that way. . . . He didn't like it, but he liked even less being blamed for doing what he had to do in order to feed his family. . . .

"As the conversation progressed," Robbins writes, "I actually began to develop some sense of respect for this man whom I had earlier judged so harshly. There was decency in him. There was something within him that meant well." And still later, when Robbins and the farmer were out walking, the farmer broke down in tears and talked about how intelligent and sensitive pigs were, and how, as a child, he had had a pet pig whom he had cherished, and whom he had been forced by his father to slaughter.

Robbins again:

I had thought he was a cold and closed human being, but now I saw the truth. His rigidity was not a result of a lack of feeling, as I had thought it was, but quite the opposite: it was a sign of how sensitive he was underneath. For if he had not been so sensitive, he would not have been hurt, and he would not have needed to put up so massive a wall. . . . I had judged him, and done so, to be honest, mercilessly. But for the rest of the evening I sat with him, humbled, and grateful for whatever it was in him that had been strong enough to force this long-buried and deeply painful memory to the surface. And glad, too, that I had not stayed stuck in my judgments of him, for if I had, I would not have provided an environment in which his remembering could have occurred.

We talked that night, for hours, about many things. I was, after all that had happened, concerned for him. The gap between his feelings and his lifestyle seemed so tragically vast. What could he do? This was all he knew. He did not have a high school diploma. He was only partially literate. Who would hire him if he tried to do something else? Who would invest in him and train him, at his age?

These serious problems were not to be immediately resolved, but Robbins and the farmer maintained their friendship over the years—and years later, Robbins reports, the farmer wrote him and said that *he had gotten out of the hog-farming business entirely and was now growing organic vegetables*. This was obviously a huge triumph, not just for Robbins, and of course the pigs, but for the farmer himself—and a classic example of how, as discussed in Chapter 1, progressive activism heals not just society as a whole, but the individual you are asking to change.

The question hardly needs asking, but I will ask it anyway: do you think Robbins could have gotten the farmer to make such a major life change if he had judged him or shamed or blamed him?

Robbins concludes:

Do you see why I carry this man with me in my heart? Do you see why he is such a hero to me? He dared to leap, to risk everything, to leave what was killing his spirit even though he didn't know what was next. He left behind a way of life that he knew was wrong, and he found one that he knows is right.

When I look at many of the things happening in our world, I sometimes fear we won't make it . . . but then I remember how wrong I was about the pig farmer when I first met him and I realize that there are heroes afoot everywhere. Only I can't recognize them because I think they are supposed to look or act a certain way. How blinded I can be by my own beliefs.

Some people are fortunate enough to be born with the ability to like and relate to a wide range of humanity, while others are taught to do so by parents, friends, teachers or mentors. If you would like to improve in this area, the best way to do so is to do some work (including, of course, activism or volunteerism) alongside people whose backgrounds and/or attitudes differ from your own. You can also read books about psychology or sociology to gain insights into human nature; and, finally, Buddhism and some other spiritual practices offer meditations and other techniques specifically designed to help you become more accepting of others.

EXERCISE

Get in Touch With Your Inner Strict Father

According to George Lakoff, author of *Don't Think of an Elephant!,* everyone uses both the nurturant parent and strict father models. As a progressive, your strict father model is probably relatively quiescent, but you might want to tap into it in your quest to feel non-judgmental compassion for conservatives. This is a very practical exercise that will also provide you with powerful ammunition for your activism, since understanding the logic behind your opponent's position will obviously make you much more effective in countering it. As Lakoff advises: "Understand where conservatives are coming from. Get their strict father morality and its consequences clear. Know what you are arguing against. Be able to explain why they believe what they believe. Try to predict what they will say."

CHAPTER 13

More on Deep Needs

Deep needs, as you will recall from Chapter 8, are those that exist on an emotional, as opposed to pragmatic, level. There are probably hundreds of them, including:

- Adventure
- Aesthetics (love of/craving for beauty)
- Beauty (related to one's personal appearance)
- Community
- Conformity (need to fit in)
- Consistency (e.g., "If I believe in 'this,' then I should also believe in 'that.'" Particularly useful when selling to people who already hold progressive views other than the one you are espousing. People like to feel they hold a consistent set of thoughts and beliefs.)
- Excitement
- Fun
- Happiness
- Health
- Hipness or Trendiness ("I'm up to date!")
- Hope (*very* important—see below)
- Identity (i.e., ethnic, religious or national background)
- Inspiration
- Intellectual stimulation or gratification
- Joy
- Love
- Safety/Security (for self or loved ones—a *very* powerful motivator)
- Self-Esteem
- Self-Expression and Self-Actualization (Maslow!)
- Sexiness
- Status ("keeping up with the Joneses")

- Success
- Uniqueness/Importance ("I consume this unique or important-seeming product; therefore I must be unique.")
- Virtue ("I need to feel like a good person.")
- Youth

Entire books—and, in some cases, entire libraries—have been written on the concepts underlying each of these needs, but I won't go into detail here, not just for space reasons, but because of the simple fact that neither my nor any other expert's interpretation of a deep need is very relevant. As you will learn in Chapter 16, the only relevant interpretation is the customer's, and you learn it not by consulting books or experts, but the customer himself. He is, after all, the reigning "expert" on his own needs.

Then, when you uncover the specific nature of your customer's needs, you can sell effectively to him using the sales process described beginning in Chapter 24. This is a highly powerful technique . . . but is it ethical? That's what I discuss in the next chapter.

"ABOVE ALL, SELL HOPE."

In *Selling the Invisible,* Harry Beckwith makes a statement of such astonishing profundity that you would sooner expect to see it in a psychological or spiritual text than a marketing one. That statement is: "Above all, sell hope."

Think of all the times activists offer their audiences little beyond gloom and doom. Sure, there are plenty of reasons to feel gloom and doom, but if we let that hopelessness penetrate our hearts and dominate our messages, we lose much of our ability to influence people. In any situation, we must always strive to fill the customer's deep need—craving—for hope.

True leaders and inspirers understand this. "Let us not wallow in the valley of despair, I say to you today, my friends. And even though we face the difficulties of today and tomorrow, I still have a dream." Dr. King's famous speech at the August 28, 1963 March on Washington for Jobs and Freedom was, in fact, one long evocation of hope.

I have the words "Above all, sell hope" taped to my computer monitor where I can see them and contemplate them every day. I believe that every activist, teacher, coach, social worker and anyone else who seeks to influence people, should do the same, and that we should all, above all, sell hope.

CHAPTER 14

The Ethics of Marketing to Customer Needs

When activists question the ethics of marketing and sales, what they are often questioning is the ethics of appealing to someone's deep needs. I understand that concern. I also understand that marketing and sales can be conducted exploitatively or even coercively. I hope no one reading this book thinks that I am advocating that.

My view is this: there is nothing wrong with appealing even to the deepest needs, provided you do so honestly and responsibly.

"**Honestly**" means you don't slant or shade the truth at all, not even a little, no matter how high the stakes are or how much you might want to. Not only is slanting unethical, it is also bad activism, for two reasons:

- Your audience will invariably find out that you lied, with dire consequences to both your reputation and your cause.
- Your opposition will also invariably find out, and when that happens, then you're really cooked. Lie once, even a tiny "white" lie, and your opposition will take that lie to the bank, using it to discredit you and your cause for years afterwards. In fact, your opposition is probably waiting for you to slip up in just this way.

The fact that your opposition may be lying, by the way, does not in any way justify your doing the same—or make it any less risky a tactic.

Not lying doesn't mean that you have to divulge every single aspect of the topic under discussion. It means not leaving out the big or meaningful things—or, if you are leaving something big out, acknowledging that fact. Many activists feel that admitting to the weaknesses in their argument undermines them, but the opposite is usually true: telling the whole truth confers a lot of credibility on you as a speaker. It is a powerful persuasive tool.

Sometimes activists don't mean to lie, but they neglect to be absolutely clear and unambiguous about the dividing line separating fact from opinion, so that their audience becomes confused. Try to avoid that mistake.

Selling to deep needs "responsibly" means, first of all, not pushing anyone further than they are comfortable going, especially if you are not trained to handle the consequences. Deep needs often exist at a semiconscious or subconscious level because they are too intense or painful to confront head-on. Forcing someone to confront a deep need who is not fully prepared to do so is an aggressive and often abusive act. Alinsky again:

> There are sensitive areas that one does not touch until there is a strong personal relationship based on common involvements. Otherwise the other party turns off and literally does not hear.

Since you don't want to be too timid in promoting your viewpoint, and also don't want to risk harming someone by being too aggressive, it's important to locate the middle ground. A good way to do this is to let the person you're talking with lead the conversation as much as possible. Let her introduce personal topics, and when you question her about those topics, do so delicately and a little at a time. If you notice her pulling back, or looking angry, fearful, sad or otherwise uncomfortable, back off immediately.

At their worst, dishonesty and irresponsibility become a form of bullying, a topic serious enough, and detrimental enough to progressive movements, that it merits its own chapter.

CHAPTER 15

On Bullying

Many activists seem to operate under the principle that if they just badger people enough, or make them feel guilty or ashamed enough, then those people will finally see the error of their ways and embrace the activist's viewpoint. A word for this behavior is "bullying," and there are (at least) three problems with it:

1. Bullying is not marketing and sales. It is, in fact, the antithesis of marketing and sales, which seeks to build a strong *positive* relationship with the customer. Even the stereotypical manipulative used-car salesman acts like he is your best friend, at least until you buy the car.
2. Bullying, even for the noblest of reasons, is cruel, and therefore not consistent with progressive ethics.
3. Bullying doesn't work. It is, in fact, more likely to motivate people away from your viewpoint than toward it.

Bullying can masquerade as activism, but is in fact antithetical to it. If you spend a lot of time talking *at* people instead of listening *to* them, you should give serious thought to the question of whether you are, in fact, bullying. And even if what you're doing doesn't quite cross the line into actual bullying, it probably isn't the most effective activism, which, as you now know, involves gentle Socratic questioning.

Many of us know activists who bully others. And, perhaps because bullies tend to be fearful and timid at heart, they often tend to bully not the opposition or the unconvinced, who probably wouldn't put up with that kind of treatment anyway, but other activists, and their own family members. They blame and shame and hector their victims for committing "the crime" of only agreeing with them 50 percent or 70 percent or 90 percent of the time. Here's Alinsky again:

> I detest and fear dogma. I know that all revolutions must have ideologies to spur them on. That in the heat of conflict these ideologies tend to be smelted into rigid dogmas claiming exclusive possession of the truth, and the keys to paradise, is tragic. Dogma is the enemy of human freedom. Dogma must be watched for and apprehended at every turn and twist of the revolutionary movement. The human spirit glows from that small inner light of doubt whether we are right, while those who believe with complete certainty that they possess the right are dark inside and darken the world outside with cruelty, pain, and injustice.

Rampant bullying also leads to the kinds of ongoing sectarian wars that can suck the very life out of a social movement. Todd Gitlin, in *Letters to a Young Activist*, points to what I would characterize as a disparity in internecine bullying as a key reason for the Right's recent successes and the Left's corresponding failures. "The fanatics of the Right . . . believe in submerging differences for the sake of victory," he says. And elsewhere:

> The activists of the right are, above all, practical. They crave results. They are not terribly interested in pure parties or theoretical refinements, not even in ideas or morals as such. Once the Christian right decided to launch out of their churches and work the political arena, they preferred actual political and judicial power to private rectitude. To agree on a few central themes—military power, deregulation, tax cuts, tort reform, cultural rollback on abortion, gay rights, and affirmative action—was enough.

Don't bully.

Bullying v. "Hardball"

When I say not to bully, I am not saying that you shouldn't fight as hard as you can for what you believe in, or use every non-bullying tool and tactic at your disposal. How could I, when Dr. King himself said, "Freedom is never voluntarily given by the oppressor; it must be demanded by the oppressed," and Fredrick Douglass said, "Power concedes nothing without a demand; it never has and it never will."

Let's remember, however, that when you're trying to influence an organization, what you're really trying to do is influence the individuals within that organization—and that you gain nothing if you wind up alienating them. Expert activists make it their business to learn the fine art of opposing someone without alienating them—an art that begins with progressive values such as respect, compassion and tolerance. Recall Nicholas Wade's observations on activist Henry Spira, quoted in Peter Singer's *Ethics Into Action*: "I think he was effective because he was such a friendly, outgoing moderate sort of person. He wasn't strident. He didn't expect you necessarily to agree with everything he said." Later, Singer quotes an executive from Revlon, Inc., on Spira, who was working to convince the company to stop testing cosmetics on animals: "On the top management floor...there wasn't one person who didn't get to personally know Henry, and like him."

There's one important thing you should notice about both Henry Spira's and John Robbins's approach to activism: that while they moderated their behaviors, they did not moderate their viewpoints and goals. **The idea that to achieve radical goals you need to employ bullying methods is a fallacy, and a self-defeating one.**

Don't bully.

CHAPTER 16

The Bitterest Truth: It's Not about You

In *How to Win Friends & Influence People*, Dale Carnegie writes, "If out of reading this book you get just one thing—an increased tendency to think always in terms of other people's point of view, and see things from their angle—if you get that one thing out of this book, it may easily prove to be one of the building blocks of your career."

Bitter Truth #2 says that people buy to fill a need, with the implication being that you need to sell to their needs. This can be hard to do if we succumb to the all-too-human temptation to place our own needs front and center. Most people have a tendency toward that kind of egocentrism—to be "the star of the movie," as I like to put it—but serious activism demands that you learn to subordinate your needs to your customer's, at least during the sale.

Here's Carnegie again:

Thousands of salespeople are pounding the pavements today, tired, discouraged and underpaid. Why? Because they are always thinking only of what they want. They don't realize that neither you nor I want to buy anything. If we did, we would go out and buy it. But both of us are eternally interested in solving our problems. And if salespeople can show us how their services or merchandise will help us solve our problems, they won't need to sell us. We'll buy.

And here's Beckwith in *Selling the Invisible*:

The most compelling selling message you can deliver in any medium is not that you have something wonderful to sell. It is: "I understand what you need." The selling message "I have" is about you. The message "I understand" is about the only person involved in the sale who really matters: the buyer.

And so, we arrive at our final Bitter Truth:

BITTER TRUTH #3

In any sale, the customer's needs and viewpoints count far more than yours. In fact, yours hardly count at all.

Here's how Bitter Truth #3 plays out in a business context:

- A "fashionista" opens a clothing store and stocks it only with clothing she likes—and is surprised when her sales are meager.
- A chef opens a restaurant whose menu consists solely of his favorite dishes, which tend toward the complex and esoteric. He also refuses to compromise his culinary standards and therefore uses only the most expensive ingredients, even in dishes where his customers can't tell the difference. His restaurant runs at a loss until, less than two years after it opened, it is forced to close.
- A freelance programmer takes pride in her elegant and "tight" code. Only, her projects frequently take too long and go over budget, so her customer list is dwindling.

Each of these entrepreneurs has put his or her needs—or ego, if you prefer—before the customer's. The fashionista's shoppers want to see clothes that *they* like in her store. The chef's diners want comfort food—and don't bother with the truffles. And the programmer's clients don't care about elegant code, or code at all: they are not buying code but an inventory-management program. They just want it delivered on time and within budget.

Placing your needs ahead of the customer's is a common reason for business failure—and also for activist failure, as we'll see in the next chapter.

CHAPTER 17

Why You're Not Getting Through

Have you ever spoken to someone with utter passion and conviction about your cause, and watched helplessly while his eyes glazed over? Beckwith explains why this happens:

> A salesperson has something to sell you. "Blah, blah, blah," you hear. He continues. Same thing. You hear the melody but not the lyrics. . . . You know why his pitch failed. Because the person did not talk about *you*. His entire pitch was about *him* and what he had, not about you and what you need. It was all about him. But what you cared about was you. [Italics his]

Like Bitter Truths #1 and #2, Bitter Truth #3 applies just as strongly, if not more so, to activism as to business. Even when what you're selling is the most unambiguous social good, you always need to keep the customer's needs front and center. If you do, you'll be able to accomplish astounding feats of persuasion. It you don't, your activism won't be nearly as effective. Peter Singer, in *Ethics Into Action*, says:

> Too many activists mix only with other activists and imagine that everyone else thinks as they do. They start to believe in their own propaganda and lose their feel for what the average person in the street might think. They no longer know what is achievable and what is a fantasy that has grown out of their own intense conviction of the need for change. . . . [Activist] Henry [Spira] grabs every opportunity to talk to people outside the animal movement. He'll start up a conversation with the person sitting next to him on a bus or train, mention an issue he is concerned about, and listen to their responses. How do they react? Can they feel themselves in the place of the victim? Are they outraged? What in particular do they focus on?

Later, he writes:

When Henry wants to get someone—a scientist, a corporate executive, a legislator, or a government official—to do something differently, he puts himself in the position of that person: "[The question to ask yourself is:] If I were that person, what would make me want to change my behavior? If you accuse them of being a bunch of sadistic bastards, these people are not going to figure, 'Hey, what is it I could do that's going to be different and make those people happy?' That's not the way the real world works...you want to reprogram them, and you're not going to reprogram them by saying we're saints and you're sinners, and we're going to clobber you with a two-by-four in order to educate you."

Once you've used Socratic questioning to learn the customer's viewpoint and needs, it's your job to rise above your own viewpoint and needs and put the information you've gotten to use. In the vegetarian/animal rights movement, for example, our primary goal is to convert as many people as possible to a vegetarian lifestyle in which animals are not used for food, clothing or other purposes. This has four main advantages:

- It alleviates cruelty to animals, many of whom live lives of unspeakable suffering in factory farms. Factory farms are nothing like the quaint family farms of yore: they are gigantic warehouses in which tens of thousands of animals are crowded together in unspeakable conditions, often living out their whole lives without ever once stepping outdoors or even outside of their tiny cages.[6]
- It offers profound environmental advantages, since factory farms are notorious polluters.[7]
- It also helps on the labor/human rights front, since factory farms and slaughterhouses tend to be exploitative employers.[8]

And, finally,
- It offers enormous health benefits to the individual involved, not just because a plant-based diet is inherently healthier (lower fat, no cholesterol, more vitamins), but because, by not eating meat, eggs or dairy, a person is also not ingesting the hormones, antibiotics, pesticides and other chemicals which factory farms feed to their

animals or treat them with—and which frequently wind up as residues in the food product.[9]

So, the vegetarian activist has many angles he can use in communicating his message to his customer. Many activists choose the "cruelty to animals" angle, perhaps because the depth of suffering the animals experience seems so immediate and awful. I, too, am moved and angered by what the animals endure—in many cases, for something as frivolous as foie gras—but in my experience many people are simply not moved by the cruelty argument, or at least not moved enough by it to give up eating animal products. The reasons for this are complex, and probably include the fact that the animal industries' operations are so far removed from most people's daily experience that they can't viscerally "feel" the problem of animal suffering. Of course, the meat and other animal industries like it that way, and do everything they can to obscure the bloody realities of their product, including setting up factory farms in underpopulated areas—and, increasingly, in developing countries with little government regulation—and packaging their products in ways that disguise their origins.

The one pro-vegetarian argument that does work for many people, in my experience, is the health one—probably because everyone experiences their health and health problems viscerally (literally!). While activists who argue for vegetarianism based on anti-cruelty, environmental or labor grounds do important work, so do the many activists—and the huge numbers of non-activist doctors, nutritionists and other health experts—who are convincing people to eat less meat, dairy and eggs so that they can avoid illness and live longer.

No matter what your field of activism, you must sell to your customer's needs, and not your own. Sometimes, those needs may strike you as unacceptably narrow and parochial, but you must avoid casting judgment on them, as that will only alienate your customer. (Even if you don't voice your judgment, people can usually tell. . . .) Casting judgment on others' motivations also signifies a certain naïveté about the fact that people's motivations are usually reasonable—if not optimal—given their situations.

Which brings us to a deep need that may be very important to *you*, and that, if it is, might be causing you to not be as effective at your activism as you might otherwise be. . . .

CHAPTER 18

The Activist's Need Not to Be Rejected

Why would activists make the mistake of addressing their needs instead of their customers'? First, because of the mistake I discussed in Chapter 9: thinking that the importance of their cause somehow nullifies the laws of marketing and sales. It doesn't.

Second, because seeing things from someone else's viewpoint is hard. It's not as comfortable as seeing things from our own viewpoint.

Finally, we often focus on our own needs when those needs are highly compelling to us. One need in particular that compels activists and salespeople to act against their success is the need to avoid rejection.

Rejection is one of the most painful of human experiences, and many people go to great lengths to avoid it—even giving up on cherished business, artistic, romantic and other dreams. Rejection is an inevitable part of sales, however—and of activism. And I believe that fear of rejection lies at the heart of much of the ineffective activism we see around us every day.

A rejection-averse businessperson usually doesn't tell herself she's rejection-averse: she just never gets around to starting her business, or starts it but busies herself with "essential" non-sales activities. She forgets that sales is one of the most essential activities of all for a new business—and that, without sales, there can be no business. So, by not-selling, she kills her business.

A rejection-averse activist can make exactly the same mistakes: either never getting around to doing activism at all, or busying himself with activities other than selling. Or, he can spend much of his time "selling" to his colleagues: not the best use of his time, since they probably already agree with him, but at least it saves him from going out and talking to people who might reject him. This is probably the genesis of many a classic "echo chamber" problem where activists spend most of their time talking with each other instead of the people they are supposed to be influencing.

It's understandable why anyone would be tempted to do whatever he could to avoid rejection, but it's a temptation that the serious activist must resist. Rejection is inevitable in activism, so learning to handle it is an essential skill. Top salespeople have an almost preternatural ability to withstand rejection: it's a cliché that, when you say "No" to one, what he actually hears is, "maybe." The remaining 98 percent of us, however, must learn to deal with the pain rejection causes. Some techniques for doing that include:

- Having multiple sales going on at once, so that any one rejection isn't too devastating.
- Remembering that the customer is rejecting the thing you are selling, not you personally.
- Being part of a supportive community that can help you cope with rejection when it occurs.
- Not being perfectionist, negative or hypersensitive. And not panicking. (See Part III.)

The best way to cope with rejection is to minimize the chances of it happening, and the best way to do that is to do your marketing and sales in a disciplined, professional way. That's because, as you'll learn when I discuss the marketing and sales processes in detail starting in Chapter 21, marketing and sales, done properly, "filter" the available customer pool so that most of the customers you come in contact with will be highly likely to buy. Your odds of rejection, consequently, are much reduced.

Before we get to the processes, however, I have a few final things to say about the Bitter Truths . . .

CHAPTER 19

Corollaries to the Bitter Truths

BITTER TRUTH #1

The success of your venture depends much less on the quality of whatever it is you are selling than on the quality of the marketing and sales you use to sell it.

BITTER TRUTH #2

People buy a product not because of its intrinsic qualities or characteristics, but because they believe it will either solve a problem or meet a need that they have.

BITTER TRUTH #3

In any sale, the customer's needs and viewpoints count far more than yours. In fact, yours hardly count at all.

These truths suggest three corollaries:

First, that **marketing and sales should not be thought of as a secondary or subsidiary activity to your activism, but as the main show.** Your projects, events and even candidates could, in fact, be thought of as "vehicles" that provide you with a reason and opportunity for marketing and selling your viewpoint.

Remember: activism *is* marketing and selling.

Second, that **marketing and sales are among the very best uses you can make of your time, money and other resources.** Don't rush them, and don't skimp on them. A good guide on how to achieve quality marketing for very little money, by the way, is *Guerrilla Marketing* (see Bibliography).

And third, that **a little marketing and sales is *way* better than none at all.** In an ideal world we would all have plenty of time, money, and other resources to market and sell our viewpoints. In the real world, however, resources are always limited, and sometimes severely so. Marketing and sales are such powerful techniques that you should never skip them, and in particular you should **never skip the marketing.** Remember: it accounts for 90 percent of every sale.

CHAPTER 20

More Marketing Basics

The marketing process, as discussed earlier, consists of these three steps:

1. **Identify** the group of customers ("target market" or "market segment") most likely to buy your product.
2. **Rework** ("repackage") your product so that it will appeal even more to those customers.
3. **Connect** the customers with your product via a marketing campaign consisting of advertising, public relations, Internet marketing, word of mouth and/or other tactics. A good distribution strategy—so that the customer can actually get her hands on your product—is also an important part of this step.

Done right, these steps accomplish the following:

- Creates or strengthens the customer's sense of need. As discussed earlier, most people will be motivated by a combination of surface and deep needs. The surface need might be, "I need to do something about global warming" or "I need to help a progressive candidate be elected." And the deep need might be one or more of the following: "I need to feel hip," "I need to feel safe," "I need to feel successful," or "I need to feel like a good person."

- Presents the product in such a way that the customer *immediately and easily* sees that it fills her needs. The customer shouldn't have to do any work (or much work) to see that the product is right for her. Consciously or subconsciously, the customer should look at the loving couple in an ad for a diamond engagement ring—or the sexy couple in an ad for a bottle of liquor, or the affluent couple in an ad for a mutual fund—and immediately, almost reflexively, think, "That love [or sexiness or affluence] is what I want, and if I purchase this product I will get it." Likewise, the customer should look at a flier for an activist organization and immediately, almost reflexively, think, "I need to feel like I'm doing something good for the world. This organization looks as if it will let me do that, and also as if it will provide me with the fun community experience I have been craving."

- Gives the customer an appealing view of your product, and also of the company that makes it. "Appealing," of course, means different things to different people. Some might find the laid-back, countrified persona (or "**brand**," in market-speak) of companies such as Ben & Jerry's or L.L. Bean appealing, while others might respond more to the youthful or hip brand of companies such as Sony, Nike or Apple. Brands, by the way, don't arise spontaneously: companies create them carefully and deliberately, often over many years and using many millions of dollars. Most marketing texts define a brand as a kind of shortcut message that conveys many points at once to the customer. Disney's brand is wholesome, yet sophisticated family entertainment. *The New York Times*'s brand is comprehensive news presented seriously; it is, after all, the "paper of record" that gives us "all the news that's fit to print." I'm not saying that these companies live fully up to their brands, by the way; most, or perhaps all, companies do not. But the brand generally describes the company both to itself and its customers.

  Activist organizations are also branded. The smart ones choose and create their brand, the way corporations do; while the naïve ones don't, and let the public—or, worse, their opposition—brand them. Some organizations project a serious, mainstream brand (Sierra Club, Amnesty International), while others project a more radical, hip or edgy one (PETA), while still others project a more scholarly (Union of Concerned Scientists) or legalistic (Southern Poverty Leadership Council) one. If you and your colleagues are wondering which brand you'd like to project, you've forgotten Bitter Truth #3: it's not about what brand you'd like, but which will most powerfully attract your customer.

- Tells the customer that people like her are, indeed, buying your product. Contrast the people you see in, say, Mountain Dew ads with those you see in Starbucks or Budweiser ads. The importance of this message—that "people just like you are buying our product"—cannot be overemphasized. As discussed in Chapter 7, there's a natural fear barrier that must be overcome for most sales to take place, and showing that people like the customer have, in fact, overcome that barrier is one of the strongest persuasive messages you can send. The same holds true for activism. One of the strongest persuasive arguments you can make to get someone to support, endorse, vote for or donate to your cause is to show him that people *just like him* have already done so.

- Provides the customer with all the information she needs to locate and buy the product. In an activist context, this could be as simple as listing your organization's Web address and phone number on a flier. Always list your contact information on *every page* of *every document* you distribute. Your audience should never have to hunt to find out how to reach you.

All of these goals, taken together, help the customer be less afraid of you and your viewpoint and, hence, more likely to buy it. In fact, as discussed earlier, marketing, done properly, makes the customer *wild* to buy your viewpoint, in which case sales becomes a snap.

The next chapter begins our in-depth discussion of the steps of the marketing process as applied to activism. It is followed, in Chapter 24, by an in-depth discussion of the sales process.

CHAPTER 21

The Marketing Process in Detail I: Choose the group of customers ("market segment") most likely to be receptive to your product.

Recall that the point of activism is to influence people to get them to change their behavior in a way that you desire. Influencing people is not easy, mainly due to the "fear factor" discussed earlier, and the best route to success is usually to focus your marketing and sales efforts, especially early in a campaign, on those customers who are most likely to buy.

Many activists don't get this. They either go after random (not targeted) customers, or tough ones in preference to easy ones. The former is often due to a lack of knowledge about marketing, while the latter is often due to bad strategy (i.e., inept marketing) or even a misplaced desire to be "challenged." You should always focus on easy customers, however, particularly at the early stages of a campaign, for these reasons:

- It makes marketing and sales much less stressful.
- It helps raise your success rate and boost your morale.
- It lets you practice your pitch on those customers who are most likely to be tolerant and forgiving of your mistakes.
- Your easy customers, once sold, can help you sell to the tougher ones. As discussed in the last chapter, people often find it very persuasive when they see someone who they think is like them embracing a product.

At each stage of a campaign, therefore, you should focus on the easiest subset (or market segment) of customers. Once you are consistently selling into that segment, you can then divert some of your attention and resources to the next segment: customers who are a somewhat harder sell than Segment 1. You continue that process through Segments 2, 3, 4, etc., never abandoning the easier segments until you've made all the sales you think you can make in them—until, in marketing parlance, you have "saturated the market."

This is true for all activism, by the way. It's true even if you follow Abigail Kelley Foster's dictum to "go where you are least wanted." Even in that lonely, frightening place, there will still be some segment of customers who are more likely than all the others to buy your viewpoint, and those are the customers you should start with. In a union campaign they could be employees who are parents of young children and who need better health insurance. In an electoral campaign, it could be people with a need for the types of improved public services your candidate is promising to deliver. In a vegetarian campaign, they could be loving pet owners who only need a little encouragement to widen their circle of compassion to include farmed animals.

How to Segment

Segmenting is easy, really: you let your potential customers do it for you. Talk to a diverse set of them and ask them to tell you about themselves: who they are, what their situation is, what their thoughts are about your cause, and, especially, what their needs are. Ask them *without pressuring them* how likely they would be to sign on to your viewpoint, and the reasons for their willingness or reluctance to do so. Then ask for their advice on how you should sell your viewpoint to people like them.

After several discussions, you should start to have a good sense of:

1. Who is in the most "pain" from the status quo, and therefore could be most likely expected to embrace change.
2. What specific messages and framing of your viewpoint would be most likely to encourage those people to take the action you desire.

That pain referred to in the first point, by the way, could be economic, emotional or even literal physical pain. An example of the last would be someone whose employer isn't providing health insurance and who can't afford to see her doctor when she needs to.

Segmenting is an art more than a science. Marketing expert Geoffrey Moore, author of *Crossing the Chasm* (see Bibliography), says you do it using "informed intuition" based on your historical and experiential knowledge of which people in which situations are most likely to want to sign on to your cause. The crucial thing is that you confirm your hunches using **market research**, including talking with your customers. There are other types of market research, including trends analysis and demographic analysis, but getting first-hand input directly from your customers is by far the most valuable.

When You Let Your Customer Do the Talking . . .

What you're doing, really, is letting your customers design your marketing and sales campaigns for you—under your oversight, of course. This clever strategy accomplishes four very positive things:

1. It takes a lot of the uncertainty and guesswork out of marketing and sales.
2. It saves you a lot of time, money and stress.
3. It helps you create an absolutely killer campaign.
4. It makes the customers you've been talking with partners in your effort. They will be your very first customers, and you won't even have to sell them because you will have let them sell themselves. And then they'll help you sell to others . . .

This is powerful, powerful magic. It is also a very progressive methodology: you are not acting "on" your customers, after all, but acting in partnership "with" them. You are treating them not as stereotypes or passive targets, but as individuals worthy of compassion, consideration and respect.

You don't let your customers make all the decisions for your campaign, of course: it's still your campaign and you need to take responsibility for it. But you should carefully consider everything they say, and only deviate from it with good reason.

The big mistake activists and other marketers make is that they don't ask their customers, they tell them. This may be from ignorance, shyness, fear of rejection, or arrogance. Even the most experienced activist is likely to screw up if he doesn't get his customer's input, however—and most experienced activists wouldn't make that mistake anyway.

Talk with your customers. Or, more precisely, listen to them. That's your main job as an activist. As Saul Alinsky writes in *Rules for Radicals*:

[The organizer] is constantly moving in on the happenings of others, identifying with them and extracting their happenings into his own mental digestive system and thereby accumulating more experience. *It is essential for communication that he know of their experiences. Since one can communicate only through the experiences of the other*, it becomes clear that the organizer begins to develop an abnormally large body of experience. (Italics added.)

In *Bridging the Class Divide*, Linda Stout tells how, during the Vietnam War era, she struggled to have her Quaker "Meeting" (the Quaker equivalent of a congregation) provide a counseling service for young men who wished to be conscientious objectors or otherwise avoid the draft. A couple of members of the Meeting objected, including an African-American man who disagreed with the idea of advising people on how to break the law. Because Quakers use a consensus decision-making process in which a single "No" vote can stop a proposal, this man was able to single-handedly block the counseling service. Stout writes:

> I was horrified that someone could come in and stop the work. . . . I brought it up constantly at every business meeting and would argue about it. In anger, I finally decided to give up and not raise the subject again. . .
>
> There was another person at the Meeting retreat who had studied the history of the Quakers. . . . He said Quakers had struggled with the issue of breaking the law when they decided to teach Charleston slaves to read and write. He pointed out that Quakers had taught Nat Turner how to read and write when it was illegal to help any slave become literate. Afterwards, this African-American man decided he would no longer block my efforts to organize a military draft counseling service. . . .
>
> . . . [T]hat retreat taught me an important lesson in patience and about people's processes of change. I learned how important it was to hear people's concerns and fears, instead of challenging them with my beliefs. I also discovered the importance of education—especially a knowledge of history—in helping people gain a context for their beliefs and learn to make connections. Most of all, I saw the need for us to really listen and share our personal feelings with each other.

There is no substitute for talking one-on-one with a few members of your audience while planning your campaign. Every conversation will be like gold, filled with valuable insights and tips that will help you design a more effective campaign. Some conversations may even wind up upsetting you: for instance, if someone tells you that you're making the wrong assumptions or thinking about things the wrong way. This is painful but wonderful! Better to learn it now than later on, after you've invested your heart, soul, time and money into a failing campaign. It's never pleasant to hear that you're on the wrong track, but it is the mark of a professional that (a) she seeks out people who can give her a strong and informed critique of her plan, and (b) when she does get some useful criticism, she grits her teeth, shelves her ego, and makes the required changes.

Conversational Pointers

Here are some pointers for holding your conversations:

- Be sure to talk with a diverse range of people, and not simply those whom you are most comfortable around or who are most like you. Otherwise, you are almost guaranteed to miss out on important information, and you might even miss out on learning about an unexpected market segment that is strongly receptive to your message.

- Remember: at this stage you shouldn't be actively trying to sell to the people you're talking to. That's because you haven't yet established the positive relationship needed for someone to feel comfortable buying from you, and any effort you make to sell is likely to backfire. Your goal at this stage is simply to ask questions and listen respectfully to the answers. The wonderful thing is that, by doing so, you are establishing the very relationship you will later need to make the sale.

- Take your time. Don't just fire off ten questions, listen impatiently to the answers, say thanks and leave. This will leave many people feeling used—quite the opposite impression from what you intended. Instead, allow plenty of time and converse in a relaxed fashion. Take time out for small talk and digressions; digressions are great, as they indicate the person you're speaking with is starting to feel relaxed around you. Also, some of the most interesting and useful bits of information can come from so-called digressions: for instance, that someone's favorite aunt or uncle or grandparent was a progressive activist.

- Don't forget to ask the person you're speaking with not just what he thinks of your cause, but what he thinks about the opposition and opposing viewpoint. This is one of the best ways to uncover your opposition's weaknesses and learn how to most clearly present those weaknesses to your audience.

- Listen to your audience not just at the beginning of a campaign but throughout it and on into the future. They'll provide valuable ongoing feedback and help you stay on track. Remember that, even though it may not seem this way when you first meet them, you almost certainly have lots to learn from them as well. (That's one of the joys and rewards of activism: befriending, and learning from, many different types of people.) Remember: your ultimate goal is not simply to sign people onto your cause, but to convert them into activists *for* your cause. Staying in touch with them as a mentor/coach/teacher/friend will facilitate that.

The next chapter offers some more tips to help you segment your market.

THE 10% OFF RULE AND THE IMPORTANCE OF FOCUSING ON JUST ONE OR TWO SEGMENTS AT A TIME

A common mistake activists and salespeople make is to go after more than two market segments simultaneously. As I hope I've conveyed by now, it does take time and effort to market and sell well, but it's an investment that pays off. It takes even more time and effort to market and sell *excellently*, but it's an investment that pays off even more. When your marketing hits the center of the target—meaning, when you get the segmenting, message and delivery exactly right—you can make an astonishing number of sales and make them astonishingly easily. Be just ten percent "off," however, and you've probably lost a lot of those sales and made the overall sales process much more difficult. I call that the 10% Off Rule.

Excellent marketing and sales pretty much mandate different materials and pitches for each segment you target. Even if two segments appear to be very similar, you will probably still need different materials and pitches, since, according to the 10% Off Rule, even a single less-than-apt word or image can cost you sales. More on this in the next chapter.

Because it will take a lot of time, energy and other resources to market and sell effectively into each segment, I recommend you confine your marketing and sales to no more than two segments at a time.

This instruction often scares novices. They think that by limiting their activities to such a seemingly small "slice" of the market they will miss out on lots of potential sales. The opposite is usually true, however: it's the salespeople (and activists) who focus on one or two segments, and therefore have the time and resources to develop a fabulous strategy and materials targeted at those segments, who wind up making the most sales. In contrast, salespeople who try to sell to everyone frequently wind up making only a vague, generalized pitch that isn't highly persuasive to anyone. Sure, they may win a few sales across a wide range of customers, but in the end they probably won't make as many sales as their more focused colleagues.

Add to that argument the plain fact that most small and even some medium-sized organizations don't have the money, time and other resources to do a good job at marketing and selling to more than two segments at a time. So, even if you're skeptical about the value of keeping to one or two segments, give it a try.

CHAPTER 22

The Marketing Process in Detail II: Adapt your message and message "packaging" so that it is the strongest possible "sell" to your chosen market segment.

Now that you've identified the market segments you are going after, and gotten feedback from members of those segments as to the best way to sell to them, it's time to put that information to use. Specifically, you will adapt your message and materials so that you can make the strongest possible sell to your segments. The things you should pay attention to are the:

- Content of your message
- Form of your message, including appearance
- Your pitch (i.e., the specific request that you are making of your audience)

Content of Your Message

Content of your message. If you're selling unionization to people who value higher pay above everything else, then you should emphasize that benefit relentlessly in all of your speeches, fliers, posters, table displays, publicity and other outreach. *Relentlessly*: with big fonts, relevant images, etc. There should be no doubt at all in your customers' minds that higher pay is the primary thing that you're selling.

Conversely, if health insurance is most important, you should emphasize that relentlessly.

Getting the content of your message right is also about making sure your message is phrased in such a way that your audience can relate to it. **Getting the language and phrasing exactly right is enormously important in marketing, since even a single "off" word can greatly decrease your message's effectiveness.** Remember: bad marketing actually repels people. You need to be particularly careful about this when addressing people of a different age, sex, class, ethnic, national or religious background than you. One of my (white) colleagues once referred to people of color as "minorities" in a press release he wrote and got an angry letter back. (In marketing, by the way, you assume that for every angry message you get there are ten or twenty other angry people who didn't bother to write.)

In *Bridging the Class Divide*, Linda Stout writes, "The first step in bridging class barriers that keep us apart is to respect each other's languages. Language creates probably the biggest barrier to building an inclusive movement, and overcoming this barrier is absolutely critical to success in organizing."

You should show *every* piece of marketing "collateral" you generate— every flier, brochure, video, poster, etc.—to several trusted audience members, friends or colleagues and get their feedback and suggestions before you use it on your audience. Showing it to a diverse group of people is best, since some may catch problems that the others may miss. You may often feel that you don't have the time to do this, but it is vital that you not skip this step. It is the easiest way to ensure that your marketing is effective, and that you don't inadvertently repel people.

Another way to match your message to your audience is to explicitly reference the group you're targeting in the text of your message. Businesspeople know that even a tiny bit of personalization can greatly increase sales over a generic message. For example, a flier with the headline, "Special Deal on Cell Phones for North Beach Residents!" will typically sell many more cell phones, in North Beach, anyway, than a flier whose headline reads, simply, "Special Deal on Cell Phones!"

This works just as well for activists. So, instead of advertising your next film event as, "Wilderness Preservation," advertise it as, "Wilderness Preservation in North Beach and Beyond" or, better yet, "How Preserving the North Beach Woodlands can Help Maintain Your Property Values." The last one, as I'm sure you recognize, is not just personalized, but directly addresses what is probably an urgent need for the audience.

Form of Your Message, Including Appearance

Getting the form and appearance of your message right is as important, or more so, than getting the words right. That's because many people will glance at your materials and make a snap judgment, based on its appearance, on whether they even want to bother reading.

Look at any popular consumer product, such as a can of soda, and what you are seeing is literally the result of hundreds or thousands of carefully considered decisions. The size, shape and weight of the can; the design, colors and fonts used; and, of course, the color, taste, carbonation and other attributes of the beverage itself: all were extensively researched and tested on actual consumers to make sure that the end product would sell as well as possible.

You should take similar care with any materials you use as part of your activism. The color, fonts, layout and other attributes of printed materials are important, as are the production values of any audiovisuals. If your document is jammed full of text, with narrow margins and little white space, few people will bother to read it. And if your film has a pounding hip hop audio track, it's likely to repel a lot of older audience members.

Again: what's important here is what *your audience* likes and responds to, not what you do.

Your Pitch

Professional salespeople, when confronted with a tough sale, always break it down into smaller, easier ones. Then they make those smaller sales one at a time, until they have accomplished their big sale.

Social change, by definition, is a tough sell, and so almost every activist sale should be broken down into smaller ones. If you're running a union drive, for example, the first sell might be to get the person to talk with you for five minutes; the next might be to get them to read your literature; the next might be to get them to attend a meeting; the next might be to get them to sign the organizing petition; and the next might be to get them to advocate to a couple of coworkers. If you ask for these things one at a time, you are likely to get what you want. If you ask for them all at once, you're likely to frighten, offend or alienate your audience.

When I sell vegetarianism to my audiences, I never ask them to stop eating all meat, dairy and egg products immediately. That would be an unreasonable, not to mention disrespectful, request, and it would most likely kill the sale. Instead, I ask them to replace just two meals or ingredients a week with vegetarian alternatives. Then, when they've accomplished that, I ask them to replace two more. And then two more. . . .

I also provide my audiences with all the information and resources they need to make the change. For instance, I usually give out a handout with some suggestions on it: that they replace ice cream with Tofutti or sorbet, for example; or butter (one of the unhealthiest foods around, after all) with healthy olive oil or butter-like "vegan spread"; or meat dishes with vegetarian ones the next time they order Chinese or Indian take-out. I even tell them the exact brand of vegan spread I prefer and where to find it in the supermarket refrigerator section. It's important to give your audience all the information they need to take the action you desire, because even a slight amount of confusion or uncertainty can kill a sale.

Peter Singer reports about Henry Spira devising a similarly carefully crafted pitch during his demonstrations against the American Museum of Natural History:

> The demonstrators carried placards and gave out leaflets describing the experiments. They did not ask people to refuse to go into the museum. That would have put most visitors in a difficult situation, since the visitors had come there, often with their children, looking forward to seeing the museum's displays. Instead the demonstrators made use of the fact that the museum had no fixed charge. Admission was by donation, but the museum suggested a donation of $3.00. The picketers gave visitors a penny and suggested that they use it as their donation. In that way, the visitors could show in a tangible way their opposition to the experiments, save themselves some money, and still see the museum.

Brilliant. And I *love* that Spira and his group actually gave the visitors the penny.

Always make it as easy as possible for your customer to take the action you desire.

CHAPTER 23

The Marketing Process in Detail III: Connect the customers with your product in a marketing campaign.

Now is the time to start contacting your customers and educating them about your cause. It is also a point in the marketing process where we see yet another key difference between successful and failed marketers: the ability to create, and follow, a plan. As discussed in Part I, Chapter 18, your plan doesn't have to be fancy or complex, but it should include these parts:

- Your **goals**, delineated in great detail, and preferably **quantified** and **deadlined**.
- The **steps** you need to take to achieve your goals, also delineated in great detail, and quantified and deadlined if possible.
- The **resources** required to achieve each step. This could be money, your time, others' time, information, equipment and materials such as office or art supplies.
- A statement of the **risks**, **problems** and **obstacles** you might encounter, and how you will overcome them.

Then, you start executing on the plan, always taking time, throughout the campaign, to stop and review what you have done, assess how effective you have been, and what changes you can make to the plan or your actions to be even more effective in the future.

Follow-Through is Key

Most of the things that can go wrong in a marketing campaign come down to this: not following through.

So, you talk to your customers and gain lots of information on what they want and doesn't want, but fail to do your segmentation or frame your message based on that information.

Or, you don't come up with a plan—or you come up with one, but don't follow it.

Or, you follow it, but don't take time out to periodically assess your level of success.

Or you do measure success, but don't get around to changing the plan to improve its effectiveness . . .

Etc.

There's an old joke that 90 percent of success is just showing up. Well, 90 percent of marketing success is just following through.

MOVING ON TO SALES . . .

Good work—we're done with our discussion of marketing! Now let's move on to sales. . . .

Let's assume you've done your market segmentation, message framing and strategic planning, and are starting to follow through on that plan. As a result, you're starting to see some lively interest among members of your audience. The remaining chapters of *The Lifelong Activist* show you how to "close" these sales and get your customers to sign on with enthusiasm and commitment to your cause.

CHAPTER 24

Sales 101 for Activists

Sales, as discussed in Chapter 2, is the work you do to persuade a customer to take an action you desire. It typically follows marketing, the process by which you attract the right customers to you in the first place. Marketing is what gives your customers a positive impression of you, your cause, and your activities. It also convinces customers that what you have to offer is exactly what they need to fill an urgent need or solve an urgent problem that they have. Once your marketing has successfully communicated these messages, then the sale itself—the finalizing of the transaction—becomes much easier.

The goal of every sale should be to get the customer to take an *action*. A car salesperson wants his customer to pull out her checkbook and pay for the car. An activist wants his customer to vote for his candidate, participate in an event or make a "lifestyle" change such as eating more vegetarian meals or conserving more energy. If the action doesn't take place, the sale isn't complete. **While it's gratifying to get your customer to agree with your viewpoint, that's only an intermediate step in the sale. The sale isn't considered accomplished until you get your customer to change his or her behavior.**

Although many people try a "seat of the pants" approach to sales, it is actually a complex process consisting of several well-established and highly studied and refined steps. Experts break the process down in different ways, but most agree that it comes down to something like this:

- Prospect
- Qualify
- Needs Assessment
- Restate
- Ponder & Present Solution
- Ask for the Sale & Supervise the Result

Prospect means creating a list of potential customers. If the list is good, a lot of people on it will be likely to buy. If not, if the list is "low quality," then few people will be likely to buy.

Qualify means separating out the small number of people on your prospect list who are ready to buy NOW from the much larger number who aren't. People who are ready to buy now are called "qualified."

Needs Assessment means talking to a qualified customer to find out who she is, what her situation is, and what her needs or problems are. The goals here are to (a) build the kind of positive relationship that facilitates a sale, and (b) gather the information you need to actually make that sale.

Restate means you repeat what the customer has told you in your own language. This confirms for her that you really have been listening to what she is saying—another relationship-building action—and also helps ensure that you correctly understood her.

Ponder & Present Solution means taking a moment to ponder what the customer has told you, and then presenting your product (or viewpoint) to her in such a way that she perceives it as meeting her needs.

Ask for the Sale & Supervise the Result. Asking for the sale means that you explicitly ask the customer to take the action you desire. Beating around the bush doesn't work! You always have to ask.

Supervising the Result means that once the customer says "Yes," you make sure she follows through—handholding her, if necessary, throughout the process.

If what you're selling is simple and/or inexpensive, like a bag of potato chips, this process can take as little as a few seconds, and you may be able to skip some steps. But if what you're selling is expensive or complex, like a house or car, the process can take days, weeks, months or even years. Progressivism is more on the complex side, so it pays to learn, practice and use the above steps. In the following chapters, I'll be discussing how each works in an activist context, but first let's discuss the preparation, skills and attitudes and aptitudes that top salespeople bring to their work.

CHAPTER 25

In Sales, Preparation + Practice = Success

It is fascinating to watch an expert salesperson at work. He seems totally confident, and totally at ease talking with the customer. He has all the facts, figures and documents he needs at his fingertips, and can handle most any question or objection the customer throws at him. On those rare occasions when he does falter, he recovers quickly and smoothly. Customers love dealing with him, and at the end of many interactions, the sale is made and everyone walks away happy.

Performance like this doesn't happen by accident; nor is it a fluke of personality or talent. It takes a lot of training, preparation and practice to operate at this level of peak sales performance, just as it takes a lot of effort for an athlete or musician to operate at peak. Because sales "looks" easy, however, and because there are a lot of inept salespeople around, most people don't realize how much work it takes to do sales right.

Here is what you need to become a great salesperson for your progressive values:

Training. The best salespeople have been intensively trained. Many corporations send their salespeople out regularly for classes and workshops, and many salespeople supplement their classroom training with books, tapes, and DVDs. Top salespeople study not just sales technique, but also topics such as psychology, teamwork, leadership and organizational dynamics.

You can often take inexpensive sales classes at community colleges and vocational schools. Some experts also specialize in teaching marketing and sales skills to activist and nonprofit organizations. (See page 386, or www.lifelongactivist.com for more information on the classes I teach.)

Information. Because uncertainty and confusion can unsettle customers, top salespeople make sure they have a detailed knowledge not just of the products they are selling, but of all of the relevant issues, surrounding those products. And they not only know everything about their industry, but about their customers. A kitchen-supply salesperson who sells to bakeries, for instance, will make it his business to be on top of all the bakery industry news and gossip.

Top salespeople also make sure they're aware of the day's headlines, and possess a good overall knowledge of current events and popular culture. You never know how a piece of news will relate to your sale, after all, or what may happen to come up in a conversation.

Attitude. Most salespeople work conscientiously to cultivate a positive attitude, both because they need it to weather the inevitable rejections, and because a positive attitude is highly appealing and persuasive to customers. Salespeople tend to be big fans of self-help books and motivational tapes and DVDs, which they often listen to while traveling from appointment to appointment. They'll even choose their music to help maintain a positive mood: loud, energizing music for when they are feeling low; and calm, soothing music for when they are feeling stressed.

Many salespeople, like many athletes and performers, also have rituals that they use to psych themselves up prior to an important sales call. One person might do some deep, calming breathing and relaxing stretches, for example, while another might do some vigorous air punches, and a third might recite a few inspirational lines of poetry. Whatever works for you is OK.

If you develop the Empowered Personality I described in Part III, Chapters 27 and 28, you will have a good attitude for doing sales.

Preparation. Preparation means having everything you need to complete the sale at your fingertips. That includes all relevant facts and figures, as well as all documents, fliers, brochures and other sales literature.

It also means that any materials you present to the customer are attractive and appealing, and free of typos and other mistakes.

It also means that your sales pitch is well crafted and to the point. Many salespeople write or purchase actual scripts for their pitches, which they memorize and rehearse exhaustively. (See below.)

Finally, it means making sure that there are no unnecessary distractions to, or interruptions of, the sales process. That means, for instance, that your e-mail and voicemail work flawlessly and professionally, and that your personal appearance and manner are pleasing to the customer.

Practice. Practice, practice, practice, practice, practice, practice, practice, practice, practice, practice. That's ten "practices," and I would write twenty if my editor would let me get away with it. Top salespeople practice selling all the time. They practice on their family, friends and colleagues— even the dog or cat, if no one else is around. They practice in front of a mirror, and videotape themselves so that they can see their mistakes on film. (Ouch!) They practice during their commutes. They practice constantly, even for just a couple of minutes at a time while waiting for a phone call or riding in an elevator. (Recall Henry Spira's constant discussions of animal issues with random strangers on the subway, bus, etc.)

They don't just practice their pitch, but how they will handle any objections a customer might raise. That way, when an objection is voiced, the salesperson will not be caught off guard and can easily deal with it. The expert salesperson's ease, when confronted with an objection, is tremendously persuasive to the customer.

The more sales technique you employ, and the better you get at employing it, the more powerful and effective your activism will be. So, be sure to pay your sales dues in terms of training, information, attitude, preparation and practice.

OK, now let's look at the sales process . . .

CHAPTER 26

Sales Process #1: Prospecting

It's a cliché that sales is a "numbers game." Basically, that phrase means that the more people you try to sell to, the more sales you will make. Experienced salespeople know their "ratios": for instance, that they will have to make X numbers of calls each month, in order to have Y express interest in their product, and Z who actually buy. A sample ratio calculation could be:

I need to call 1,000 customers a month—or 50 calls each and every workday—so that 100 (10 percent) express a positive interest in my product. Out of that 100, 25 (2.5 percent of the original 1,000) will agree to let me come to their offices and make a presentation, which means I need to make at least 7 office visits each week. [Actually 6.25, but you need to round up to make your quota.] Out of those 25 presentations, I need to close at least 5 sales (.5 percent) of at least $3,500 each, for a total of $17,500 in sales, or I won't meet my target.

Note how small the ratios are: only 2.5% of the customers she calls agree to a meeting, and only .5% will wind up buying. And in some businesses and activist organizations, the ratios are far smaller. Activist Linda Stout reports in *Bridging the Class Divide* that she had to call "fifty or sixty" people to find eight ministers who would meet with her to discuss holding a regional peace conference—a "yield" of about 15%. That doesn't sound so bad, all of a sudden, does it? It's not—but we also don't know how many of those ministers stayed with her until the project's completion . . .

All this is an argument for getting *very* good at weathering rejection, and it also means that you need a very large pool of "prospects" from which to draw your customers. Most salespeople's prospect lists contain hundreds of names, and many contain thousands. All of those listed should, at least in theory, be willing to buy your product at some time. Some may be ready to buy this year, some next year, some two years from now, and a relatively small percentage should be statistically likely to buy NOW. That last group is obviously of the greatest importance to the salesperson who has a monthly quota to make, and all of the hundreds of calls he makes each week are made with the single aim of locating them. The process of making hundreds of calls to locate the few likely customers resembles gold mining, where you sort through tons of gravel just to get at the few valuable nuggets. Hence the sales terms "prospecting" and "prospect list."

Why would someone be ready to buy at one time and not another? It happens all the time. Some sales are seasonal; for instance, most swimsuits sell in spring and early summer, and most computers sell either during the holiday season or before school starts.

We also tend to buy certain products or services at different life stages. Someone who has just gotten engaged is probably looking to rent a reception hall and purchase flowers, catering, music, etc. A year ago, she didn't need those services, and a year from now (hopefully) she won't, either. It's all in the timing.

USE QUANTITATIVE GOALS
TO STAY FOCUSED

If you do what professional salespeople do and set quantitative goals for your activism—i.e., "I need to get 100 signatures today" or "I need to get 12 people to come to this week's meeting"—that will help you keep focused on those activities and customers who are likely to pay off, and avoid those who aren't. Be sure to set ambitious but reasonable goals, and not to berate yourself harshly if you fail to meet them.

How to Build Your Prospect List

Activists, too, should work from a large prospect list. You build your list as part of your marketing—in fact, the list should consist, as much as possible, of people from the market segments you are focusing on. Your list should be as large as possible—at least hundreds of names, and thousands, or even tens of thousands, is better. You should also be constantly adding to it.

You can build your list from many sources, including union rosters, liberal religious congregations, community organizations, university clubs, online communities, petitions and people who sign up for more information while you're tabling or doing demonstrations. Other sources include the phone book and lists of property owners (available as public information at most town halls). Be creative in building your list, and remember that lists of names from organizations and online and offline communities should only be used with the official permission of the leader of the group—who should have gotten prior permission from the members to give out their information.

Trading lists with other organizations is also a good idea—but again, make sure you have your members' permission to give out their information before you do so.

If you've got some money, most magazines will rent or sell you pieces of their subscription lists, and many organizations will do the same with their membership lists. Rented lists are generally provided in the form of stick-on labels that you can just use once, while sold lists are generally provided on a CD that you can use over and over. Rates vary widely, and range from two cents to five dollars a name, depending on how valuable the list is considered. If you are serious about paying for lists, you may want to seek the help of a professional called a List Broker who specializes in helping organizations buy the right combination of lists for their needs. Check the Yellow Pages or the Web for more information.

Many salespeople consider their prospects lists, which they may have built up over years or even decades, their most precious career asset, and you should, too. That means that you should maintain your list on professional software, keep it up-to-date, and back it up constantly and redundantly—with one backup copy residing in a bank vault or similar secure location.

OK, so now you've started to build your list. The next chapter tells you how to use it.

CHAPTER 27

Sales Process #2: Qualifying

Sorting out the relatively small number of people on your prospect list who are ready to buy NOW from the much larger number who aren't is called "qualifying," and the people who are ready to buy now are called "qualified." The term sounds judgmental, as if qualified customers were somehow better people than unqualified ones. But salespeople don't use it judgmentally: they just use it to indicate whether someone is likely to buy or not.

Many salespeople consider qualifying the most important step in the sales process because it helps them determine how—or, more precisely, on whom—they should spend their time. A salesperson should be spending most of her time selling to people who are ready, willing and able to buy *now*. (Some time can also go toward maintaining contact with people who are likely to buy in the future, and to scouting out new prospects.) Otherwise, she'll waste too much time, and possibly her whole sales career, on the far greater pool of people who don't intend to buy now no matter how great her product is, or how good a job she does at selling.

A qualified customer is often one who has an urgent need for your product—or, more precisely, who experiences his need as being urgent. Someone who feels slightly inconvenienced by the status quo is likely to be less qualified than someone who feels seriously oppressed by it. Qualifying is, in essence, "re-segmenting your marketing segment." It's the process of choosing "the likeliest of the likeliest to buy." So if you segment and qualify properly, you should see a lot of sales successes.

How to Qualify

Salespeople qualify in different ways:

- The perfume and makeup saleswomen in the department stores qualify passersby in a few seconds by observing their hair, makeup, clothes, shoes and jewelry. They even check out the names on the shopping bags the shoppers are carrying! All of this information tells the saleswomen which customers are most likely to buy some expensive perfume or makeup—in other words, who to approach with a perfume squirt or a free sample.

- Car salespeople pay close attention to sex, age, marital status and the presence/absence of kids, and various socioeconomic cues (clothing, jewelry) of people entering their dealerships. Parents with kids will probably get directed to the minivans; affluent-looking types might get shown the sports cars or luxury sedans; and young adults might get shown the cheaper sedans. The salesperson will also ask questions about the customer's budget, lifestyle and familiarity with the make and model of the automobile he is selling, to ascertain whether the customer is a serious prospect (i.e., qualified) or just a "tire-kicker." If the salesperson thinks the customer is serious, he will lavish attention on him. But if he decides the customer isn't ready to buy now, he will spend much less time with him.

- A computer consultant may ask a detailed series of questions to determine whether a particular small business would be a good client for her. In particular, she asks what its needs are and how urgent those needs are, to see if they are a match for her skills and availability. But—knowing that having an urgent need does not by itself make a good customer (see below)—she also asks about the business's budget for computer programming services, its financial stability (to make sure it can pay her), how organized its office operations are, and why it's no longer working with its previous computer consultant. (Back when I was a computer consultant, a business owner told me of his former consultant, "He was ripping us off and I threw him out of here bodily." He might or might not have been telling the truth, but I got out of there as soon as possible. . . .)

Good salespeople qualify throughout the sale. They ask questions and make observations that help them determine if the customer is likely to buy now, and which messages are most likely to work to persuade him or her. If, at any point, they decide the customer is not qualified—i.e., not ready to buy now—then they end the sales process as quickly as possible so that they can move on to another, presumably more qualified, customer.

The cardinal rule of qualifying is:

It is *far* better to qualify too zealously—thereby risking that you accidentally weed out a few good prospects—than to not qualify zealously enough, and consequently spend a lot of your time trying to sell to people who aren't likely to buy. In fact, experienced salespeople *expect* to "over-qualify" and lose a good prospect once in a while. If they don't, they know they aren't qualifying zealously enough.

Qualifying for Progressivism

Qualifying works exactly the same way in activism as it does in business. It's a process of looking for characteristics or clues that your customer is, indeed, ready to buy. For example, someone might be qualified if you learn that:

- His or her parents were union members. (If you're running a union drive.)
- He or she has beloved companion animals. (If you're doing vegetarian or animal activism.)
- He or she was born in a particular foreign country, or his or her ancestors came from that country. (If you are doing human rights work related to that country.)
- He or she has donated money to Greenpeace or some other environmental organization. (If you are doing environmental work.)

How exactly you qualify someone depends on your specific circumstances, of course. It's also something people tend to get better at as they gain experience. Mentors can also provide useful guidance, here.

Qualifying does not mean you wind up preaching to the choir—i.e., spending your time talking to people who already agree with you. It means going after the people who don't agree with you now, but are the most likely to be easily convinced: the "low-hanging fruit."

As in business, you qualify throughout the sale, and are always prepared to abandon ship if the person you're talking with reveals themselves to be unqualified. Your foreign-born customer may reveal herself to be an arch-conservative and isolationist who couldn't care less about human rights. If so, thank her for her time and move on. .

Sometimes you invest weeks or months in a contact before you realize that they are not qualified. That's something you want to avoid, but it happens even to the pros. Just face the truth and move on.

An Urgent Need Isn't Enough

All qualified customers need to have an urgent need, but not everyone with an urgent need is a qualified customer. The customer also needs not to be truly willing and able to take the action you desire. In business, a customer could be unwilling or unable if she is takes forever to make up her mind; is unable to pay, or pay promptly; or is constantly second-guessing the businessperson on his work. In activism, a customer could be unwilling or unable if she:

- Harbors unreasonable doubts and/or suspicions about you or your cause.
- Teases or game-plays instead of works in good faith with you to achieve a win-win outcome.
- Has a Hamlet-like inability to make up her mind.
- Has unreasonable expectations of the benefit she will receive by embracing your viewpoint.
- Seems inappropriately or excessively angry, resentful or bitter, or generally emotionally unstable.

Customers such as these can sap your time and energy and drive you crazy in a hundred ways. They can also do great damage to you and your cause by badmouthing you to others. Some will string you along and tease you by acting very interested in your viewpoint, but then they never seem to move ahead toward taking the action you need them to take. They always have a million questions and concerns that they need addressed—and which you already addressed. Or, they miss phone calls or meetings. Or, they don't do the things they agreed to do, or do them late and/or poorly. In short, they're not working with you as a partner toward the desired outcome; you're laboriously dragging them along.

It is important to end the sales process *immediately* if you sense that a customer may be stringing you along. Don't wait for her to behave egregiously—she probably has already behaved badly in small ways, which is why your suspicions have been raised in the first place. Trust your gut and end the interaction, as nicely as possible, of course. Yes, this suggestion is rather draconian, and if you follow it you will probably eventually prejudge someone who is innocent. But believe me: it's better to miss out on ten potentially good customers than to fall prey to one who behaves destructively.

There's one group of people who seem like they should be qualified, but aren't. Many activists work very hard to try to convince this group, often with heartbreaking results. I discuss this "non-qualified" group in the next chapter.

CHAPTER 28

About Your Family

Many progressive activists are brought to the edge of despair, and beyond, trying to convince their parents, siblings, aunts, uncles, cousins and other relatives to embrace their values. But guess what? Nothing in any sales book I've ever read says that your family are automatically qualified just because they happen to be your family.

In fact, the opposite appears to be true: that your ideas are held in lower regard by the people who watched you grow up, and who in some cases diapered you, than by the general population. This doesn't just apply to activists: many artists and intellectuals throughout history have also had to leave home to find an appreciative audience.

I was discussing this topic with a friend who is an observant Christian, and he commented, "Even Jesus had to leave Nazareth to preach!" And guess what? He's right. Here's the text, from Matthew 13:

> And when he was come into his own country, he taught them in their synagogue, insomuch that they were astonished, and said, Whence hath this man this wisdom, and these mighty works?
>
> Is not this the carpenter's son? Is not his mother called Mary? and his brethren, James, and Joseph, and Simon, and Judas?
>
> And his sisters, are they not all with us? Whence then hath this man all these things?
>
> And they were offended in him. But Jesus said unto them, A prophet is not without honour, save in his own country, and in his own house.
>
> And he did not many mighty works there because of their unbelief.

That passage cracks me up. It also helps me to feel better about my own family's occasional imperviousness to some of my own fabulous progressive wisdom. Hopefully, it will do the same for you.

If your family is resistant to your progressivism, my suggestion is not to sweat it. It's not that they are dumb or that they don't love you; it's that they are not qualified customers. Give up on your efforts to sell to them, and try to influence them by joyful example, instead. I know, I know—it can be hard to watch loved ones embrace views or behave in ways that you find inappropriate or even unethical. But what's your choice? You can't force them to adopt your views. So follow the ancient wisdom of "live and let live," and save your sales efforts for qualified customers who are more likely to be convinced.

Also be alert to the possibility that unresolved personal issues between you and your family are muddying your efforts to influence them. If you already have a contentious relationship with your family, don't further complicate it by dragging your politics into the mix. Instead, take the initiative to work on repairing the relationships, and you may find that your family magically becomes more receptive to your values.

As discussed earlier in *The Lifelong Activist*, if your family is actively hostile to you, or undermines you, then separate yourself from them and interact with them as little as possible.

Spouse and Kids

I was mostly talking, above, about your birth family, but what if your created family—your spouse and kids—resist your progressive values? This is a much trickier situation. For those of you who aren't yet partnered, I reiterate the crucial advice from Part II: choose your mate wisely, since that choice will likely be one of the key determinants of your success as an activist and as a human being.

If you are already partnered with someone who doesn't support your progressive values and this situation is causing you pain, consult a therapist or other professional. If it's not causing you pain, but is merely an annoyance, then you should probably treat it like all the other minor annoyances of couplehood and "live and let live."

Kids are, in a way, simpler, since your responsibilities as a parent trump those as an activist. There is a natural tendency for kids raised by progressive parents to be progressive themselves, but if your kids don't happen to agree with you, or go through a period of rebellion, your responsibility as a parent *and* a nurturant progressive is to respect their independence, individuality and self-determination. If you don't try to bully them, but instead model for them the joyous progressive life, there's a good chance they will eventually return "home" to your values. If not—well, rejoice in their independence, and base your relationship not on your differences but on your areas of commonality. Chances are, you'll discover that your kids are not actually as far to the right as you feared.

Now, back to the sales process. . . .

CHAPTER 29

Sales Process #3: Needs Assessment

The Needs Assessment is a conversation you have with the customer, during which you work to gain an understanding of who he is, what his situation is, and what his thoughts and feelings are around your cause. While the market research conversations you conducted earlier were focused more on general questions of how to reach your audience, now you're homing in on the specifics of how to reach the individual customer you're speaking with. All of the information you collect is designed to answer the two most crucial questions you need to address in any sale:

- What needs or problems does my customer have that my cause might help address?
- What's the best way I can frame my cause so that my customer perceives it as fulfilling his need or solving his problem?

The answers to those two questions are the "gold" you're seeking in the Needs Assessment, as that is the information you need to straightforwardly make your sale.

The Needs Assessment is a conversation, but buried within the conversation is an interview. You will be asking a lot of questions, but be sure to keep the conversation light and natural so that it doesn't come across as an interrogation. Use small talk to break the ice, and observe the other social niceties as well. A good strategy is to begin by discussing the many *non-political* things you and your customer have in common: for example, a sports team you both like, a town you both lived in, the fact that you admire his beautiful garden, or the fact that you both have companion animals. Then, use these commonalities to form the basis of a positive relationship that's strong enough to accommodate a shift to discussing the "scary" subject of politics or morality.

Simple Questions, Complex Answers

A Needs Assessment lasts anywhere from around a minute to many hours or even days. It's generally the part of the sales process that takes the longest. Especially if the salesperson is selling something complex or expensive, there are literally dozens or hundreds of questions he can ask, including:

- Can you tell me a little about yourself?
- What do you do for a living? How did you get into that job or career? How do you like it?
- What's your living situation?
- Do you rent or own? Who else lives with you?
- Can you tell me about your family?
- What is your national/religious/ethnic background?
- What do you like to do in your free time?
- Where were you born? Where have you lived? Did you like those places?
- What is your educational background?
- What do/did your parents do?
- What do you think of Issue X?
- Have you ever known anyone who was [Democratic/vegetarian/gay/etc.]?
- What do you think of that person?
- Do you practice a religion?
- What are your goals, dreams and aspirations—for you and your loved ones?

Note that while the questions tend to be simple, the answers should not be. Since it's the details of a person's story that often provide you with the strongest clues as to how to frame an issue for them, it's important to get at those details. They will also be useful in helping you see the person as a unique individual, and not merely a target or stereotype.

Don't rush the Needs Assessment: the more information the person is willing to share with you, the better. Rushing can also make the person you're speaking with feel disrespected, which obviously works against your purpose. Many activists, especially when they are just starting to use sales techniques, rush nervously through the Needs Assessment and reflexively start pitching their solution, i.e., their cause. This inevitably brings on the "glazed eyes" reaction discussed in Chapter 17, and the way to avoid it is to practice doing Needs Assessments on colleagues and friends until you are comfortable enough to take the technique out into the field.

The next chapter offers more tips for doing a good Needs Assessment.

CHAPTER 30

Eight Tips for Conducting a Good Needs Assessment

The Needs Assessment, as I discussed in Chapter 29, is a conversation with an interview hidden at its core. Here are seven tips for conducting a good one:

1. **Remember: You're Selling Throughout the Process**
    A sale's success or failure doesn't occur at the moment when you finally ask the customer to take the action you require; it happens in degrees throughout the sales process. Throughout the Needs Assessment and other steps, the person you're talking with is consciously and unconsciously gathering information and impressions about you and your cause. Each little bit of information and each impression inclines him closer to, or further away from, accepting your viewpoint. **This means that you should be the best possible advocate you can be, not just at the end of the sale when you explicitly ask the customer to take your action, but throughout the sales process.** Waiting until the last minute to "turn on the charm" is not just duplicitous; it doesn't work.

2. **Remember: You're Still Qualifying**
    Somewhere during the conversation you may learn that the person you're talking to is implacably against your cause, or for some other reason is not in a position to take the action or make the behavioral change you seek. At that point, you should end the conversation gracefully and move on.

3. **Remember: You're Primarily Selling *Yourself***
    In any sale, the first and most important thing you need to sell is *yourself*: if the customer feels comfortable buying from you, you've probably made the sale; and if he doesn't, you've probably lost it, no matter how badly he needs whatever it is you're selling.
    As discussed in Chapter 7, more than anything else the customer needs

to feel **safe**, especially when what you're selling is something as "scary" as an alternative social or political viewpoint. If the customer feels you're using or exploiting her, or that she otherwise can't trust you, you've lost the sale (deservedly).

The customer also needs to feel **respected**. Remember the story from Chapter 5, about the culture clash between the Iowa caucus voter and the "Deaniac"? Showing up on a stranger's doorstep and behaving in ways that conflict with the local customs and mores is disrespectful.

You also have to be **attractive**, not in the fashion sense but in the pleasant/personable/good company sense. At the very least, you shouldn't be a person who repels others. Attractiveness has many components—including at least a minimal standard of personal grooming—but an important one is to have an appealing personality. Professional salespeople, as discussed in Chapter 25, work conscientiously to cultivate one, but many activists do not. Many activists, in fact, manifest a repellent personality, in the literal sense: unhappy, sour, judgmental, bitter, alienated or angry. And then they wonder why they have such a hard time selling their viewpoint!

I'm not saying that any given activist, or activists in general, are not justified in occasionally having those feelings; only that exhibiting them excessively or inappropriately is detrimental to your success in activism and other areas of your life.

Another aspect of selling yourself is **professionalism**. Always be calm and cool and in control. Show up on time, fully prepared and fully rehearsed. Make sure that any materials you use are polished and 100 percent accurate, since even trivial mistakes can seriously undermine your credibility.

4. **Employ Active, Non-Judgmental Listening Techniques**

Most people listen passively, meaning they don't really give the person they're speaking with their full attention. They hear at least some of the words, but their mind is off wandering in different directions. They may be thinking about what is being said, how they feel about it, how they will respond or even something totally unrelated, like what they are having for dinner that night.

Active listening, in contrast, is the process of listening with deep focus to what the other person is saying. That means that you're not distracted by your own thoughts, and therefore able to more fully understand what is being said.

Your goal, during the Needs Assessment, is to ask questions and then listen actively and non-judgmentally to the customer's answers—and then, to use those answers to shape the rest of the conversation so that it speaks even more strongly to his individual situation and needs.

Active listening is more difficult than passive listening, and many of us need to practice it to get good at it. Do that by using active listening in all of your conversations, including casual ones with family and friends. You will probably notice an immediate, positive shift in the relationship as the person you are speaking with registers, perhaps only subconsciously, your greater level of interest in their situation and needs.

5. **Make Sure Your Language Supports Your Viewpoint**
George Lakoff, author of *Don't Think of an Elephant!*, warns against adopting the opposition's linguistic constructions (or "frames," as he calls them), because when you do you automatically reinforce that construction in the mind of your listener. The minute an environmentalist mentions the conservative frame of "conservation versus jobs," for instance, she's put herself at a huge disadvantage. The frame she should be using, over and over again, is, "conservation means jobs."

Similarly, a reproductive rights advocate should never refer to the opposition as "pro-life," as it likes to designate itself. They should only be referred to as "anti-choice."

So, work to develop powerful frames for your issues, and to enforce "message discipline" in yourself and the others you work with. Make sure it is your frame, and not the opposition's, that is activated in your audience's mind.

6. **Use Your Customer's Language and, Whenever Possible, Refer to His Experiences**
You should be doing more listening than talking during the Needs Analysis—the talking comes later, during the Restating and Presenting Solution steps of the sales process—but when you do talk you should use your customer's language, and speak in terms of his experience, as much as possible. "[The organizer] learns the local legends, anecdotes, values, idioms. He listens to small talk. He refrains from rhetoric foreign to the local culture," says Alinsky.

Let's say you're giving a talk on climate change at a local church. The audience looks bored: they've heard it all before. Then you mention the word "stewardship" and everyone snaps to attention. That's because stewardship (a.k.a. "taking care of God's creation") is a fundamental obligation under the Christian faith. The topic may not have changed, but by simply adopting your audience's language, you've made it extremely relevant to them.

7. **Ask Open-Ended Questions**

Open-ended questions elicit a detailed response: i.e., "What do you think about Candidate X's economic views?" Close-ended questions, in contrast, typically elicit only a brief—often yes/no—response: i.e., "Do you like Candidate X's economic views?"

Open-ended questions tend to move the conversation along and open it up in new directions, whereas close-ended questions tend to shut it down.

Use open-ended questions whenever possible.

8. **It's Okay to Take Notes**

Unless the conversation is highly personal or sensitive, it's perfectly okay to take notes. In fact, doing so makes you look professional and organized. Before you break out the notebook, though, ask the person you're speaking with whether they mind.

In my experience, by the way, audio recorders make people *much* more nervous than a simple pen and paper.

CHAPTER 31

Sales Process #4: Restate the Customer's Problem

After you've conducted the Needs Assessment and feel you have a good understanding of your customer, his situation and his needs, you should **restate** what he has just told you in your own language.

Restating is an extremely powerful technique that is used not just in sales, but in coaching, teaching, therapy and other fields. It is the most direct and powerful way of demonstrating that you've actually been listening to the other person—and, by extension, that you respect and care about them.

Restating also gives you the opportunity to make sure you accurately understand the customer's situation. Since getting even one detail wrong can jeopardize a sale, you need to make sure you get as much right as possible, and especially that you don't proceed based on erroneous information or assumptions.

It is not a problem, by the way, if you get a detail wrong. If you do, the other person is likely to say, "Well, no, that's not what I meant." That's okay: simply ask him to correct you; and then restate his statement until you get it right.

Here's how restating works:

Activist: So, what you're telling me is that you like our candidate's stand on gay rights and the environment, only you're not sure whether you could vote for a third-party candidate. Is that right?

"Customer": Yeah, and I didn't like that she voted for a property tax increase, either.

Activist: Okay, I'm sorry I missed that. So you're saying that you would vote for our candidate because you like her stand on gay rights and the environment, only you're not sure whether you could vote for a third party candidate and you also didn't like her vote to raise property taxes. Is that right?

"Customer": Yes.

What the activist needs to do now is to continue to use gentle Socratic questioning to determine what, specifically, he means by "third-party candidate" and "raising property taxes," and what his objection is. Hopefully, the process of questioning will be enough to help him clarify his thoughts and defuse his objections. It might uncover, for instance, that although he clearly objected to having his property taxes raised, it was only a .25% raise that cost him less than $80 a year, and that the taxes paid for improvements in the community recreational facility that he and his family use regularly. These facts and the "more taxes = better public facilities" frame may defuse that particular objection.

As always, the key to moving the sale along will be not to lecture the customer, but listen to him.

Restating Works Magic

Restating someone's thoughts and feelings can have amazing, almost magical effects. For instance, when you restate, the customer often corrects *himself*. In other words, once he hears his thoughts and feelings reflected back at him, he realizes that those are not his thoughts and feelings after all.

"Customer": Actually, you know, the property tax thing was no big deal. And, you know, come to think of it, I did vote for a third-party candidate a while back.

Believe it or not, something like this frequently happens.

Another magical thing that can happen is that the customer may spontaneously embrace your viewpoint without any further action or persuasion from you:

"Customer" [*thinking aloud*]: Gee, those are not very good reasons not to vote for someone I otherwise like, are they?

This also happens frequently.

Only after you've used restating to demonstrate that you understand your customer's thoughts and situation, should you begin—very gently—to ask questions and make statements that challenge his views relative to your cause.

The next chapter tells you how.

CHAPTER 32

Sales Process #5: Ponder & Present Solution

This situation happens many times each day: someone approaches someone else with a problem. Maybe it's a child approaching his parent. Or a person approaching her partner. Or a corporate employee approaching his department's computer person.

The person starts to describe a problem, and the person they approached interrupts and says, "Oh, I know what that is. Don't worry, it's no big deal. All you have to do is. . . ."

Most people *hate* being on the receiving end of that kind of treatment. It's not just rude, it's dismissive and devaluing, as if the person's problems, and by extension the person himself or herself, are not worthy of serious consideration. (It is particularly wounding if the adviser dismisses what the asker considers to be an important problem.) More fundamentally, it deprives the asker of a feeling of specialness or uniqueness—of self-esteem, really.

Most people have an innate need for—or, more precisely, craving for—esteem, including self-esteem. Psychologist Abraham Maslow wrote about esteem at length, ranking it second only to self-actualization itself in his famous Hierarchy of Human Needs. Professional salespeople and activists know this, as do teachers, coaches and others who work with people. They also know that showing esteem for someone is not just a humane and compassionate thing to do, but creates a strong bond with her that makes her much more receptive to your viewpoint.

Is this manipulation? As with all moral questions pertaining to marketing and sales, the answer is: not if you do it honestly and responsibly. You should strive for an expansive world view that allows you to respect and value a wide range of people, including those who happen not to agree with you politically. And if you do respect and value someone, you should be willing to tell her so, if not explicitly in words—although that's frequently required in sales—then at least implicitly in your actions and the way you treat her.

If I were teaching a course on "Life Success" and the textbook could only contain two sentences, those sentences would be: "First, learn to feel good about yourself, no matter how flawed or imperfect you may perceive yourself to be. Next, work to help everyone around you feel better about themselves, and never stop searching for opportunities to do so."

How to Convey Respect

The entire sales process is designed to convey your respect, caring and concern for the customer, along with other goals such as qualifying and gathering information. The Ponder & Present Solution step, however, is where you most clearly convey your respect.

Here's an example of how to do the Ponder & Present Solution, from one of my former businesses:

Back when I was a freelance computer consultant, at least half the people who called me seeking help had one of the same few problems: a bad cable, a virus, a printer problem, a failed hard drive or a deleted file they needed to recover. One of the worst things I could have done, during such a call, would be to tell the customer, "Oh, that's not so bad! I've seen it a million times. I know exactly what you need." That would make them feel as if I didn't see their problem, or them, as unique and important.

Instead, I learned to first Restate the Customer's Problem, as described in Chapter 31, and then to Ponder and Present my Solution to that problem, which in this case goes like this, "Well, that sounds like a terrible problem. I can see why you'd be upset. Let me think about it for a moment." (Pause.) "Did you try swapping in another network cable?"

Here's an analysis of that response:

Well, that sounds like a terrible problem. I can see why you'd be upset. This is the truth told not from my perspective, but from my customer's. To her, the problem *is* terrible and upsetting, no matter how routine it may seem to me. As Bitter Truth #3 (Chapter 16) teaches us, it's the customer's viewpoint and not your own that's most important.

Whereas during the Restatement part of the sale, I was restating the factual truth of my customer's situation, now I am restating the *emotional truth.* Psychologists call this "mirroring," and it conveys a lot of respect and compassion for the person you're speaking with.

Let me think about it for a moment. This further reinforces the fact that I think the customer and her problem are important. By pausing to think her situation over, even if I'm pretty sure I know what's going on, I'm paying her the respect of giving it serious consideration.

Pause. During the pause, I make good on my stated intention "to think about it for a moment."

If you don't use this "pondering" time to actually consider the customer's problem, but simply to count the seconds before you start talking again, the ponder becomes a duplicitous tactic: you're only pretending to care. Given that, and given that people who make snap judgments are frequently wrong, you should always use the ponder to try to view the customer's situation through fresh eyes. This is especially true if you're one thousand percent sure you know what's going on, since it's typically in situations such as these that we make our most embarrassing mistakes.

Did you try swapping in another network cable? Finally, I propose my solution; and because the customer feels much more valued and respected by me than if I had simply thrown the solution at her first thing, she is far more likely to actually take my advice or hire my services to fix the problem.

Please reread that last sentence: " . . . she is far more likely to actually take my advice or hire my services." In other words, by showing my customer that I valued her, I was far more likely to elicit the behavioral change I desired from her.

It works exactly the same way in activism. Say you're trying to convince someone to vote for a Democratic candidate when that person has voted Republican his whole life, along with the rest of his family and most of his community. Those are the facts of his situation; this Ponder & Present dialogue narrates the emotional truth:

Activist: You said earlier that although you really like our candidate, it would be tough for you to vote Democratic for the first time. Can you tell me why?

"Customer": Well, my family and the people at church are bedrock Republicans, and they wouldn't think too highly of it.

Activist: So you're afraid your vote might alienate your family and the people at church?

"Customer": Yes.

Activist: That's a tough one, a really tough one. Let me think about it for a moment. [*Pause.*] Are you really sure that there isn't *anyone* in your family or church community who has voted Democratic?

"Customer" [*thinking*]: Well, there is my cousin Jack. He lives in the next town over, and he votes Democratic a lot. In fact, he's active in the local Democratic committee.

Activist: Really?

"Customer": Yeah. Funny, I forgot about him until just now.

Activist: How do people feel about Jack, knowing that he's an active Democrat?

"Customer": Okay, actually. He doesn't push his politics down people's throats. He's just one of us, only he votes differently.

"Activist": Hmmm . . . [*Pause.*] How do you think your family and friends would react if you took the same approach as Jack? Voted Democratic but didn't shove it down their throats?

"Customer": Probably not too badly. Yeah, it probably wouldn't be so bad at all. . . . In fact, my family wouldn't mind too much: it's my wife's family I'm more worried about. They're *really* bedrock Republicans. But they live on the other side of the state and we don't actually see them that much . . . and, actually, I don't really care what they think, too much, anyway. My wife can handle them . . . she's pretty tough. [*Laughs.*]

The Path of Persuasion

In the above example, the Restate and Ponder & Present Solution steps help the activist demonstrate his honest understanding of, and respect for, the customer and his situation—and therefore, implicitly, his esteem for the customer. In doing so, he not only forges a bond with the customer, but helps him feel safe enough, psychologically speaking, to contemplate adopting the activist's viewpoint and taking the action the activist desires. The "path of persuasion" that leads to a customer's taking a desired action often looks like this:

1. The customer begins with a natural distrust or suspicion of, if not the activist himself or herself, the thing the activist is trying to sell him.

2. After some discussion, the customer starts to trust the activist, and perceive him as an ally in making the difficult decision of whether

or not to take the action. He sees that he can draw on the activist's strength and support, as well as other resources the activist may provide, such as information.

3. The customer gains a fuller appreciation for the rightness of the activist's position. He may or may not see the action the activist wishes him to take as necessary or desirable, however—or the negatives of it may still outweigh the positives.

4. The customer starts to see himself as being on the same side of the question as the activist. The action the activist wishes him to take now starts to seem increasingly sensible, if not imperative.

5. At some point, the customer starts to view the positive consequences of taking the action as outweighing the negative ones. The action, therefore, seems increasingly doable. At some point, discussion may shift from theory and philosophy to planning—i.e., a detailed examination of the actual steps needed to take the action—and to ways any obstacles can be avoided or overcome.

6. The customer agrees to take the action.

7. The customer takes the action. The activist continues to support him.

8. The customer has taken the action. The activist continues to support him.

9. At some point after the action has taken place, the customer is ready to consider taking a new action. The path of persuasion begins anew—only this time, it is likely to go easier and more quickly, thanks to the strengthened relationship between the customer and the activist, and the fact that the customer is now more fully on the same side of the issue as the activist.

That's the sales/activism process at its best, and it is fueled by the simple but powerful act of honestly esteeming someone.

CHAPTER 33

Change is Hard

A naïve or inexperienced activist would handle the situation in the previous chapter by telling his customer, "Oh, just go ahead and vote Democratic! It's not such a big deal. In fact, it's easy! I do it all the time, and my folks are Republicans, too!"

But we already know why many people have trouble switching political parties, joining a union or making some other important change: change is hard and often painful. Even a seemingly benign act like voting for a Democratic candidate can be fraught with danger. It could, for example, be perceived as a betrayal of one's family or community. (Recall, from Chapter 7, the violent reaction of Mississippian Rhonda Nix's neighbors to her public declaration that she would be voting Democratic.) Or, it could be perceived as the first step down a slippery slope where the customer will be forced to painfully confront many of his long-held and cherished convictions, as well as many of his past actions.

Can you imagine John Robbins telling his pig farmer, "Oh, come on, it's easy to stop slaughtering pigs! Just give it a try." Or Henry Spira, talking to his vivisectionists, "Oh, come on, just come up with an alternative to the animal experiments. It's easy!" Of course not. And can you imagine what the result would have been if they had said those things?

The minute you start thinking that the action you're asking someone to take is easy, you're demonstrating a lack of empathy and compassion for that person that will almost certainly cost you the sale. In contrast, when you mirror someone's emotional truth by telling them, either explicitly or implicitly, "I understand how difficult this change must be for you, and I respect how brave you are for even considering it," you are in essence standing up with them against their fears. With your empathy and compassion, as well as other forms of support, they might well succeed at winning out over their fears and making the change you wish.

CHAPTER 34

Sales Process #6: Ask for the Sale & Supervise the Action

In the end, you have to ask your customer for the sale:

- "Will you vote for my candidate?"
- "Will you sign my petition?"
- "Will you donate to our cause?"
- "Will you help out on our campaign?"

Many salespeople and activists get right up to this point and then choke. They do a great job at prospecting, qualifying, interviewing, restating, pondering and presenting their solution. They get the customer all excited about what they're selling.

But then they don't ask for the sale.

It's not hard to see why: we're not accustomed to making important requests of strangers, or even of friends and family members. It can seem rude, or like we're imposing on them.

Also, asking is the heart of the sale, the do-or-die point at which you either achieve or don't achieve your goal, where you either "succeed" or "fail." It's a scary moment; and it's no wonder many people seek to avoid it.

But you have to push through your fears and ask for the sale. Because, although it might seem like it would be enough to make your point persuasively, it's not.

You need to ask.

Ask in a Way that Presumes Success

Here are better ways to ask the questions listed above:

- "Can I put you down on my list as a vote? What time will you be voting? Will you need a ride? Can I help in any other way?"

- "Great! It sounds like you really do agree with our position. Are you ready to sign the petition? Here's my pen!"
- "So you do find our cause compelling. How much of a donation can I put you down for? Fifty dollars? Twenty? Okay, twenty's great! Will you be paying cash, or by check or credit card? Here's the form . . . "
- "We have a volunteer training session for our campaign next Thursday. Can you come? No? How about the following Tuesday? Great! Do you need a ride? No? Okay. I'll call you that morning to remind you, and I'll look forward to seeing you there."

Each of these formulations presumes that the sale was a success, and each provides a little extra encouragement to the customer at a critical point in the sales process. If you've done your marketing and sales correctly up until this point, most customers will be poised to buy. Phrasing your "ask" as if they've already decided provides the tiny bit of extra push needed to close the sale.

You may find these formulations manipulative or overbearing. I can respect that, and personally would never use them with customers I felt were too intimidated or confused or uninformed to say no. But most customers are perfectly capable of saying no, even in response to a strong ask.

Don't use these formulations if you're not entirely comfortable doing so. You will probably find, however, that after a little sales practice you'll start to feel comfortable enough to ask in a way that presumes success. Your cause is important, after all, and you shouldn't be shy about advancing it.

If You Get a "Yes"

If you get a **"Yes"** at this point, congratulations! You've "closed the sale," in business parlance. At this point you need to:

1. Congratulate your customer *immediately* for agreeing to take such an important, worthwhile, brave action.
2. *Immediately* work to secure her commitment, signature or donation. This probably entails supervising the action she has promised to take to ensure that she does indeed follow through. And, of course, providing whatever support she requires to do so.
3. Begin working on a follow-up sale. Once someone agrees to buy something from you, they are receptive to making additional purchases. This is why fast food restaurants ask if you want fries with

your burger, and the boutique owner shows you jewelry after you've decided to buy the blouse. If your customer has agreed to sign your petition, maybe you can ask her to attend your next meeting, make a donation or get three of her neighbors to sign. Again, if this tactic seems too pushy and/or manipulative, feel free to omit it. But most customers will be at least receptive to hearing about more ways they can work with you, even if they ultimately choose not to do so.

If you get a **"No,"** the sales process continues, as described in the next chapter.

CHAPTER 35

How to Handle a "No"

You always need to ask (not assume) why you got a "No."

Usually it's because you made one of these two mistakes:

1. You screwed up on at least one of the steps in the marketing and sales process. For instance, if you didn't segment or qualify properly, you might be talking to someone who never intended to buy your viewpoint and take the action you want. This would be akin to the Mercedes salesperson spending a lot of time with someone who only has $10 in the bank. Or you could have screwed up on the needs analysis, and wound up making the wrong pitch to the customer. This would be like the salesperson trying to sell a tiny sports car to a couple looking for a family vehicle.

Or,

2. You short-circuited the sales process by asking for the sale prematurely—i.e., before you established a positive and trusting relationship with the customer.

Even if you think you know what went wrong, however, it's still important to ask the customer what he thinks. That's because (a) you want to make sure your assumption is accurate, and (b) in discussing the situation with the customer, you may get a chance to defuse his objection(s) and turn the "No" into a "Yes." You do this not by arguing with him or lecturing him, but by assuming that you've made a mistake somewhere in the sales process. If the customer permits it, go back and repeat the Restate, Ponder & Present Solution and Ask for the Sale steps, and see if you can do better.

No one likes to hear a lot of "No"s, but they do go with the territory.

Salespeople and activists both need to develop a thick skin so that the "No"s just bounce off. (In any case, you should not take them personally!) Remember that a disciplined approach to marketing and sales can help minimize the number of "No"s you wind up hearing, and also make those "No"s you do hear easier to deal with.

CHAPTER 36

A Day in the Life of a Successful Activist

A day in the life of a successful activist could be a day in which she or he:

- Won a significant victory in a campaign.
- Didn't win a victory, but participated in a series of productive activities related to the campaign.
- Experienced a "defeat" or "failure"—but handled it well.
- Spent the day doing paperwork. It wasn't too exciting, but it wasn't that stressful, either, and it had to get done.
- Procrastinated on work for four hours—but not five!
- Procrastinated for five hours—but not six!
- Finished one-tenth of what she had planned to do—which is still better than not doing any of it!
- Didn't shame, blame or criticize herself for any of the above or other perceived "failures."
- Didn't do much, or any, activism, but performed well and in a low-stress way at her classes or day job.
- Spent the day working mainly on health and relationship goals, or reworking her Mission or Time Management.
- Didn't work on any goals at all—just had fun!
- Didn't do much of anything—was feeling stressed out, so stayed home and took a low-stress "mental health day."

A successful activist will experience all of these types of days, and many more. Some days will seem more productive than others—although you should be careful about defining productivity too narrowly, since a day spent catching up on paperwork or taking a needed break definitely qualifies as productive. You should also avoid labeling days "good" or "bad," since almost every day, no matter how much it may seem to tilt in one direction, will probably be a mix of both.

Of course, the secret that all empowered activists know is that every day you spend fighting the good fight—no matter how "much" or "little" you achieve—is a good day.

CONCLUSION

Why We Will Win

CONCLUSION

Why We Will Win

It is a marvelous thing, the malleability of the human soul. Healing, growth, and the capacity for joy are available to all of us, no matter how old we are or how oppressed or unhappy we have been. Some of the best activists are people who have suffered tremendous loss, wounding or oppression, then cultivated within themselves the vision and strength to emerge from that dark place and help others. Remember that, and don't ever set a limit on what you or anyone else can achieve.

Human societies are also malleable, and have the capacity to grow and heal. As discussed earlier, it took little more than a hundred years for slavery to go from being an accepted practice throughout much of the world to being outlawed throughout the world. It is an evil that continues to be fought to this day, in Sudan and elsewhere, but no society claims that it is legally or morally defensible to own slaves, the way many societies did as recently as 150 years ago.

Remember, always, that "in dreams begin responsibilities." Dream boldly; then act responsibly to make your dream a reality. Remember, also, to "be regular and orderly in your life like a bourgeois so that you may be violent and original in your work." Manage your mission, time, fears and relationships.

Devote yourself whole-heartedly to your self-actualization, and never feel guilty for doing so. And never, ever blame, shame or criticize yourself or others: these behaviors accomplish nothing and are, in fact, undermining. Focus on your strengths and achievements, be a compassionate observer of your weaknesses and mistakes—and then go out and do the same for others.

Surround yourself with a supportive community and stay away from people who put you down, no matter how well-meaning they say their intentions are, or how close you've been to them in the past.

Strive to treat everyone you encounter with empathy, respect, compassion and love. Strive, especially, to treat conservatives that way. Don't dismiss them as intellectual or moral lightweights, but listen carefully to what they are saying and their reasons for thinking the way they do: first, because in doing so you will gain a better grasp of their reasoning—and, hence, be better equipped to counter it—and second, because sometimes the conservatives are actually right. Remember, also, that often when conservatives are wrong, they are wrong for innocent reasons. Also keep in mind that the world is complex enough that often progressives and conservatives will each be right, and wrong, about different aspects of the same problem.

Above all, don't worry about whether you are destined to make a monumental contribution such as Gloria Steinem's or only a smaller one. As the brilliant English novelist George Eliot wrote in *Middlemarch*, a novel whose main character, Dorothea, is an activist, the smaller contributions are vitally important. Here is Eliot's description of the impact of Dorothea's life:

> Her full nature, like that river of which Cyrus broke the strength, spent itself in channels which had no great name on the earth. But the effect of her being on those around her was incalculably diffusive: for the growing good of the world is partly dependent on unhistoric acts; and that things are not so ill with you and me as they might have been, is half owing to the number who lived faithfully a hidden life, and rest in unvisited tombs.

Don't worry too much about the big picture; just keep doing your work, and doing it as joyfully as possible.

The last few years have been difficult for American progressives, but the truth is that, while we may have been losing elections, we have been winning the far more important values war. David Brooks, in his book *Bobos in Paradise: The New Upper Class and How They Got There* (New York: Simon & Schuster, 2001), documents the ongoing blending of "bourgeois" and "bohemian" culture in the United States. ("Bobo" is a contraction of "bourgeois bohemian.") What he's really saying is that even the most conservative (i.e., bourgeois) communities are embracing progressive (i.e., bohemian) values. He's also saying, of course, that bohemian communities are embracing bourgeois values, but in my view that's a much less meaningful "win," since progressives have always had to coexist with capitalism.

Brooks, a self-described conservative, even admits to being a Bobo himself:

> Let me say first, I'm a member of this class. . . . We're not so bad. All societies have elites, and our educated elite is a lot more enlightened than some of the older elites, which were based on blood or wealth or military valor. Wherever we educated elites settle, we make life more interesting, diverse and edifying. . . . On balance I emerge as a defender of the Bobo culture.

Public policy expert Richard Florida documents a similar trend, which he calls the "Big Morph," in his book, *The Rise of the Creative Class . . . And How It's Transforming Work, Leisure, Community, and Everyday Life* (New York: Basic Books, 2002). "At the heart of the Big Morph is a new resolution of the centuries-old tension between two value systems: the Protestant work ethic and the bohemian ethic." Florida is very clear that this is a permanent and radical change in the American psyche:

> The great cultural legacy of the sixties, as it turned out, was not Woodstock after all, but something that had evolved at the other end of the continent. It was Silicon Valley. This place in the very heart of the San Francisco Bay area became the proving ground for the new ethos of creativity. If work could be made more aesthetic and experiential; if it could be spiritual and "useful" in the poetic sense rather than in the duty-bound sense; if the organizational strictures and rigidity of the old system could be transcended and **if bohemian values like individuality—which also happens to be tried-and-true all-American value—could be brought to the workplace, then we could move beyond the old categories.** And though the Valley itself has now mushroomed into something quite different than it was, the ethos that it pioneered has spread and endured, and continues to permeate our society. (Emphasis added.)

As our final example, see Rod Dreher's book *Crunchy Cons*, which extols for his conservative audience the virtues of (among other good things) organic food, environmental stewardship, anti-consumerism, anti-corporatism, local economies, and—yes—even granola and Birkenstocks.

"It is impossible to be truly conservative nowadays without being consciously countercultural," he writes.

The truth is, this drive toward freedom, individuality and other progressive values is bigger than all of us. As the World Values Surveys demonstrate, it's even bigger than American culture and society itself. It is, in fact, the "arc" that Martin Luther King, Jr., famously referred to when he said, "The moral arc of the universe is long, but it bends toward justice."

Note that King wasn't just talking about America or civil rights: he was talking about the universe and all social justice movements everywhere. He could do that because his arc derives from the universal and powerful hunger all humans have for freedom, love, esteem and self-actualization. It is the inevitability of that arc, and the consequent inevitable triumph of progressive values, that, more than anything else, may be driving the Far Right to such hateful extremes. The Right knows that its survivalist, strict father values will be left in the dust as societies around the globe become more prosperous and enlightened.

In a kind of desperate last stand, arch-conservatives around the world are doing their best to foment the kinds of hatreds and fears that they hope will allow them to stay in power. But hate-mongering has always been a temporary solution at best. King's moral arc prevailed over such horrors as Nazism and the European and American slave trades, and it will prevail over today's fascists.

Never forget that, as Richard Florida points out, America was founded on the *progressive* values of freedom, equality and individuality. As activists, it is our obligation and privilege to help America recognize and reclaim its vibrant progressive heritage. So . . .

Be happy.

Celebrate and honor your needs, and work hard to meet them.

Celebrate and honor the good in your society, and work hard to increase it.

Create a joyful, loving and supportive community around yourself.

Free yourself, so that you may better help others become free.

Start now.

—Duxbury, MA
and Boston, MA
March 2006

NOTES

INTRODUCTION

1. Throughout *The Lifelong Activist*, except where specifically indicated, I use the word "career" not in the formal or corporate sense, but simply to indicate long-term activist work. This work can be full- or part-time, paid or unpaid. If your activism is important to you, I call it a career.

PART ONE

1. Burnout is also a symptom of Compassion Fatigue, a secondary traumatic stress disorder whose other symptoms include fear, dissociation (disconnection from the immediate environment), obtrusive daydreams, disrupted sleep patterns and hypersensitivity. Compassion Fatigue afflicts activists and other "frontline workers" who regularly work with people or animals who have been traumatized either by violence or by having been caught in a terrifying situation such as a natural or manmade disaster. Compassion Fatigue can also afflict family members or friends of those who are traumatized. If you think you may be suffering from Compassion Fatigue, you should seek prompt help from a psychologist who specializes in treating it.

2. We're not even accounting for the huge role luck played in Steinem's career: specifically, the fact that she did her activism at a time in which our society was unusually receptive to new ideas and lifestyles. This is not to denigrate her and the other Second Wave feminist activists' achievements at all, but simply to point out that you yourself might not be so lucky.

3. To learn why good nutrition means vegetarian nutrition, see Bibliography.

4. I empathize if you object to giving money to the insurance industry. Moreover, you don't want to fall into the clutches of this country's healthcare system if you can possibly avoid it. The right strategy is to employ good preventative self-care (see Chapter 10) and to carry enough health insurance to get you *comfortably* through an accident or serious illness. Please don't stint: you are too valuable an individual, and have too much work left to do, to be unnecessarily incapacitated. Oh, and you'll probably want disability insurance, too. Sorry.

5. Don't be put off by the title: *The Millionaire Next Door* mostly deals not with those who inherited wealth, but those who accumulated it over their lifetime. It actually has a strong anti-consumerist theme that should be palatable to most activists.

6. Throughout *The Lifelong Activist* I quote from books written for artists, and I also list several such books in the Bibliography. Activists and artists are such similar types of people—individualistic, creative, risk-taking, etc.—that advice for artists often applies equally or nearly as well to activists. There are also many more self-actualization-themed books out there for artists than there are for activists, so why not borrow some wisdom from our artistic friends?

7. In their research, Stanley and Danko, the authors of *The Millionaire Next Door*, found that adults who regularly receive cash infusions from their parents tend

to become, over time, less and less able to live independently. Specifically, they tend to spend more, save less and get into more debt than adults who are self-supporting.

PART TWO

1. If you are younger, unmarried or male, you may have trouble identifying with these examples. Try to do so, however, because they illustrate what is perhaps the most common road to burnout: conformity with prevailing materialist/consumerist values. In other words, even if these examples are not pertinent to you right now, they may well be in a few short years. These examples also assume that neither activist is able to do full-time activism, as is the case with even many dedicated activists once they have a family.

2. This example assumes that both Alyssa's and Chris's husbands are willing to shoulder their fair share of the childcare and housework—an assumption, alas, that is still not valid in even many progressive households.

3. More companies offer flex-time than you might think, and even those that don't will often make accommodations for a good employee. Sociologist Arlie Russell Hochschild, author of *The Time Bind: When Work Becomes Home and Home Becomes Work* (New York: Henry Holt/Metropolitan Books, 1997), has done research showing that the vast majority of people who work for companies offering flex-time and other family-friendly benefits fail to take advantage of those benefits. For one reason why, see the next chapter.

4. "Cruelty-free" means the product wasn't tested on animals and, in some cases, contains no animal-derived ingredients. The website of In Defense of Animals, www.idausa.org/facts/crueltyfree.html, offers lists of companies whose cleaning, cosmetic and other products are cruelty-free. Also, look for the "leaping bunny" logo that a growing number of cruelty-free products now carry: see www.leapingbunny.org.

5. Electronic versions of all the forms mentioned in this section of *The Lifelong Activist* can be found at www.lifelongactivist.com.

PART THREE

1. Why would someone who procrastinates, and who is made miserable thereby, want to maintain the status quo? See Chapter 11: Fear.

2. The philosophical issues are important, but schedule them in; don't let them interrupt other work.

3. Frankl's wife died in Bergen-Belsen in 1945.

4. There are actually discussions, among activists, on whether it is ever appropriate to say we've "won" on a particular issue or event. The theory, apparently, is that since all victories are temporary or partial, it's somehow misleading to use the "V" word. C'mon!!!! I can't even begin to tell you what's wrong with that attitude, beginning with the fact that it is psychologically undermining. If you can't claim your victories, then what are you working for? How do you hope to inspire others? Do the New York Yankees, or any other sports team, refuse to celebrate their victories because they know they could have won by a wider margin, or could lose the next game? Of course not! And, of course, many of the same activists who are so reluctant to declare victory seem to have no problem at all declaring defeat.

5. A disproportionate number are computer geeks, engineers and other technical types, by the way. There are many reasons for that, including the fact that technical people are trained to hunt down the flaws in their projects so that they can

then fix them. That flaw-finding tendency comes in handy when you're design-ing, say, a bridge or a computer program, but it can be a pain in the interperson-al sphere

6. If you don't like to write, try journaling anyway; it's much easier than the kinds of writing you probably had to do for school. If writing still doesn't work for you, you can dictate an "audio journal" into a tape recorder, or call a friend and have a "journalistic," by which I mean focused and analytical, conversation. But please try writing—it offers many advantages, not the least of which is conven-ience.

6. As cited in Eric Maisel, Ph.D., *A Life in the Arts*, Chapter 3. (See Bibliography.)

7. Baum, Kenneth. *The Mental Edge: Maximizing Your Sports Potential with the Mind-Body Connection*. (See Bibliography.)

8. Csikszentmihalyi, Mihaly. *Flow: The Psychology of Optimal Experience*. (See Bibliography.)

PART FOUR

1. Some contemporary psychologists are reinterpreting and building on Maslow's model to make it more relational. See, for example, Steven J. Hanley and Steven C. Abell's article "Maslow and Relatedness: Creating an Interpersonal Model of Self-Actualization." *Journal of Humanistic Psychology* 42.4 (2002): 37–57.

2. In this chapter and elsewhere in *The Lifelong Activist*, I use the terms "conserva-tive," "Right," and "Far Right" interchangeably. This is for rhetorical conven-ience only, and not to deny the fact that conservatives, like progressives, vary enormously in their thinking and viewpoints.

3. An article entitled "Sex-Ed Class Becomes Latest School Battleground," in the March 30, 2006 *Wall Street Journal*, discusses the controversy surrounding abstinence-based sexual education programs that are being widely promoted by the Right, and funded by our currently conservative federal government. The article reports: ". . .sex-ed classes that discuss birth control as a way to prevent pregnancy and sexual diseases are increasingly being replaced or supplemented by curricula that promote abstinence until marriage and discuss contraceptives primarily in terms of their failure rates." Said one parent of the curriculum her child was taught: "It was fear- and shame-based. . . . There's nothing in there talking about sex as a natural part of a healthy loving relationship."

4. Of course, throughout American history the "enemy" has also been people of color who didn't obey the "rules."

PART FIVE

1. This includes the evangelical churches that have recently been winning many con-verts in the United States and abroad. See, for example: Symonds, William C.; Grow, Brian; and Cady, John. "Earthly Empires: How Evangelical Churches are Borrowing From the Business Playbook." *BusinessWeek*, May 23, 2005, cover story.

2. Green, Jesse. "When Political Art Mattered." *The New York Times Magazine*, December 7, 2003. Green writes: "I sometimes wonder what would have happened if instead of emerging among urban gay men, AIDS had first burrowed its way into the sexual lives of, say, accountants. On the one hand, the world would surely have responded with more kindness. But could the accountants have organized and responded to the crisis the way some gay men eventually did, using their profes-sional skills to alter policy and in the process change their culture?"

3. In a December 2005 *Atlantic Monthly* article on chess champion Garry Kasparov's courageous political campaign to replace ex-KGB agent Vladimir Putin as presi-

dent of Russia, the author describes Kasparov's confrontation at a rural campaign stop with five thuggish young men who were members of Nashi, a pro-Putin youth group. He asked them to consider why Putin had awarded the highest medal of honor in Russia, the Order of the Hero of Russia, to a Chechen rebel leader and his son, whom he described as "bandits and murderers of our Russian soldiers." The article reports, "The hall was silent. The Nashi members dropped their eyes to the floor. 'Why? I ask you again, why did our president cheapen our award by giving it to the murderers of our soldiers, of guys your own age? Answer me!' 'We'll ask him when we see him,' one [Nashi member] grumbled, eyes downcast."

4. "Problems" and "needs" typically go hand-in-hand, in that when someone has a problem she usually also has a need. Hereafter, for simplicity's sake, I'll mostly use the word "need," but when I do so, I'm also always implying a "problem" as well.

5. See, for instance: George Lakoff, *Moral Politics: How Liberals and Conservatives Think* (Chicago: University of Chicago Press, 2002); David Brock, *Blinded by the Right: The Conscience of an Ex-Conservative* (New York: Crown, 2002); Michael Lind, *Up From Conservatism: Why the Right is Wrong for America* (New York: Free Press, 1996); and John Micklethwait and Adrian Wooldridge, *The Right Nation: Conservative Power in America* (New York: Penguin, 2004).

6. For more information on how animals suffer in factory farms, visit www.factoryfarms.com.

7. See www.sierraclub.org/factoryfarms/

8. Numerous citations exist. Here are three: In an article entitled "Finger-Lickin' Bad" in the February 21, 2006 issue of the online environmental publication *Grist*, author Suzi Parker documents the exploitative and antiquated sharecropper-type business model used by poultry agribusinesses to dominate the small farmers who actually raise many of the birds sent to slaughter. And an article entitled "The Chicken Hangers," in the February 2, 2004 issue of the online publication *In the Fray* documents not only the horrific working conditions in the poultry industry, but management's hostile (and often unlawful) resistance to unionizing efforts or even basic workers' rights. Finally, a January 26, 2006, *New York Times* article entitled "Rights Group Condemns Meatpackers on Job Safety," begins, "For the first time, Human Rights Watch has issued a report that harshly criticizes a single industry in the United States, concluding that working conditions among the nation's meatpackers and slaughterhouses are so bad that they violate basic human rights."

9. Lantern Books author Michael Greger, M.D., has written extensively on the chemical and biological contamination of industrial meat, dairy and egg products. See the "Selected Writings" section of his Website, www.veganmd.com. And Will Tuttle, Ph.D.'s book *The World Peace Diet* (Lantern Books, 2005) provides an excellent overview of all of the issues.

BIBLIOGRAPHY

Note 1: although the books cited below are organized into the general categories of Mission, Time, Fear and Relationship Management, many pertain to more than one category.

Note 2: many of these books merit repeated reading.

MISSION MANAGEMENT

Revolution From Within: A Book of Self-Esteem by Gloria Steinem. A unique and inspiring blend of autobiography, self-help guide and meditation on how we can work together to achieve a progressive society. Steinem not only writes candidly about her life and her successes and failures as an activist and human being; she also discusses the larger forces of power, self-esteem, spirituality, compassion and love as they play out in our lives and across society as a whole. New York: Little, Brown, 1993.

Letters to a Young Activist by Todd Gitlin. Gitlin was a leader of the 1960s Students for a Democratic Society (SDS) movement, and he has been doing, writing about and teaching activism and progressivism ever since. His book is packed with great advice and perspectives, including difficult topics such as anger, self-indulgence and what he calls "the discipline gap" between the Right and the Left. New York: Basic Books, 2003.

Why Are Artists Poor?: The Exceptional Economy of the Arts by Hans Abbing. A fascinating book by an author who is both an economist and an artist. Abbing answers the title question in part by analyzing the economics of the art world, and in part by analyzing the psychology of artists. Briefly: the art market is irrational, and artists tend to be more motivated by internal rewards (as opposed to external ones such as status and paychecks) than most people. Artists are also prone to a "gambler" mentality that hopes for easy success and is not good at weighing the benefits, costs and risks of certain behaviors. Much of what Abbing says also applies to many activists. Amsterdam: Amsterdam University Press, 2004.

Money Drunk, Money Sober: 90 Days to Financial Freedom by Julia Cameron and Mark Bryan. This eye-opening book, co-authored by Julia Cameron, author of the classic *The Artist's Way*, is essential reading for all activists. It discusses the ways people tend to make themselves poorer, focusing on five common dysfunctional attitudes toward money: Compulsive Spender, Big Deal Chaser, Maintenance Money Drunk, Poverty Addict and Cash Codependent. The book also offers a plan for recovering from poverty. New York: Ballantine/Wellspring, 1999.

The Millionaire Next Door: The Surprising Secrets of America's Wealthy by Thomas J. Stanley and William D. Danko. Ignore the hype-y title. This book is useful because it deals mainly with those who accumulate wealth, not those who inherit it. It shows how, through frugality and wise investing, you can parlay even a moderate income (for example, a teacher's income) into a comfortable living and retirement. (Hint: it's more about how little you spend than how much you earn.) New York: Pocket Books, 1999.

Rich Dad, Poor Dad: What the Rich Teach Their Kids About Money—That the Poor and Middle Class Do Not! by Robert T. Kiyosaki and Sharon L. Lechter. This popular book explains which habits lead to wealth accumulation, and which don't. Short, to the point, and easily understood. New York: Warner Business Books, 2000.

How to Get Out of Debt, Stay Out of Debt, and Live Prosperously by Jerrold Mundis. The classic guide to getting out of debt and living a debt-free life, based on the methodology and teachings of Debtors Anonymous. The beginning chapters help the reader recognize if he or she has a "debting" problem—symptoms include unopened mail, unbalanced accounts and soliciting family and friends for loans—and explain how it could have arisen. Later chapters offer a plan for "recovering" from the debt. New York: Bantam Books, 2003.

What Color Is Your Parachute? 2006: A Practical Manual for Job-Hunters And Career-Changers by Richard Nelson Bolles. Another classic guide— this time, to looking for a job and planning a career. Bolles recommends starting with your values and Mission (a word he, too, uses) and working outward from there. Goes into each phase of the job hunting process in useful detail. Berkeley, CA: Ten Speed Press, 2005.

The Ultimate Fit or Fat by Covert Bailey. There are a zillion health and fitness books out there, but I like Bailey's for its exceptional clarity and straightforward approach. Bailey, who has a master's degree in biochemistry from MIT, also knows the science behind fitness better than many authors, and that lends the book some added heft (so to speak). Boston, MA: Houghton Mifflin, 2000. (P.S. Ignore Bailey's nutritional advice and go vegetarian! See next entry. . . .)

Vegetarian/vegan resources: To learn why good nutrition means vegetarian nutrition, read Brenda Davis and Vesanto Melina's *Becoming Vegan: The Complete Guide to Adopting a Healthy Plant-Based Diet* (Summertown, TN: Book Publishing Co., 2000) and T. Colin Campbell and Thomas M. Campbell II's *The China Study: The Most Comprehensive Study of Nutrition Ever Conducted and the Startling Implications for Diet, Weight Loss and Long-Term Health* (Dallas, TX.: BenBella Books, 2005). And to learn why vegetarianism is in line with fundamental progressive values, read Pamela Rice's *101 Reasons Why I'm a Vegetarian* (New York: Lantern Books, 2004); Erik Marcus's *Vegan: The New Ethics of Eating* (Ithaca, NY: McBooks Press, 2000); Will Tuttle's *The World Peace Diet: Eating for Spiritual Health and Social Harmony* (New York: Lantern Books, 2005); and John Robbins' *The Food Revolution: How Your Diet Can Help Save Your Life and Our World* (Berkeley, CA: Conari Press, 2001).

TIME MANAGEMENT

The Effective Executive Revised: The Definitive Guide to Getting the Right Things Done by Peter Drucker. First published in 1966, it remains one of the most-read management guides. Its emphasis is on goal setting, time management and prioritizing your activities so that you invest your time on those activities that best support your mission. Drucker's advice applies not just to executives, but anyone shouldering a lot of responsibility. New York: HarperBusiness Essentials, 2006. Also recommended: *The Essential Drucker: The Best of Sixty Years of Peter Drucker's Essential Writings on Management.*, New York: CollinsBusiness, 2001.

The 7 Habits of Highly Effective People: Powerful Lessons in Personal Change by Stephen R. Covey. A perennial bestseller, it offers tons of useful advice pertaining to Managing Your Mission, Time, Fears and Relationships. Covey's "four quadrants" method for organizing your time and tasks is particularly useful; and I also like the way he advises you to work toward effectiveness in both your professional and personal lives. New York: Gardners, 2004.

FEAR MANAGEMENT

The War of Art: Break Through the Blocks and Win Your Inner Creative Battles by Stephen Pressfield. I recommend this book to everyone, and everyone I know who's read it says it has changed his or her life. This is not just a book for artists; it's for anyone with an ambitious goal. On top of its many other virtues, it's also a short, pithy and entertaining read: you can finish it in an afternoon. New York: Warner Books, 2003.

A Life in the Arts by Eric Maisel. Maisel is a psychotherapist who specializes in helping artists and performers, and his book dissects the motivations, attitudes, rewards and punishments of the artistic life better than anything else I've read. It goes into great detail on topics such as talent, isolation, moods and "obscurity and stardom;" and he also includes a "transition program" for moving into and out of a professional art career. Because of the similarities between art and activism, and because so many activists are also artists, I have no hesitation in recommending this book to activists. New York: Tarcher, 1994.

Flow: The Psychology of Optimal Experience by Mihaly Csikszentmihalyi. "Flow" is the feeling of being fully and happily immersed in whatever you're doing, so that time appears to stand still, the rest of the world recedes, and you are maximally effective. Others call the same phenomenon "being in the zone" or "peak performance." Whatever you call it, you probably want to experience it as much as possible, and *Flow* will help. It begins with a discussion of what flow is, then moves on to what causes it, what impedes it, and how you can encourage it in different areas of your life. New York: Harper Perennial, 1991.

Are Your Lights On? How to Figure Out What the Problem *Really* Is by Donald C. Gause and Gerald M. Weinberg. The first and most crucial step to solving any problem is determining what exactly the problem actually is—

often a tougher challenge than it might seem. This book discusses this subtle topic in simple language and using fun examples. I'm partial to Weinberg's work ever since having taken a class on Problem-Solving Leadership with him that changed my life. New York: Dorset House, 1990. Also recommended: Weinberg's *Secrets of Consulting: A Guide to Giving and Getting Advice Successfully*. New York: Dorset House, 1986.

Addictive Thinking: Understanding Self Deception by Abraham Twerski, M.D. If you have an active addiction, deal with that problem before all others and seek professional help. This book will provide insight into some of the probable causes of your addiction and the mindset that keeps you addicted. Topics covered include self-deception, impatience (a warped time sense), denial, guilt, shame and hypersensitivity. If you don't believe you are an addict, but any part of your life feels out of control, or any serious problem you have seems intractable, then you should also read this book. Center City, MN: Hazelden, 1997. Also recommended: *The Addictive Personality: Understanding the Addictive Process and Compulsive Behavior* by Craig Nakken. Center City, MN: Hazelden, 1988; and *The Heart of Addiction: A New Approach to Understanding and Managing Alcoholism and Other Addictive Behaviors* by Lance M. Dodes, M.D. New York: Harper Paperbacks, 2002.

There Must Be More Than This: Finding More Life, Love, and Meaning by Overcoming Your Soft Addictions by Judith Wright. Wright lists more than forty "soft addictions"—everything from compulsive video game playing and email checking to fantasizing and hair twirling—that can interfere with your success. Although not as dangerous as traditional "hard" addictions like alcoholism, soft addictions can nevertheless impair your life and success. This book tells you what causes soft addictions and how you can deal with them. New York: Broadway Books, 2003.

The Myth of Laziness by Mel Levine, M.D. An important book for anyone who is having trouble getting his or her work done. Such people are often called "lazy," but, as the title implies, Levine considers laziness a myth at best, and an improper diagnosis at worst: he says many underperformers actually suffer from "output failures" linked to learning disabilities or poor educational support. His book focuses on those topics, but he also discusses how underperformers use, or misuse, time and other resources. Levine writes mainly about children, but much of what he writes can be applied to adults as well. He pays particular attention to writing blocks and problems, since he considers writing the most challenging project most kids tackle, or, as he puts it, "the largest orchestra a kid's mind has to conduct." New York: Simon & Schuster, 2003.

The Mental Edge: Maximizing Your Sports Potential with the Mind-Body Connection by Kenneth Baum. Tips from a top sports coach that can help you attain both your athletic and non-athletic goals. Baum's approach is similar to *The Lifelong Activist*'s in that he advises you to work to envision your goal in great detail, and plan for how you will get there. He also emphasizes the importance of maintaining a positive attitude and not arbitrarily setting limits on what you can achieve; and also offers useful tips for improving your ability to focus and concentrate and stay "in the moment." New York: Perigee Trade, 1999.

RELATIONSHIP MANAGEMENT

Rules for Radicals by Saul D. Alinsky. A unique and irreplaceable classic. Alinsky spent decades doing labor and other activism, chalking up many victories. His book contains a wealth of pragmatic wisdom on not just how to create change, but how to live as an activist. It is distinguished by a very plain-spoken and candid approach, and Alinsky is not just forthcoming in his opinions—writing in 1968, he accuses the hippies of "copping out"—but fearless in tackling some *very* tough questions, including, in a long chapter entitled "Of Means and Ends," the appropriate uses of propaganda and violence. New York: Vintage, 1989.

Ethics Into Action: Henry Spira and the Animal Rights Movement by Peter Singer. Probably the best activist biography, it also explores the attitudes and behaviors that contributed to Spira's many successes, as well as his preferred strategies and tactics. I was struck by how, though an avid coalition builder, Spira preferred to work solo or with just a couple of part-time assistants, to avoid what he considered time-wasting bureaucracy and meetings. The book is also a guide to what it's like to live as a truly dedicated activist, and the rewards of such a life. Lanham, MD: Rowman & Littlefield, 2000.

Bridging the Class Divide and Other Lessons for Grassroots Organizing by Linda Stout. This activist autobiography is filled with practical advice and inspirational stories. Stout grew up poor and, as the title states, a major theme of her book is how activists can reach out to, and connect with, people of other classes. Some of the stories she relates of activists who failed to do so—or, worse, failed to even try—are painful to read. Boston: Beacon Press, 1997.

How to Win Friends & Influence People by Dale Carnegie. An easy book—or title—to mock, but this may be the best book ever written on how to get along with people and, yes, influence them. Critics consider some of the techniques manipulative, but they can be used manipulatively or sincerely—take your pick. If every progressive activist put the techniques described in *How to Win Friends* to work, the world would be a much better place. New York: Pocket, 1998. Also recommended: everything else by Carnegie.

How to Talk So Kids Will Listen & Listen So Kids Will Talk by Adele Faber and Elaine Mazlish. I *love* this book. It's a parenting book that has sold millions of copies, but I recommend it to everyone, whether they have kids or not. It is basically about how to deal with people and get them to buy into your agenda without exploiting or undermining them. (That's what good parents seek to do with their kids, after all.) Topics discussed include praise, compromise, effective communication and the dangers of shame, blame and negative labeling. Also, good stuff on effective problem solving. New York: Collins, 1999.

Conscious Loving: The Journey to Co-Commitment by Gay Hendricks and Kathlyn Hendricks. One of the best guides to building successful long-term intimate relationships, it takes the approach that, to build such a relationship, we must overcome any ingrained, often unconscious, thought patterns and behaviors we have that can sabotage relationships. The book offers a process for doing so, and also discusses the "upper limits problem," the common misconception that we are not supposed to be feel good much of the time. New York: Bantam, 1992.

Overcoming Your Strengths: 8 Reasons Why Successful People Derail and How to Remain on Track by Lois Frankel. A guide to avoiding self-sabotage in your job and career. Frankl, a corporate coach, says talented people often make the serious mistake of over-relying on their core talent, and neglecting other important talents and skills (think of your typical activist geek who knows everything about strategy, social movements, etc., but can't get along with people). Frankel also discusses common problems underachievers have, including overlooking the importance of people, inability to function effectively in a work group, failure to focus on image and communication, and insensitivity to the reactions of others. Pasadena, CA: Corporate Coaching International, 2003.

Outing Yourself: How to Come Out As Lesbian or Gay to Your Family, Friends, and Coworkers by Michelangelo Signorile. The definitive guide to coming out as a gay man or lesbian, but it can be used by anyone who wishes to live a more authentic life and speak the truth about himself or herself. I love its systematic, commonsense approach that begins with coming out to yourself, and then to other gays, friends, family, coworkers and strangers. New York: Fireside, 1996.

Crunchy Cons: How Birkenstocked Burkeans, Gun-Loving Organic Gardeners, Evangelical Free-Range Farmers, Hip Homeschooling Mamas, Right-Wing Nature Lovers, And Their Diverse Tribe Of Countercultural Conservatives Plan To Save America (Or At Least The Republican Party) by Rod Dreher. A terrific and fun book that may profoundly change your view of the "opposition." Many principled conservatives, it turns out, like many of the same things we do, including an honest government, healthy food, a clean environment and a reduction in the role of corporations in American society, politics and culture. New York: Crown Forum, 2006.

Don't Think of an Elephant!: Know Your Values and Frame the Debate—The Essential Guide for Progressives by George Lakoff. Many readers of *The Lifelong Activist* are probably already familiar with Lakoff's work on the different ways progressives and conservatives use political and social language. *Don't Think of an Elephant!* discusses how conservative politicians have made far better use of language than progressives, in recent decades, and how this has been a major reason for the Right's electoral victories. It then goes on to discuss what progressives can do to correct the problem. Every activist should read this. White River Junction, VT: Chelsea Green Publishing Company, 2004. Also recommended: Lakoff's longer, more scholarly work on the same topic, *Moral Politics: How Liberals and Conservatives Think*. Chicago: University of Chicago Press, 2002.

Selling the Invisible: a Field Guide to Modern Marketing by Harry Beckwith. A terrific book that distills the essence of effective marketing into 250 short and entertainingly written pages. Beckwith often disdains things that other marketers hold dear, such as focus groups and the idea that "strategy is king." That doesn't mean he's wrong, however, and most of the things he disdains are money— and time-sinks that most grassroots activist organizations shouldn't be bothered with in the first place. That, plus his focus on marketing and selling "intangibles" (in his meaning, services, but it also applies to ideas and ideals such as progressivism) make this valuable reading for any activist. New York: Warner Business Books, 1998.

The 22 Immutable Laws of Marketing by Al Ries and Jack Trout. A short and easy read. The examples are somewhat dated, but the principles the authors write about—e.g., that marketing is more about perception than reality—still very much apply. New York: Collins, 1994.

Crossing the Chasm by Geoffrey A. Moore. Another marketing classic, this time in the field of high tech. It should be of interest to activists because marketing high tech and marketing social ideas are both about marketing *innovation*. *Crossing the Chasm* is perhaps the best-known high tech marketing guide, and the one that popularized the term "early adopter," meaning a "mainstream" (non-geek) person who is highly receptive to new ideas and products. Its market segmentation approach (dividing your market into Innovators, Early Adopters, Early Majority, Late Majority and Laggards) is particularly useful. New York: Collins, 2002.

Guerrilla Marketing: Secrets for Making Big Profits from Your Small Business by Jay Conrad Levinson. The classic book on how to market cheaply yet effectively. It's been around forever, and has probably contributed to the growth and success of thousands, if not tens of thousands, of activist and other endeavors. Levinson offers good explanations of marketing strategy, and good discussions of the pros and cons of various traditional marketing techniques, including public relations, advertising, flyers and postcards. Boston: Houghton Mifflin, 1998. The book's coverage of the Internet and online technology remains a weak spot, so you may want to read additional books specific to that topic, such as Holly Berkley's *Low-Budget Online Marketing for Small Businesses.* Bellingham, WA: Self-Counsel Press, 2003.

INDEX

The Lifelong Activist Workgroups Program

www.lifelongactivist.com/workgroups

Thank you for reading *The Lifelong Activist*. I hope you found it a worthwhile experience and are ready to begin Managing your Mission, Time, Fears and Relationships. I urge you not to work in isolation, but as part of a supportive community, as that will make your work easier and more fun, and help you succeed more quickly.

The Lifelong Activist Workgroups Program is a FREE program that can help. I started it to help activists find, or build, communities, and to help the communities themselves be more effective. A Workgroup consists of two or more activists who are committed to working together on the Lifelong Activist program, and generally supporting each other in their self-actualization. Any two or more activists can create a Workgroup: you don't have to be in the same movement or organization; you don't have to be in the same location; and you certainly don't have to be of the same age, sex, race or religion. (In fact, it's usually an advantage to have some diversity.) The only important requirement is that all Workgroup members be committed to not just to their own success and self-actualization, but that of the other Workgroup members.

If you wish to **start** a Workgroup, you'll find lots of information, exercises and other resources to help you do so at www.lifelongactivist.com/workgroups. If you wish to **join** a Workgroup, you'll find a list of existing Workgroups at www.lifelongactivist.com/workgroups/workgroupslist.htm.

I also invite you to visit *The Lifelong Activist* blog at www.lifelongactivist.com/blog. There, you'll be able to share your experiences with, and seek advice and assistance from, other activists.

I welcome your comments and feedback on *The Lifelong Activist*, as well as on activism in general and your activist career, either at the blog or at lifelongactivist@yahoo.com.

—Hillary

The Lifelong Activist Coaching and Consulting/Training Programs

www.lifelongactivist.com/coaching
www.lifelongactivist.com/consulting

Individual coaching in the areas of mission, time, fear and relationship management is available from Hillary Rettig or one of her associates. Please visit www.lifelongactivist.com/coaching or email lifelongactivist@yahoo.com for more information.

Organizations seeking consulting and/or training services related to the topics covered in *The Lifelong Activist* are invited to visit www.lifelongactivist.com/consulting or email lifelongactivist@yahoo.com for more information.